Benedict Allen is one of the UK's most prominent explorers. Wherever possible, he prefers to travel alone, immersing himself in alien environments having first learnt survival skills from indigenous peoples.

He read Environmental Sciences at the University of East Anglia, and in his graduation year joined expeditions to Costa Rica, Brunei and Iceland. In 1983, aged 23, he crossed the remote rainforest between the Orinoco and Amazon, on foot and by dugout canoe: a journey that became the subject of his first book *Mad White Giant: a Journey to the Heart of the Amazon Jungle*.

Following this, he underwent a gruelling 6-week initiation ceremony in Papua New Guinea, chronicled in his second book *Into the Crocodile Nest*. Subsequent expeditions have included a search for ape-men in Sumatra (*Hunting the Gugu*), a trek through New Guinea and to Australia's Gibson Desert (*The Proving Grounds*) and a 3600-mile journey across the Amazon Basin (*Through Jaguar Eyes*).

In recording his third Amazon expedition for the BBC, Benedict developed a filming technique new to television, his use of just a hand-held camera allowing millions of people to share the ups and downs of remote travel for the first time. There followed his pioneering series *The Skeleton Coast* (a journey with three camels through the Namib Desert), *Edge of Blue Heaven* (from Siberia across the Mongolian steppe and alone through the Gobi Desert), *The Bones of Colonel Fawcett*, and *Last of the Medicine Men* (a study of shamanism in Haiti, Siberut Island, Siberia and Mexico). Recently he returned from Siberia with frostbite having undertaken his latest BBC project, filming a 1000-mile trek with a reluctant dog team.

Hunting the Gugu

In search of the lost ape-men of Sumatra

Benedict Allen

faber and faber

First published in the United Kingdom in 1989
by Macmillan London Limited

This paperback edition first published in 2002
by Faber and Faber Limited
3 Queen Square London WC1N 3AU

Printed in England by Mackays of Chatham, plc

A CIP record for this book
is available from the British Library

ISBN 0–571–20627–1

2 4 6 8 10 9 7 5 3 1

Contents

To the generous peoples of Malaysia and Indonesia

Acknowledgements

'Theodore Hull' was very gracious in allowing me to write about him, his Malay, Chinese and British friends, and the expedition to find his Missing Link. I am also indebted to cousins 'Alex' and 'Henry' and their families, and to the Ambassador and the Fathers and Brothers of the Xaverian Mission and MEP, for being so hospitable in Thailand and Sumatra and so tolerant of all my teasing in this book. In addition I would like to express thanks to my astute and tireless editor Brenda Thomson, and to Sue Kennett for letting me be her 'slacker in the attic' and for her sound advice downstairs across the kitchen table. Finally, thanks to her local vicar, the Reverend Theo Hull of the parish of St Mary and St John, Balham, for the loan of his name.

For Theodore's sake I have reworded any quotations from his thesis 'Hope at Large', to enable him to publish seriously under his real name should he ever wish, and on his request I have altered a few personal details to protect his own and his friends' privacy. I have also changed the name of the housing project on the Sumatran Highway, and those of 'Agga', 'Uhu', 'Telee' and the enigmatic female 'Segma'. Want of space has led to my excluding any account of my very long-suffering travelling companion in Thailand, Siobhan Quin, who instead gains mention and thanks here.

Benedict Allen
May 1988

Foreword

Every corner of the globe has its Wild Man. There is the snow-resilient Yeti, there is the cumbersome Bigfoot, and on the rarely trod slopes of Bhutan there is the elusive Migu; closer at home, there are the agile Pixie, the troublesome Troll, and the rather irritating-at-times Leprechaun. Walking through the Gobi Desert, I heard several Mongol nomads muttering that the Almas would surely get me. In the swamps of the Sepik, New Guinea, I found myself with an eye out for the Wunjumboo; in the Gibson Desert there was the creepy Featherfoot of the Aborigines.

So are these Things just the product of superstitious minds? Are they merely the religion of the so-called 'primitive' and 'backward'? After all, these hairy humanoids only ever seem to crop up in the back of beyond – whether the bogs of Ireland, or, in the case of the Gugu (the *orang pendek* or little man who is the subject of this book), in the tropical forests of Sumatra. If so, if they are indeed only the creations of 'simple' people's minds, then we are all, perhaps, simple. For surely these ape-men are not so very different from angels – though often rather more hairy. They are not giving expression to God above, as the Angel Gabriel did so proficiently, but rather to a landscape that remote people utterly depend on. Nature can destroy life, or it can choose to succour it. And though few of us now believe in angels, we do still believe in their modern equivalent – they don't speak for God, but do speak for values sacred to us. These are our modern heroes – say a campaigning journalist, Mother Teresa or an elected President. Just like our arch villains, they become more than mortals, as we discover from our shock when we lose them. I heard of Lady Diana's death from Mongolian nomads, of all people – even they were a little distraught. These characters we've more-or-less created ourselves seem to live to define our hopes, symbolize our fears – as the orang pendek might for the Sumatran forest dwellers. They are not God, they are not spirits, they are much more like us, bringing a face to a bewildering world.

Or, of course, the Gugu might be 'real'. This book comes to no definitive conclusion – and I hope this is of no consequence to the reader: This is not a scientific investigation. That said, after *Hunting the Gugu* was first published, a more dedicated *orang pendek* researcher called Debbie Martyr did approach me saying that she was off herself to find what evidence she could. That was the last I saw of her, and she may be still there in the dank forests. I know only that, since having met her then, she has come up with some startling first-hand accounts – and more than that, with physical evidence. Most importantly, she took a plaster cast of a 'Gugu's' print. But that's a story for her, not me, to tell.

Hunting the Gugu is the story of my own journey, and my journey wasn't, in the end, a 'Who Dunnit?'. This was a quest in the classical sense, the archetypal tale of the boy who is sent away by an elder to find his place in the scheme of things. It's an odyssey in the universal tradition – the young Sioux Indian sent away to find wisdom, a Dyak headhunter dispatched through the Borneo forests for his first head, Arthur the apprentice to the sorcerer Merlin, the teenager who leaves home and squanders his allowance, and even perhaps Lara Croft, the heroine of computer game Tomb Raider. They come home – hopefully – and like the Prodigal Son, they have learnt.

At this level, it doesn't matter what battle honour I myself came home with – whether I had come face to face with the creature. The importance lay in journeying, in what happened along the way. Of course, I didn't realize this at the time I was busy hunting that infuriatingly elusive Gugu – and come to think of it, what would I have done with a Gugu anyway? But by now I was trapped in a story just like Odysseus or all the others who have to act out an immortal tale; and there I now remain, just one more young warrior sent on a quest by a Wise Old Man, named Theodore Hull; once home, my education completed, he breaks my bow. It's all over. Suddenly, the quest gives way to the realization that the answer, after all that sweat and bother, lies much nearer at hand.

Benedict Allen
October, 2001

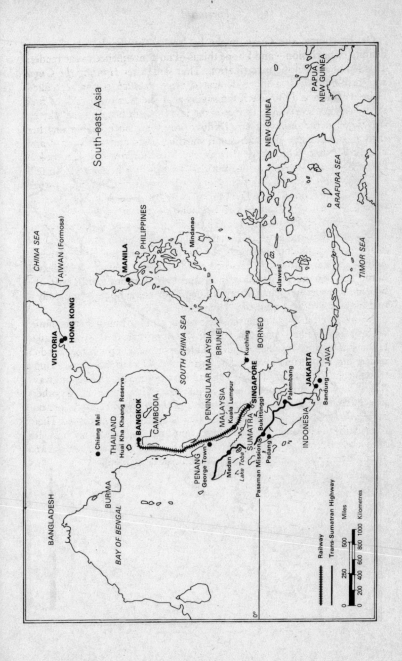

South-east Asia

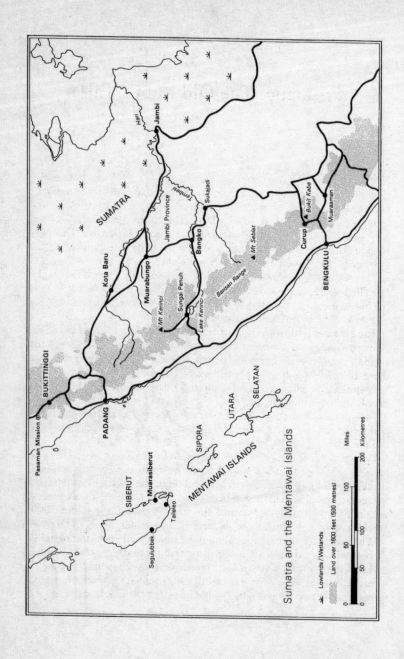

Sumatra and the Mentawai Islands

Prologue: The Old Man's Tale

The thorns should have ripped open the creature's bare skin but instead they skidded lightly over it, accommodating themselves to the animal's curves. Birds which should have shrieked and clattered through the branches merely hunched down a little. The animal parted the saplings and spiralling creepers as if to avoid creasing the leaves. The only obvious disturbance to the jungle was in its wake: leaves lifted in the gust; gnat clouds were momentarily unbalanced.

This was what Pastaran saw, and he tightened his grip on his single-barrelled shotgun. He would have made a run for it, but he could not: his boots would not budge. It might have been mud that gummed his feet down, but more likely it was fear.

The creature had stopped in its tracks; it must have caught his scent. Now it was behind a web of vines. Pastaran could not actually see the animal, but the vine clump had a new solidity about it. The beast was there all right, standing – or stooping, or hanging, or whatever it did – only spitting distance away. Any minute it might bound over the clogged brook and gore him.

Mosquitoes were sucking on Pastaran's legs. He let them. They plopped to the ground, incapacitated by the ingestion of so much blood; he did not care.

Perhaps the beasts were all around him. Pastaran listened. The jungle's clicks and buzzes spilled down on to him – the accumulated racket of a million fidgeting crickets and bugs, the footsteps of a billion foraging ants. He had never been able to put names to the forest inhabitants. Normally he lumped the sawings and gratings under the label 'cicadas' – the male ones serenading their mates, he thought.

What was the animal? An orang-utan which walked too upright? A gibbon which had been swinging in its tree carelessly, taken a tumble and was living down here while its bones were on the mend?

Pastaran tinkered with these plainly inadequate explanations, trying to maintain a grip on himself. His ignorance of the jungle stemmed, he had always considered, from his over-enthusiasm for it as a boy. So often he had tugged his father's fingers, begged to be taken right into the *hutan*, into what he supposed were the jungle's dank, secret innards, where devilish spirits loomed from deep nooks. Come midnight, he knew, men who had been bewitched would loiter there – men who under favourable lunar conditions were transformed into tigers; they would lollop through the trees, their roars chased by an echo with a soft, plaintive edge . . . But when, at long last, he *had* been escorted deep into the *hutan*, he found nothing but disappointment. Mud had almost sucked the toes off his feet. When he had stroked a hank of grass, it had lacerated his hand. He had developed raised, red sores where the insides of his legs rubbed. Suddenly he did not like the place. Leeches careered at you across the fallen leaves, sniffing you out, or dropped from branches and stalked noiselessly through your hair. He had learnt that some were fastidious in choosing where to syphon your blood, and would take a wander round, maybe sauntering up a nostril, while others would just sink their heads into you without hesitation. Talk of long forest snakes had, he had found, been greatly exaggerated; the first he had glimpsed was on his third trip to the *hutan* and it had slunk away guiltily. That was another disappointment: the danger of snake bite and/ or strangulation had held a certain glamour.

Later he realised that this boyhood, Javanese jungle had been only a slither of woodland park, which had since been replanted with office blocks. With the help of the government resettlement scheme, he had moved here, to the less populous island of Sumatra. This forest was quite a different matter. The trees, amassed around his farmstead, were one vast, whistling, hostile organism with a wet, stale breath.

For another ten minutes Pastaran stood sweating in his boots, cast-offs of a passing Dutch map surveyor. Still no movement from the animal, just the weight of its preying eyes. This feeling of being watched was almost worse than the threat of death by ape-beast bite. It was almost as if by standing its ground, invisibly, a few paces away, the animal was saying that it belonged in the forest – whereas he, an honest farmer, did not. This thought roused a sudden madness in him. Why should he be made to feel a foreigner here? The animal was smug, mocking, telling him he was not part of the forest, with his anti-insect, anti-thorn boots. He was being humiliated; this was just how he felt when urchins yelled through the dust smoke after his buffalo cart, 'There goes Pastaran, the *orang gila*! Pastaran the buffoon!' An animal should not be able to do this to him. Not an animal, Pastaran thought. But then this was not a normal animal, was it? He had caught the brief wind which the creature left in its wake: it was lightly scented with woodsmoke.

Pastaran looked at the shotgun in his hands. Usually matters of the forest were dealt with simply: if he required firewood, he despatched a handful of his children, of which he had twelve. But today he had entered the *hutan* himself – a secret assignation with his best friend's daughter. Within half an hour, Pastaran had realised that the romantic liaison was not such a good idea. The girl, of course, had not turned up. Or, if she had, she had totally mistaken the rendezvous point. Or he had. He had stood there for a little while, cursing the creeper-draped trees. And now this . . .

Suddenly Pastaran knew he must kill the beast. He was not so afraid now. The animal was a menace – a deviation from the natural order. It must be destroyed. He scratched away the bark splinters itching at the crest of his neck, thinking ahead to the triumphant press photo of himself hugging the mocking beast's black rug of a body. The proof would be vital. He was not renowned for his honesty. He tried to count the number of lies he had told his wife that very morning. Four, he thought. No, five. But that did not matter now. He switched the gun's catch away from 'S' for 'safety'. As he raised the barrel, he uttered a few pertinent prayers to Allah – in particular that the weapon should strike down the beast in one go. What would happen if it was only grazed and went berserk? In his mind he saw dirty claws slashing the air, finding his neck. If only he had thought to bring the heavier-gauge cartridges.

If the ape-beast saw the leaves shivering as Pastaran clumsily arranged himself, it gave no sign. He removed his finger from where it rested along the guard, and curled it up around the trigger. Only as he jerked that finger back did he see, in his sights, mottled by thin shadows, a face. As the barrel directed the explosion into it, and Pastaran's scrawny shoulder bucked, he met eyes. The gaze was spread wide in childish innocence – nostrils expanded in fear, a small face so wide open, a flower spread to the sun, vulnerable, shivering. A human face – a girl's. *This* was not a beast! Not a proper one: tears were racing down her cheeks. He was committing murder.

The explosion seemed to leave a hole of shocked silence in the forest and into this the hairy girl released a soft groan. But Pastaran gaped. Where had she gone? She should have been thrown backwards a foot or so by the blast – a heap of wet hair and torn guts studded with hot lead shot. Instead there had been a flick of a golden mane, and she had melted into the leafscape. His feelings of near remorse changed first into confusion as he could discover only a light sprinkling of blood; then into frustration as he failed to spot a single footprint; finally into a boiling anger as his incompetence mocked him again. There was no proof, no nothing. He had hoped at least to scalp the ape-girl, bring back her feet and hands.

Late in the night the dogs of the neighbourhood barked, reporting a disturbance on the forest perimeter. Pastaran was finding his way home. And what a change had come over him! He had never cut a dashing figure, but as he dragged himself right through the taro crop he was like a maimed cockroach feeling for its crevice. Finally he made it to the steps of the verandah. Indoors, he slumped over the table. His wife patted his back. She was quite fond of him, but she could not help but grimace at the first touch of his film of running sweat.

Perhaps it was because Pastaran, all of a flutter, now began to confess his adultery to his whole family that his story rang true. They gathered round to listen. His son Raden cut in with a pitying snigger: the stupid old twit had seen an *orang Belanda*, a Dutchman – most likely had chanced on him naked, scrubbing himself in the brook. That accounted for the blond mane that Pastaran had spotted as 'she' vanished beyond the gunsmoke. At this, the peasant rapped his brass ring so hard on the table that the large, inlaid pebble shattered. 'It must be', said his wife, who could sometimes but not always be counted on to deliver a dramatic line, 'that Allah's hand is in this.' The ape-girl had been sent to Pastaran in place of his lover. Divine punishment, that's what it was. The naked furry female was a grotesque parody. Yes, said Pastaran, remembering another cruel detail – the hairs as thick as thread which sprouted from her bosom. Yes, it stood to reason.

And so, uneasily, the story is laid to rest. As for Pastaran, the world raises not a single protest when, in 1959, some twenty years on, workmen raise their pickaxes and incorporate his grave into the foundations of a third-rate hotel.

Part 1

A Certain Lack of Understanding

Chapter One

Thorns. They are what come to mind whenever I think back to the events of last year. Dull, smooth palm thorns – and then an ape-girl flitting so easily through them. I picture them, and usually sooner or later I end up wondering how I came to be in Pastaran's neck of the woods in the first place, hunting out things called Gugu. My thoughts skip to the train ride, the start of it all, and before I can help it I am in a kind of stupor, reliving the whole episode . . .

The honking snores of the youths were boxing me in. As I sweated the night out, each one of these snorers was an extra degree of heat. The air of the carriage was a blanket stitched tightly around me. I wanted to peel it away with the wet bedsheets and take a stroll. But mine was the uppermost bunk. If I lifted my head an inch through the dark my nose met the hot paintwork of the ceiling.

It was my cousin Alex who had told me about him, this man I was going to meet the next day. Theodore Hull, now getting on a bit, had knocked about South-east Asia for years and in the war had survived on numerous occasions when he shouldn't have. We had something in common, Alex had said, and I took him to mean our time spent in jungles. I would find him good company, he continued. He had been a name in the spice trade. He was a man of action, and knew every ripple of the South China Seas. What is more, Theodore, of no fixed abode, was a thinker, and had his own thoughts on the nature of man's existence. An understanding, a realisation, an insight – call it what you want. *I* called it an understanding. It had come to him as he lay in prison. It was only a *personal* understanding, Theodore apparently insisted, a little guiding lantern which had helped him along through life. 'What was it?' I hear you ask. I did not know. And finding out was another good reason for making this detour from my expedition to New Guinea – suffering like this in a broiling train.

So, I had written to him, care of his Penang haunt, explaining that I was an explorer likely to be dropping by George Town, Penang, for a visa stamp – this November and, if he chanced to be in Malaysia, could I pay him a visit?

'Dear Benedict Allen,' Theodore had replied, 'With regret, must explain that aged widowed sister-in-law from France with her already aging son Roderick have recently informed me by 'phone from Marseilles of their fixed intention almost immediately to flop upon me (or should I say "grace this small establishment"?) for an unspecified period. Hence, as my Penang abode is a doll's house, I shall be unable to put you up. I shall of course be delighted to meet you and suggest nearby accommodation at any rate you may fancy from around 12 bucks (Malaysian) a night to as high as you like to go . . .' The keys of his typewriter had been punched so hard that the 'o's had dropped out of the paper.

The train jolted to a halt. The guardsmen walked outside, whistling and swinging their hand lanterns. The scent of flowers drifted in through the window slits. The honey odour was lost in diesel as we rattled on again. Lying in the wet bunk of a red train, the air tight, the night black, I was thinking: Solitary confinement; week after week, waiting for his execution. Was the air this thick and black in Hull's prison cell? Probably it was worse.

A long time later there was a shudder – one worse than usual. I opened my eyes and it was daylight. Malays, fresh-eyed from a good night's sleep, were tackling shirt buttons, perching on the lower bunks as they wriggled into their underpants. This must be Kuala Lumpur. I would have to change trains for Penang. First I ran to the market. It might have been sleeping pills that I was after but I was thinking of a gift for this man Hull. Flower-sellers sat in the road twining blooms into wreaths with the help of their toes. Apothecaries dispensed dried-snake cure-alls; tea was served by the glass; under the level sunlight, mosque roofs glowed molten. So this was Malaysia. This morning she had a breeze that sucked on your skin, leaving it not cooled but hot and wet.

Being an expatriate, Theodore would like a little something from the UK – a packet of PG Tips, a bar of Lux, a jar of Marmite. The market offered blue crabs which clicked and bubbled, turtles which blinked and cried in silence as they dried, and scared finches hopping to death in bamboo cages. The wares were displayed on trestle tables, around which the Chinese housewives peered and mulled, scuffing their sandals along the alleyway of crunchy seashells. Over the gutters – flowing red – whiskered fish were being split on logs by girls with slender, quick hands.

I picked out two fish at random. The girl was worried by my choice, but the fish looked quite dead enough for me. I opened my book to try out some Malay. The twang of the language – it seemed to be full of 'k's and 'j's and 'g's – cried out, like a challenge. I spoke slowly and clearly. This was child's play! The Chinese girl looked a little sadly at me. She said thank-you in English and parcel-wrapped the fish corpses in newspaper. Catfish – not likely to be a very welcome present but, as I always say, it's the thought that counts.

Almost on time, my train lurched off through the corrugated shacks. This was November, and I was fresh from a blustery England. There were still chips of Hampshire clay in the treads of my shoes. After autumn's speeding clouds and soggy leaves, peninsular Malaysia was too bright and cooked. However, I guessed the scenery was dry even for here. And, what with the weight of this morning's air, the Malaysians must be expecting their own rains. Their garden fruits looked cracked and buckled in, the grasses were dirty whites and burnt yellows, the ponds sepia, shrunken and bubbling. The cows looked as if they had died from the heat – you couldn't blame them – and been cemented into the landscape, just as they stood, by quick-drying mud.

This was the singing midday and my saliva was gritty and thick, my front teeth sticky. I was gazing through the grey dirt-spots on the window, to the sunburnt fields dotted with bent-over men. The punching heat of the carriage had taken on a smell like that of a harbour at low water, only more so, as if a putrid carcass had rolled in on the last tide. I looked around at the screwed-up faces of the other passengers. Their eyes were sharp and accusatory. Some were fixed on me; most were on my baggage.

But I was trying to think. A young man on death row: the urine-tasting air, the algal walls, the Japanese boots squawking down the corridor, the reek of one's own excreta, flies fighting over it. He does not have a release date, but it is no matter. His mind is serene. Why? Because he's got his understanding, I said to myself, prising open a window, and sliding the catfish outside. They skated away and nestled into the track-side plastic litter.

The last daylight was furry and blunt. We were coming into Butterworth station, opposite the island of Penang. In a few moments I was aboard the ferry, staring across the black water towards the winking lights. I remembered another thing about Theodore. By all accounts he was a mite eccentric. For instance, according to Cousin Alex, drinking at the club late one evening he had let slip that he was convinced of the existence of monkey-men! You could not help but chuckle. However, there was obviously a touch of exaggeration on Alex's part. No one believed in monkey-men.

Chapter Two

'Mr Theodore Hull?' Ahead, under the lights of the disembarkation point, there was fast approaching a tall, rectangular form with resolute shoulders and a brazened head with hair which flowed from the parting in three crested waves. The trishaw men, who a moment ago had been badgering me for custom, were stepping back to allow the figure more room, though he was ten paces away.

'Benedict? My dear chap! Splendid. Fling your kit in the boot.' He had a solidly built face with a well-laid jaw foundation and eager eyes set in firm flesh. He steered me towards the rear of a battered yellow car. 'The Old Crate' he called it. It was certainly old; dying was nearer the mark. 'I'll take you along to your accommodation after we've had some refreshment. The relatives haven't turned up. There's just my young Chinese housekeeper Ling and his charming wife Jo – but you'll be at the Low Tide Hotel. More spacious. It's a modest pub right on the beach. All fixed up.'

I creaked open the car door. 'Don't bother with the seat belt – it's bust.' We accelerated away and a motorcyclist cut across without signalling. Theodore swerved, then bawled out of the window, 'Turn ya lantern on!' We wove between the steaming noodle-stalls and dodged trishaw drivers with legs so mat from dust that they did not reflect back the light. Motorcyclists swarmed at us like flying ants – helmets gave them domed, expressionless heads and their loose shirts and sarongs flapped like wings. George Town was scented with street-shrine joss-sticks and you could hear the smacking of Chinese men's lips over soup-bowls. Oil crackled on an Indian street stove. 'Oh damn! Oh damn!' came a sad voice from the night, 'I have bloody burnt my fingers again.'

Theodore was saying, 'And how are things in Britain? Still America's unsinkable aircraft-carrier? Can't say I like the sound of this Thatcher chap.'

'Well, I spend a lot of time abroad, as you know, off in the jungle – though there's less and less of it.'

'Ha! There's plenty more howling forest yet. But I know what you mean. Take some of these fundamentalist missionaries. I hear from your cousin Alex that you met them in the Amazon. From the Mid-West, I'll bet.'

'Yes, as it happens.'

'Why don't they stay there, where they say they're the Moral Majority? Before long they'll be like the Ku Klux Klan.' He blunted his words of any offensive edge by inserting a wry chuckle. Then he finished, 'Piss on you if you're not white!'

'I suppose they think they're on a divine crusade.'

'Religious crusades do so often seem to end in blood, don't they?'

Then we were witnesses to a tragedy. The car that was two vehicles ahead ploughed into an oncoming motorcyclist, burying him and his female pillion in its radiator. The traffic quickly congealed. Theodore sighed grimly. After a moment, he slowly pulled the car on to the grass verge. Dodging pedestrians, we continued along the pavement. 'See the motorcyclist?' said Theodore.

'Really only the dented bumper, and a girl's white sandal on the road.'

'If you look in the papers tomorrow you'll see the motorcyclist was Chinese. Dead certain. Poor chap.' Theodore drew his head back, his chest up, and clamped his hands higher on the wheel, as if bracing himself to contain something that was welling inside. 'The Chinese nature is to flow like a liquid, a supreme fluid. Any crack, and they'll slip through, seeking to advance. It's their extraordinary pedigree.'

'Pedigree?'

'For centuries the Chinese were cock of the dung heap – way ahead of the West. Still are. And they reached that prime place after millennia of striving with every toe-hold, every finger-hold. Their ability is phenomenal. Would beat Jewish chaps at business any day. And—' We thumped off the pavement, and were back on the road. 'I say, Benedict, would you mind awfully if I stopped to buy some shoes?'

'Of course not, if that's what you want to do.' It seemed a batty thing to do just now, but perhaps he wanted them for the club we were heading for. It was a great shame I had not bothered to sew up the holes in my trousers. The knees were a disgrace.

We pulled in. 'My only passable pair of shoes were borrowed from my doorstep this morning. Not by a Chinese – in their eyes it would be unlucky. Not by an Indian because the shoes were fussy ones and not so much to their liking. You know, pansy buckles.'

'Who was it then?'

'A Malay. Their atoll heritage. Wonderful. Everything was shared on their ancestral islands – Polynesia. Fortunately the trait is still very strong in them. You know, I've such a soft spot for the Malays. Always will have – and not just because we've got the same taste in shoes.'

Afterwards, we parked at the club. 'Shouldn't we lock it?' I asked, polishing my shoes alternately on the calves of my trousers. 'I mean, there's a shifty-looking boy skulking in the shadows over there.'

Theodore yelled, '*S'lamat sore!*'

The Indian's very black face split open, white teeth marking a grin out from the night. '*S'lamat sore*, Mr Hull, sir.'

Theodore said that the boy's father had been much the same – a skinny lad with scabby elbows and toes, he must mean – and he had persuaded him to attend school. The offspring, like a ghost of Theodore's past, loomed forward – he smelt of curry, but the yellow on him was street dirt. He unfurled his shirt cuff and briskly rubbed the windscreen. In the dark there was no practical point – it was a gesture of affection.

I wondered, Who is this man, of ancient English stock, named, Alex had said, after some ancestral settler of Britain's shores? This man who, in the war, found inner completeness in a stuffy tropical prison?

Theodore was taking the steps – he did it at a lumbering run, parting the air ahead with his stick. 'Come along!'

A wall of cold hit us. 'Ow!' I said. Suddenly there seemed to be a real danger of frostbite.

'Air conditioning. It's a modern gadget.'

'I've encountered it before, actually.'

'A man of the world,' said Theodore. He laughed: 'Aaaaaa!', a soft gasp through half-clenched teeth. 'Benedict, we're going to have many a good time together! And how I'm longing to hear your jungle tales! Perhaps we'll even get around to mulling over a couple of my ideas.'

'Ideas?' But he was busy finding his spectacles for the register.

Theodore hung his stick on the lip of the desk and spread his hands across the page. 'An old man's writing,' he said as he signed me in with looping, extravagant but disciplined sweeps. There was poignancy in the remark, and it lingered a bit in the air-conditioned air. But the laugh was quick to follow. 'Aaaaaa!' He charged onward, waving his stick. 'Hurry along!'

'Am I dressed all right?' I turned my knees inward to hide the holes.

'My dear fellow, don't concern yourself. The club rules are that you're not allowed into the dining room unless you wear a tie and socks. That's all they worry about. If you've got *them* on you can walk in there starkers.'

Apparently, if we now failed the inspection of the crisp-suited Malay at the stairfoot we would have to go up the back stairs to the smaller room – the children's room, Theodore called it. But the manager bowed, and Theodore bowed back. The Malay flagged his hand at the front stairs and led the way, taking smart, military strides up the steps. 'Everybody here is a gentleman,' said Theodore as we tagged on behind. 'Strikes me every year I'm here. None of those weak-kneed fellows from Milton Keynes who don't even know how to say "*S'lamat sore*".'

We ascended through the dry cool, brushing by a sequence of photos of trees and rocks, artistic statements in black and white. Theodore said, as we climbed, 'Bless 'em, they don't just cool us, they've also put in smoked glass so everyone can peer out of the windows in the searing noon and imagine that outside it's as mild as sunrise.'

As we passed under a geometric creation in metal, glinting overhead like a thousand guillotine blades, Theodore paused to say, 'My feeling is that this is Malaysia, not Britain, and that's just the way it should be. Who are ex-patriates to come here, puff themselves up, and demand decor according to Kensington's latest? It's tantamount to saying "*We're* better than you bums." Such talk is worse than shark's shit. Do you know shark's shit?'

'No, not all that well.'

'It's heavy, Benedict. Very heavy. Hardly ever stirs – sits there, the lowest of the low on the sea bed. No. Even if for some reason my younger Malaysian chums one day chose to decorate the walls like an army Naafi, that's their right. If they wanted it dressed up like a whoreshop, I'd say "Good for them!"' Theodore continued the climb. 'Fortunately, as it happens, they don't.' At the top of the stairs he said, 'Damn it, look around you. This is exciting, don't you think?' We were looking at a dining room, but Theodore was talking like a climber who had grappled his way up to the roof of the world.

'Lovely,' I said. 'Where shall we sit?'

Theodore did not move. He said, 'I could go on about it for hours.'

Granted, there was no hint of musak, of guests who smoked in each other's faces, of surly waiters, of butter in silver packets. However, when all was said and done, this *was* only a restaurant.

'What is it you see, you giant fellow?'

I was the only possible giant here – six foot four – but I looked to check that Theodore was talking to me. He was. I tried to be more intelligent. Malays occupied most tables, but there were also Chinese and Europeans – the whole lot suit-clad, neat, cultivated in Western ways. They dabbed their lips carefully with linen napkins; occasionally they clicked open briefcases, shuffled papers, berated the dollar rate. The Europeans among them were not old-timers, staying on, but sallow youths, thicker-boned than the locals from their milk diet. *They* tutted about the dollar too.

'Now. What do you see?'

'Well, it's a restaurant. Very nice too. About four stars.'

'Actually . . .'

I saw that the menus were housed in purple folders with modest tassles and a fur like antler felt. 'Five?'

'What I'm getting at is this: here we have the rapidly advancing unification of humanity. Only one fragment of it, I grant you. But you can see it. Unification is the watchword. It's happening now, right under our feet.'

I looked down at my unpolished shoes, and then at Theodore's new pair. This was all above me. Hell's bells, I had not slept a wink the previous night and was not on his wavelength.

As Theodore swayed through the room, the young Brits – apparently financiers on their two-year South-east Asia stint – looked up from their lobsters and salads and lost the threads of their conversations. As those along our route pulled in their chairs they must have wondered what an old man was doing out here, so far from home. Maybe it was a good question.

Here I was settling down to eat lavishly with a genuine seadog – one of life's veterans, you might say. For instance, the 'understanding' that I mentioned: he was meant to be festering, rotting in the foul dew of his cell; instead he was content. Why? Because somehow, in the solitude, he had learnt to redefine his life, adjust to the new, shortened horizons forced on him. This understanding affected him deeply, worked into every sinew a strength of peace.

Each day the guard would kick open the cell door, empty the prisoner's pail and chuck him a fistful of rice on a banana-leaf tray. But, from all Alex had said, Theodore grew indifferent to the possibility that he might never get around to digesting it. Each week came the echoes of the next prisoner being booted out of a neighbouring cell and down the corridor, to death awaiting him in the sunshine.

'My turn now?' he used to ask, as each morning his guard unlocked the door. The guard said yes some days; on others he said no. But always he left the cell laughing, having chucked the prisoner his rice ration. Theodore did not have a sentence to serve. He could not scratch out each day on the wall, dispose of time by dividing it into manageable units. Time was made infinite.

Theodore asked me how Alex was, and then about myself. His eyes were intuitive. 'The world is a comedy to those who think; a tragedy to those who feel.' So said Horace Walpole, and I was measuring Theodore all the time I spoke, musing on which was stronger in him – the thinker or the feeler.

I told him how the wall posters at Singapore railway station had blared warnings of the death penalty to all drug traffickers. Seeing all my jungle equipment, the customs officials had given me the full treatment. Cripes! Suddenly I was a suspect. This could be a classic case of remote border drug-running, and their blood was up. As the policemen fondled their holsters expectantly . . . But I could see that I had put Theodore in mind of something. Was it the prison cell? He leant forward, his right hand throttling a napkin.

'You know, in the 1960s I went to India. Took a coach. Found myself next to a youth with tattoos up the inside of his arms. His hair was in twisted strings. He was wearing a dhoti and singlet – that's all. As the coach climbed through the hills, he turned pale. Started to shiver. I asked him – because I wasn't sure – "Are you a hippy?"

'He said, "Yes, s'pose I am."

' "Are those drug-needle marks up your arms?" By that I meant the marks I'd taken for tattoos.

' "Yes."

' "Well, you shit! You come here from England, and throw yourself on to the streets to live like an Untouchable. What do you think the Indians think of you?"

' "Not much, I suppose."

' "You grimy bastard! Are you ill?" He was yellow now – rattling like an exhaust pipe too.

' "Yes, I've got hepatitis. The government's chucked me out."

' "God! Well, you take these, you shit." ' Theodore mimed whipping off his shoes. ' "And this." ' His shirt. ' "And these." ' His spare trousers. ' "I don't care what you do with yourself, but I can't let you die. Get back to Britain and pull yourself together. If you want to return the clothes" – and they were damn good – "here's my card. Send them to the East India Club." I didn't hear, and didn't hear. Didn't expect to. Then after eighteen months, they came. And a note. "I made a mistake. You showed me my error. No one else ever tried . . ." ' Theodore suddenly smacked the table and exclaimed, 'Jiminy cricket, what a business!' Nearby, someone upset their wine.

'What a business,' I murmured. The man who was shown the error of his ways was a junkie, and that was how the story had been prompted by my trafficking tale, but Theodore was getting at something altogether different. I could not fathom it.

We dug into our fried rice. I said, 'I've been dying – er, longing – to ask. This contentment you discovered in prison. I'm not sure how exactly you came to be captured – perhaps we'll get on to it later? – but there you were, under a heavy sentence ...' I went on gingerly, '... death in fact, and from what I gather you learnt not to mind your imprisonment one iota.'

'It was rather wonderful, in a strange way. But don't let's put a damper on the proceedings, harping on about the past. The future – that's what's in front of us. Here – another drink.'

'Wonderful, you say?'

'Well, there it is ...'

Where was what? He had not answered the question. Here was someone caught by the enemy's advance, condemned as a spy. Escape? Not a hope. Where in Sumatra would a nude Briton run to? Each day when the warder undid the lock and the door threw in light: 'My turn now?' After the clap of the cell door he would be back to awaiting death once more; and to the business of adjusting to his own company. Solitary confinement means removal from distractions, utter confrontation with yourself – no hiding place for the mind or soul.

Theodore said, 'The war was not about heroics. I rather think heroes might not exist. Just people doing their best. There were tears, misery, the occasional good laugh. Even the odd insight – that's what I had. A modest glimmer of something special.'

'And this glimmer – what I term your understanding – can you tell me what it is, in one word?'

'In one word? You mean what it was that lifted my soul out of that place and clean away? Wrapped me up in peace, embalmed me in it? No, I don't know that I can.' He was carefully placing both hands palm downwards on the table. 'But this other thing that I was getting at before: I've great faith in humanity. Expectations of it, I mean. Jesus, Mohammed, Buddha – they all had it right. Some of their supporters might have gone astray somewhat, but mankind will knit together, form something higher.' He ended, triumphantly, hands taking to flight, 'From the unwashed masses of the past, great things will come.'

The room was silent. How long had everyone been listening? They were well tuned in now, waiting for the next instalment. But Theodore said, 'Now, what are you having for pudding?'

I said, 'And does this tie in to your prison insight?'

'Benedict, what a gentleman – do you really want to hear more?' I said yes. But he did not explain about the understanding. Instead, he said enthusiastically, 'The way I see things, if we don't, if we don't continue rising from our animal state, we're done for. We will squabble a final time and exterminate ourselves. Because we can't yet escape this small planet of ours . . .' He delivered these lines with panache, no grandeur. 'Our earth,' he mused fondly, 'this little dinghy in the eternal sea and space of time . . .'

I wanted him to keep going. But Theodore said, 'Now, your pudding . . .' I had a peach melba, and the thought occurred to me: supposing, by some strange, perhaps mad, rearrangement of scientific facts, Theodore has incorporated in his personal vision of the world a belief in monkey-men – the ones that Cousin Alex mentioned. Back in England I had pricked up my ears. It had been a charming idea: a grown-up who believed in monkey-men! But now the notion was like a pesky fly, polluting with its grubby proboscis everything Theodore had said. I could not take him seriously. Any minute now he might drop into the conversation that there were sub-hominids in these parts. Yes, here, he would confide. Living locally. Just down the road. Take the first left and it's the third house along.

'In a minute I'll take you to your hotel. You must be dog-tired.'

'Yes, I am feeling tired, rather suddenly.'

'Of course, you'll have a drink first.'

I protected my glass with both hands. 'But we've been drinking all evening!'

'I'd be very disappointed in you . . .'

The fly needed swatting. Best to approach the subject carefully: if he really did believe in a modern Missing Link, he would have been laughed at about it rather a lot. 'Ever hear interesting folklore over the years? I mean, there must be loads of things waiting to be discovered – if one grubs about in the jungle.' He looked blank. I helped him. 'You know, *things* in the trees . . .'

'Depends what you mean by—' Theodore stopped.

'Yes?' He lowered his spoon and its pineapple load.

'Sir!' It was a voice from behind me – a voice from the old man's past. I know now that when you went out on the town with Hull this was what you had to expect. It was the same right up and down the peninsula. They came flooding in, spirits of times gone – banana-boat skivvies, drunken pirates, biscuit-shop proprietors, sewage-cart men, icecream vendors, itinerant oil-loggers. They came up to say hello, and they left a card, every one of them.

This caller was an Indian in a sober suit. 'Well, well . . .' Theodore was returning the greeting more with his eyes – as bright now as a child's – than with words. He used an arm to prop himself up on the table. 'How very good it is to see you after all these years! And may I now introduce my friend Mr Benedict Allen, an explorer who has agreed to look my thesis over.'

The Indian forgot to say 'How do you do.' He blurted out, 'You're taking on the thesis?'

I was confused. 'I don't think—'

'But you are so generous with your time.' The Indian swiftly slipped his hand into and out of mine as if posting a letter. 'Please take my card, Mr Allen. And if you are ever in need of my services please, you must be sure to pop in.'

The card read: 'Mr Rajiv Parnella, Advocates and Solicitors, Bombay.' But I was thinking: Thesis? What thesis?

The Indian was suddenly gone.

Theodore exclaimed, 'Now, where were we . . . ? I'm quite lost. But the main thing is that you are here. You'll be staying for a few days? Have another drink to round off the meal – ya can't fly on one wing.'

Soon I needed to visit the gents. Quite a while later, as I took my place again, Theodore said, 'You know, at my age when you go is academic.'

'To the loo?'

'To heaven. The firmament – you were asking about this matter that you are generous enough to call my understanding . . . It's selfish wondering about your own end, but it must be faced. I'm in the firing line all right.'

'Well . . .' It had to be faced. He was at least eighty years old.

'In line for promotion. Ready to be miffed.'

'You must have the stamina of an ox.'

'Aaaaaa! If anything I'm an orange dwarf!'

'An . . . ?'

'The last phase of the sun. An orange dwarf.' He was grinning, and his face was full of light, so I felt I could laugh. But I was uncertain: he was leading up to something and I was not sure that I was going to grasp it.

'Old Giant, I've told you I have my thesis. Well, if the hypothesis is proved right, then it will rock the world, and, bang! just like an orange dwarf, I'll expire with an explosion!' I was open-mouthed. The whole dining room was open-mouthed. But Theodore was uncomfortable with the weight I was giving his words. He dismissed them. 'Ha! Just the croakings of a daft old bird. Here, you're being very slow with your drink – but that's all right, each one at his own pace. Will you join me in another?'

At last we were out of town, heading through suburbs, a smiling skull on a signpost telling us about the treacherous road bends.

'I'm looking forward to tomorrow. And our discussion.'

'Our discussion?'

'Or should I say debate? Depends on how you take to my hypothesis. But only if you can spare the time.' We slowed to turn into the drive of the Low Tide Hotel. 'I'll let you have a good night's sleep. Pick you up at ten.'

I got out. The breeze was salty and I could hear the sighing of waves on the beach. I wondered how expensive the hotel was. Theodore did not even need to do a three-point turn. He swung the car round and waited for a gap in the main-road traffic. I went up to him. The road tarmac had bubbled in the heat. Sticky blobs spat and popped under my shoes. Theodore was prodding at the accelerator, rhythmically tempering his frustration as the cars ripped by. 'Doesn't do any good to buck against the tide.'

'Thanks again for the evening,' I said. 'I did enjoy our natter.'

'We haven't talked about your adventures yet. Ling and Jo are dying to hear the Amazon stories. You had to eat your dog, so Alex said.'

'Yes, my canoe capsized and I lost all my supplies. Had to live off berries and the juicier insects. That is, until Cashoe turned up. Cashoe was the dog.'

'You poor chap.'

'Well, you've been through worse.'

Theodore saw a space in the traffic. 'You must have been desperate,' he said, as he lunged into the road. The voice tailed from the window, 'because dog meat is bloody stringy, I find. On the whole.'

'Do you?' I shouted.

'Oh yes.' His voice tapered to me from the stream of traffic. 'Worse than cat even.'

That night I lay listening to the waves uncurling. I got up to look at them and at the mainland behind, a foamy spread of sparking, duelling car lamps. I could not sleep. I was sad for Theodore. He had some vision of the future and, let's be sensible, whatever it was, it was not compatible with any belief in monkey-men. In the late marvellous pipedream, to over myself, and thought, Even so, who expired with an explosion. threw a sheet fully have as an epitaph: *Like an oran*

Chapter Three

As I got up, the early sunlight was filtering across the water. I had a lemonade at the bar, which was shaded by trees with leaves like piebald cowhide. Each time one of them fell to the ground with a slap, it was booted out of sight from between the metal tables by the barman. I watched the sun rise out of the low slab of mainland and enjoyed the lick of the off-water breeze.

The terrace was just above the storm tide-mark, and grubby sand led down to surf which was not white but caramel. The water was cloudy with something, and it looked as if the something was unhealthy. Pity; I would have liked a dip. Two blonde women came up. They were tall, thinly fleshed, angular-limbed. One of them told me she was called Belinda; then she plunged into the brown water. Once in a while I waved, and once in a while their beach ball came in my direction and I put down my lemonade and tossed it back.

'Come on in! The water's lovely,' called Belinda. The girls were Australians – two parts of a Qantas flight crew.

'The water might be. It's the stuff floating in it that I'm worried about.'

'The jellyfish?'

'And those as well.'

'Spoilsport!'

'I'll help you both rub down afterwards,' I said heartily. Belinda had eyes that dodged mine. It might have been coyness, but I decided it was a game – like her bikini top, a little device which provided about as much restraint as an elastic band. As she leapt through the surf, cleaving it with her hands, it looked as if it was about to snap.

Meanwhile, ... of absorbed in astrology – not my subject. Was there actually a type of ... ... called an 'orange dwarf'? A red giant might implode or explode – bu ... lled ... was not called an orange dwarf, it was a supernova. Theodore migh ... was not called an orange dwarf, it was was just a type of condensed star. ... ant a *white* dwarf, but that surely ... ... in—

'Can I have some of yer juice?' Belinda's voice slammed into my thoughts. She was standing over my table, water surging in sheets down her belly.

'What? Oh, the lemon. Right,' I said. Belinda's throat arched towards the sky. Water flipped from her elbow as she tipped the glass back, her armpit opening to expose the smooth, fluted recess. 'See more of yer,' she said, and ran to her room.

'And more of you too,' I said.

'My God, she's beautiful,' said Theodore, arriving in time to see her bottom bounce away.

'A Qantas airline hostess,' I said.

'Then in no time she'll be swept up by a Qantas airline captain.'

Theodore took me along to the Swimming Club. Hong Kong, Jakarta, Kuala Lumpur – wherever he happened to be residing, he was always sure to search out a pool. He would visit it like a shrine at dawn, and sit there by the edge, happy just to be near water.

'It's the heat, dear chap,' he said to me from a deckchair, after I had sunk at the deep end with cramp, having tried to overtake a retired Gurkha officer. 'Later you'll have a reviving drink.'

The Major said, 'The first drink is always the best of the day,' and began accelerating. He wore a little cloth hat over his bald spot during the breaststroke. He had once led a gallant charge at Monte Cassino, Theodore told me, under the showers. While leading his charge, he had turned to urge his men on and had been shot in the back.

We lobbed the soap backwards and forwards, and I thought how incredibly well fastened together were the physical components that made up Theodore. He was in his eighties, and his muscles were as tight as hemp rope. A haze of silver body hair, but none of the usual aged man's rings of tired belly flesh. I knew the fastest and furthest of jungle marches, could do over a hundred press-ups if called to – but beside Theodore I felt a little like a wimp.

This club's bar was designed like a liner's passenger deck. It hung right over the sea, and you could feel seasick if you leant over the railings. As well as the salty breeze it had the panelling, the varnished handrails, roll-up wood blinds to keep the 'spindrift' out, and port and starboard lights behind the bar, either side of the lifebelts. But times change. Though the floorboards were still kept squeaky with polish, the squeak was not as fine as it had been. And Theodore said you did not want to come here in the evenings sometimes because, God bless 'em, they had organised 'a bloody jigajig'.

'Ah, a disco.'

As we glanced through the British newspapers, the Major cried out that his Honkers and Shankers were causing him great pain. Before I could express sympathy, Theodore said, 'Hong Kong and Shanghai Bank. Plays the world money markets. Not one of my skills – devil of a pity.'

The old soldier introduced the lad who was with him – a Nepalese boy, the grandson of his batman. He was called Gun – short for Gunbahadur or something along those lines. Sometimes, Theodore said, when you thought you saw Gun skipping along behind the Major it was actually a smaller Nepalese protégé. 'Pistol' was what Ling called him.

The Major snatched up a local newspaper, the *Star*, and collapsed into an armchair. 'From what I remember, any minute now dear Dick'll laugh himself silly,' prophesied Theodore. Major Dick let out a rip of laughter, and as he shook he buried himself deeper into the chair. 'It's the cartoons,' said Theodore, folding away the London *Times*. 'Now, you must come to my house – it's full of objects that you'd be interested in. And there's my precious "Hope at Large". Practically an antique now too. It's in the sitting room for the moment – the light's not so bright on it.'

'A watercolour? I love watercolours.'

'I don't follow you.' He took up his wet towel and trunks.

'We'll go downtown now. Get the "Introduction" photocopied. It's sitting patiently in the back of the car. In draft form. Didn't I mention it last night?'

'Not by name.'

'From my *oeuvre*. In my household that's called the family bible it's such a tome.'

'Is it?' I said warily. But I must help the old thing out. 'Well, for what it's worth, I'd love to give it a flick over.'

'You don't know how honoured I'd feel. Just to give an honest opinion. You *might* think it's a load of shit.'

'I'm sure I won't.' Though naturally, I thought, that depends if it mentions anything about monkey-men.

The ailing yellow car shuddered to a halt outside the photocopying shop. 'Looks like it's shut,' I said. 'Lunchtime?'

'Yes, she locks the door and stuffs her face for an hour. But she'll let me in. Though I don't know where on earth we're going to park.' A gangly Chinese stood by the monsoon ditch, rubbing his belly with his fingers.

'Can we park in this space?'

'Wah?' The boy began chewing into a thumbnail.

Theodore turned to me and said, 'Gormless bum.' Out of the window he said, 'We – here – park – can?'

'Yeh, yeh. Can.'

'Good-o!' Theodore said, backing the car up. 'Then we are hotsie-totsie. I'll just get the car's arse stuck in. There. Right. Hand me my stick, there's a good fellow.' He slammed the door, and the car rocked. 'Won't be a jiffy.' He skipped over the ditch, with its scum of greasy rainbow whorls and its black water which burped and emitted a steam that smelt like yesterday's Kuala Lumpan catfish.

The sun came down in a vertical blaze. The trishaw drivers were slowing. They had opened their paper sunshades. Some had parked and had their legs resting up – fat, veined calves, gristly ankles, dusty feet. A blue bus slowed to drop off a hunchback. The conductress, in her fresh white shirt, stood at the exit enjoying the breeze. As the hunchback made his flying jump, she clanged her ticket clipper on a handrail, and the bus picked up to cruising speed.

'Well, here it is. Just a few introductory pages. Cast your eyes over it and see what you think.'

'Great. I'll look forward to a good read.' I looked at the reams of dull type doubtfully. 'Back at the hotel.'

'All clear astern?' We pulled out. Theodore drove from right back in his seat, but keeping his hands alert and high on the steering wheel. The sun slanted down on the red forearm hair and freckles. We nudged through the cyclists and past two members of the old municipal band, wearing plastic topis, one swinging a cornet, the other a drum. Theodore told me that they were Tamils, who were originally sailing chaps – they had been knocking around the region since the Chulia dynasty. He seemed to be giving me a historical tour and judging by our meandering route he was going to great lengths to get it chronological. Outside the museum was a black statue, now with a cap of bird droppings. 'Francis Light. Founder of George Town two hundred years ago. He searched the seas for an island where he could settle to grow strawberries or raspberries. Tied up here. Found the perfect spot on Penang Hill. Got his spade out and began digging them in.'

Now we were winding around crumbling old houses in the Chinese quarter. The cracked plaster balustrades must have been a danger to the beggars sprawled underneath, positioned to show off their disabilities to best advantage.

'Built on the proceeds of opium.'

'That doesn't sound very nice.'

'You see, opium dens were like pubs. People came in for a natter and a quiet sit-down. Opium was only as harmful as tobacco, usually. Cleared your head, soothed your pains – shortened ya life a little maybe.'

Now we were along the seafront by Fort Cornwallis, 'built by the British around 1810 when the French were knocking the stuffing out of us'. It was a raised block with stern walls spiked with cannons and weeds, and – but we were already moving on to the present century. A quick mention of the Chinese Snake Temple, built in 1850 – red and gold, and live snakes around and about – dedicated to the deity Chor Soo Kong, and we were on to the government offices. 'See that splendid rather Germanic structure, the colonnades and monstrous porch? Resplendent guards used to stand there, marvellous chaps. In 1957, at Independence . . .'

We swerved through Penang in an arc that to me looked calculated to end at Theodore's drinks cabinet, out of town. From time to time I glanced at the photocopied sheets. Theodore drove defensively rather than aggressively – swinging to miss a rogue noodle-stall trundling in from the left, or to the right a man taking to the road with three tacky coffins stacked on his head. I was too car-sick to digest much of the 'Introduction', but, skimming through it, there was not a word of monkey-men. Phew! That was all I wanted to know. I said, 'It's a funny thing, but Alex got the idea you believed there are monkey-men in Sumatra.'

'How very strange.'

'Yes! But I must say I'm relieved to hear you confirm that. I thought you might be barmy!'

'Giant, of course you would! Monkey-men! That puts me in mind of Marco Polo. Called in on Sumatra seven centuries ago. Reported that the people of Jambi Province had tails! Should have checked his facts!'

'Ridiculous. Thought as much.'

'Yes, they weren't monkey-men at all.'

'Silly man.'

'Quite so,' Theodore said. 'They weren't *monkey*-men—' He squeezed the steering wheel excitedly. I knew he had not finished, and suddenly my car-sickness was much worse. 'No,' he said. 'More likely *ape*-men.'

'I . . . see,' I said, gripping my seat belt. 'Ape-men . . .'

'Tailless. Makes far more sense.' Theodore put his foot down, and we accelerated fiercely. 'Let's go back home for our afternoon refreshment, shall we?'

Chapter Four

On the sitting-room wall hung a Celeban model of a Portuguese carrack, banana-palm-trunk sails bent under a fair wind. By the cumbersome desk, gnarled like bark in parts, beside a dwarf Buddhist monk who was a lampstand, there was an overbearing cabinet of stinkwood with butterfly keyholes, Javanese leafy legs, and pineapples secreted in its curves. But essentially it was a Chinese room, and you guessed it was going to be as soon as you took off your shoes to enter and noticed above your head a wooden banana leaf splashed with Chinese characters. Dragons flashed from Ching vases, and foxy bats hung along panels of silk. Around you minstrels strolled among hinds, plucking mandolins, while girls were seduced by boys' flutes on rafts becalmed on heron-strewn lakes. From the fish tank squinted golden orfes and fantails, and these looked Chinese too.

We sat in cane chairs with iced whiskies. The overhead fans lifted away our perspiration in quick breaths. Beside a barrel table – chiselled vegetation and infinite mazes – lay Hoi the overweight bulldog. He was panting hoarsely, his belly carefully spread out on the cool tiles, his loyal eyes gazing upwards into Ling's bedroom, from which came deep, snoozing sighs. And, not far off, positioned centrally on an immovable-looking table in a circle of serious, stiff black chairs, was a bound manuscript, a volume a good few inches thick: 'Hope at Large'.

'First of all, the ape-men are called Gugu,' Theodore was saying. 'Now, Gugu come in two varieties. The ginger-coloured mane indicates the friendly Gugu. The one which is always ready to flee. The aggressive bugger you recognise, if he hasn't made it obvious, by the black mane down his neck. He is *quite* a different character. He is big and he is, to be blunt, nasty. You give his land a wide berth; trespassing without a guide through his neck of the woods is not a good idea *at all*, Benedict. Drink up, and I'll get you another.'

'Yes, I could do with a couple more.'

'However, when travelling in Gugu parts, it's always advisable to have something to offer as a present. If you don't, the Kubu will tell you—'

'Excuse me, but what are Kubu – Gugu that talk?'

'Kubu are the aborigines, the men of the forest. Small, curly-haired, button-nosed. There are only pockets of them. Other peoples migrated in later, and pushed them inland. These Kubu from time to time report that they've been pestered by the ape-men, the Gugu. And how! The Gugu gibber and screech all night long. They go on the rampage, they tear at your hut, they rattle every fibre of the forest, drop logs through ya thatch. Pluck away ya house stilts. So the chaps are always sure, when they pass through Gugu land, to put out presents before going to bed.'

'Like putting out milk for a cat at night?' Really, how was I meant to take this seriously?

'Precisely. Here, I'll fill ya glass.' He took the tumbler, but put it down on the table and recounted what Westenenk, a Dutch planter, had said. In Lubuksalasik, in 1910, several coolies and their overseer came across a Large Creature, 'low on its feet, which ran like a man'. It stopped, about to cross their path. 'It was very hairy and it was not an orang-utan; but its face was not like an ordinary man's. It silently and gravely gave the men a disagreeable stare and ran calmly away. The coolies ran faster in the opposite direction.'

And so I was taught about the ape-men,[1] and their Barisan mountain home – I pictured a knobbly line of blue peaks like the scaly crest of a lizard. Mr Van Herwaarden, a settler, recalled in 1923, 'the lower part of its face seemed to end in more of a point than a man's; this brown face was almost hairless, whilst its forehead seemed to be high rather than low. Its eyebrows were the same colour as its hair and were very bushy. The eyes were frankly moving; they were of the darkest colour, very lively, and like human eyes. The nose was broad with fairly large nostrils, but in no way clumsy; it reminded me a little of a Kaffir's. . . .'

The Gugu were, more often than not, small; on that, at least, there was overall agreement. Four foot six was about the usual maximum. But there were notable exceptions. And some folks insisted they walked with backward-pointing feet to confuse anyone audacious enough to track them. When it came to selecting Gugu gifts, plugs of tobacco were a popular choice of expeditioners.

You had to look on it as a tax system, explained the Kubu guides, who knew the Gugu best. Each gift was a toll charge for passage through Gugu territory. For, the forest nomads could tell you, Gugu were really very civil creatures – the black-maned ones included – and never spilt a drop of blood. Over the years, by spying through the branches on their human cousins, the Gugu had copied the peasant custom of chewing tobacco. Judging by the popularity of the narcotic, they were now hooked on it; there were even those who postulated that the Gugu were chain-smokers.

And so the tales of the Gugu had echoed in and out of the Barisan Range for centuries. 'Peasant folklore,' concluded the urban Sumatran. 'Charming, but primitive.'

'The *orang pendek* – little man? A decrepit old gibbon, half-bald with mange, too stiff with arthritis to swing in its trees.' So said one school of scientists. But if it was crippled with arthritis why was it strolling along, chin up, like a man? '*Ah*. Well, actually you'll find that most of these so-called witnesses', countered the learned men, 'are uneducated folk from the sticks.' And how could these yarns of peasants – who did not seem to know the forest fauna as well as you might expect – be trusted? Those tribesmen, the Kubu, it had to be admitted, *did* know the jungle. But they were obviously (you only had to take one look at their wiry little faces) even more simple-minded. Frankly, were *they* fully human?

In 1924 a Dr Dammerman examined a paraffin-wax mould of a 'Gugu print' from upper Palembang and proved that this was an impression of the flat hind feet of the Malayan sun bear. He noted that this species was more habitually bipedal than any other, standing at five foot. Its claws were often retracted – that was why they did not show in prints; the smaller prints discovered were not of Gugu young, as claimed, but of the squarer front paws of the bear. Any other tracks, he postulated, were the smudged amalgam of front and hind feet. The old wisdom that the Gugu pottered along with his feet turned back to front must have derived from the bear's manner of walking with toes turned inwards, thus rendering the little toe particularly conspicuous. What is more, the Dutch had, on occasion, taken pot-shots at what natives exclaimed were Gugu. The corpses turned out to be those of sun bears – balding ones, often. Dammerman had cracked it. The bear explanation was complete – except for one thing: though the bear stood erect, it went down on all fours to walk.

The Dutch had offered a reward to the first person to bring in a Gugu, dead or alive. On 22 May 1932 the *Deli Courant* was in a position to bring its readership the happy news. Sensation! Four natives had shot down a baby *orang pendek*, a little man. The body was being brought in from the back of beyond for analysis. A few days later the newspaper claimed a world exclusive – the first description of a Missing Link. The monkey-man was 16½ inches high; its skin was hairless; the hair on its head was grey. The remains were despatched to the Zoological Museum at Buitenzorg for further scrutiny. On 9 June the *Deli Courant* was pleased to provide its readers with a photo. They could see for themselves: the teeth were mature; it was not, therefore, a human baby. The arms were short, too short to be those of an anthropoid ape. Breaths were held . . .

At last the examination results came back from the boffins. The creature was a langur, a leaf-eating type of monkey. Some character had taken his razor and shaved the animal all over, except its crown, which was left with a pretty tuft. Its cheekbones had been biffed in a bit, its canine teeth sharpened with a file. To complete the monkey's transformation, its nose had been elongated with a splint. In short, it was not a Gugu, it was a fake.

No one would treat the Gugu tales seriously any more. And honestly, it just was not fair, Theodore felt.

'And what light,' I asked him, 'does the Gugu's existence – that is, just supposing they do exist – throw upon our origins?' I did so need that drink that he was meant to be getting.

'Ah! For the answer to that we must turn to the chapter "Concerning the Roots of Humanity".' Theodore put down another empty glass and creaked open 'Hope at Large'. He smoothed his hands over the pages, though they were already very flat and even – perhaps ironed by the same gesture a thousand times before, as he pondered alone in haunts throughout the South China Seas. ' "Concerning the Roots of Humanity" . . .' He put on spectacles, reminded himself briefly, and then removed them, snapping them sharply shut. He pushed the book aside, and began . . .

Theodore, it emerged after another good three-quarters of an hour, did not believe in the currently accepted theory of human evolution. In point of fact, he rejected the notion that we had a common origin at all. No, our ancestors did not diverge from a single pool of humans on the African plains who bred and travelled until they populated the globe. They probably burst on the scene out of wildernesses all over the place.

I listened on, scared for Theodore – what might he say next? By and by, he said, 'I hope you are with me so far, Benedict?'

'Oh yes,' I said. 'Just.'

'Yes, the more one sifts through the evidence, the clearer it becomes that the range of *Homo sapiens* we have here in South-east Asia is essentially home-grown. Let me give you an example,' he continued – but he had already described the physical characteristics of at least a dozen peoples – 'fellows with an easy stride', or 'folks clad with russet hair', or chaps with 'ernest browes'. He said: 'For instance, Benedict, cast your mind over the splendid array of our species inhabiting even now the glorious island of Sumatra.'

I'll try, I thought. But I had been listening for hours now, and some sentences were exhausting enough just taken individually – ape-men coming in two models, one of them nasty and with a black mane?

'The low marshes to the east of the glorious peaks of Kerinci and Seblat, for example, in the basin of the Hari river, form the land of a tribe who, if we are absolutely honest with ourselves, haven't as yet properly blossomed into a fully human state.'

'Blossomed into a fully human state,' I repeated weakly.

'These simple, coy people – Kubu by name – insist that they have lived in their forests for ever and ever, emerging as if by magic from the mists of time . . .'

A gecko fell to the floor. Splat! The stunned lizard's pale face swivelled and peered – eyes as glistening black as caviar. The creature clicked, lunged at a fly – the flash of elastic tongue, the fly gone. Pause. The clattering clicking again. Pattering onwards. Stops. Waits.

And how, wondered Theodore, could humans as primitive as the Kubu have managed the feat of toddling from our common origin in Africa to the jungles of Sumatra on one hand and to the icy sub-antarctic island of Tierra del Fuego on the other? 'Ridiculous!' he said, not waiting for an answer. A far more logical explanation was now available. That the world's races had sprung up from all over the globe. Provided with identical conditions, evolution would pursue an identical course, you see. Ending up with humans . . . 'Ah. Benedict. I see that at last your glass needs a fill-up.'

It had been bone dry for two hours and five minutes. 'Don't worry, I'll do it,' I muttered, making off. 'I'd better bring the bottle in here.' I tottered into the kitchen, smashed some icecubes out of the plastic casing, and spilled an auburn wave into both glasses. 'Your kitchen's very spick and span,' I said, coming back. 'No ants on the floor.'

'That's because of Ling's relentless war. Hates the things.' He tilted the glass into his mouth. 'I don't mind them myself. They're clean, small . . . edible.'

'So let me see if I'm getting the drift of what you're saying. Given the right stimuli, by natural selection a human could evolve from any form of life, say an amoeba, through to an ape and man, cropping up in suitable habitats throughout the world.'

'Right, Benedict.'

'And the independently created hominid forms would sometimes be so identical to each other, having been subject to identical selection pressures, that they could interbreed. Be one species, in fact.'

'Absolutely, you giant boy.'

'So where do the Gugu fit into all this?'

'My dear chap, I can't say I'm not a little disappointed. I thought you had grasped it.'

'I want to get it clear.' Or do I? I thought.

'What I've said so far is mere conjecture. Hypothesis. What I need is proof. What I need, in fact, is to find and study some form of life which is even now in an actual state of emergence into man. Creatures definitely marooned where they originated in a state of what we may call "*cul-de-sac* evolution" ' – Theodore turned to crib from 'Hope at Large' – 'having got lost along the evolutionary path through no fault of their own and so making no progress towards becoming fully fledged humans but instead petering out in dispirited clumps, unknown and unseen in the last lonely hiding places left to them around the globe.'

'The Gugu.'

'The Gugu – or any other of them. The world is brimming with stories: the Lost People of Sri Lanka, the Big-Foot of North America, the East African Agogwe – shares its meals with baboons – the Ivory Coast Hairy Man, the—'

'Abominable Snowman,' I suggested.

'Attaboy! You see? It's as plain as a pikestaff, Benedict.'

Was it? I was sure only that if I had been an archaeologist or ethnologist – or any scientist for that matter – I would have put down my drink and raised a few queries. Quite a number of them actually. Probably the hypothesis had been chucked into the waste-paper bin by intellectuals a thousand times before. However, it must be said that Theodore delivered this antiquated notion with a new, resounding authority. He had been as near to death as anyone, he seemed to be saying, and that told him more than any boffin knew about the origins of life.

'Well, what do you think of "Hope at Large"?'

'It's' – best to be sympathetic, because who was I, who had not been in a death cell, to judge? 'Theodore, it's . . . splendid.'

'You grand man. Only a nobleman of eighteenth-century sensibilities would have been so kind. That's terrific praise coming from you.' But I'm no one, I thought. He added, 'And I glory in it.'

'Forgive me for being cautious, but I must ask: why couldn't these stories just be the product of uneducated peasants' imaginations? I've heard it said that pixies, for instance, were a legend based on the Picts, the tattooed "Scottish" blokes from over Hadrian's wall.'

'That argument simply doesn't wash – not when you've got countless hundreds of these tales. But I agree. We do need that final bit of evidence.' His eyes were burnished, flaring bright, as if he was homing in, a spiralling buzzard.

'And you think Sumatra will provide it for us – I mean for you – in these Gugu?'

'Yes,' he said. He smacked a hand down on his leg. 'Yes!'

'Theodore, you've known about these stories for how long? And you've never tried to nip across the water to Sumatra to investigate?'

'Ah, but I have. Combined it with a nostalgic tour of my better prison camps. And my attempt was foiled. That was seven or so years ago now.'

'What went wrong?'

Old Theodore raised himself to his feet and limped over to the huge stinkwood cabinet. I thought he was going for a fresh icecube, but he curled his fingers over a clutch of flint axes – 'Found them on a hike,' he said, and I visualised him on a pinnacle wearing snow goggles. 'Beautifully smooth, aren't they?' He might have lugged them home in his knapsack as beauty objects, but at the moment they were serving a medicinal purpose, lowering his blood pressure. 'Yes, I might have clinched it. If it hadn't been for Millet.'

'A friend?' It could not be a Kubu guide. A Kubu would be called Anak, or Djumahat or something.

'I was going to go alone. Just potter with the companionship of my stick. Poke about a little. But Ling said I was "getting on". Would you believe it? Anyway, Ling had said I ought to take a friend along. I picked up my pen and winged a message to Ed Millet. Millet, he'd been brought up a barefoot boy, only son of a goldminer. One day his father had a strike. A strike? My God, he struck it rich! It was in South Africa; called it the Ed Mine. Millet inherited it. Had a good income in the old days. Now? Now you couldn't keep a chimneysweep on it. What else can I say about Millet? He had a bad war – minesweeping. Eventually retired to suburban Surrey. Sat waiting to die; bored blind. So I sent him an invitation to come along – see my favourite wartime punishment block, maybe the odd Gugu, I said. I looked upon it as a favour, a rescue from a long wait for the coffin among the old dears in Epsom. Saved from an autumn existence. The expedition, then: what a fiasco! We launched off to Sumatra. Got to Padang. Booked into the Grand Hotel – not so grand, mind you. Padang was pleasant enough. The taxis were pony traps; the ponies wore the dearest of pompoms and bells between their ears – yes, you'll like those, Giant.'

'Actually, I'm not going to Sumatra,' I said. 'Actually.'

'Nor you are. My mistake . . . Now in Padang I had my first stroke of luck. It was at the Catholic cathedral, run by a squad of Italians, the Xaverian mission. Found a priest there – riddled with malaria, a fag from his mouth, and a white frock with a line of buttons from top to bottom hem. What an outfit – like a precious dressing-gown. The fellow was certain: the Gugu existed all right. He gripped my arm like a lunatic.'

'Perhaps he *was* a lunatic.' I had to remain sceptical. It was a way of pretending to myself I was making a thorough critique.

Theodore laughed. 'Yes! Maybe the sun had addled his brain!' He had thought I was joking. 'His cheeks were sunken,' Theodore recalled. 'He was wasted, unshaven. His feet – he wore sandals – were like underdone steaks. His English was lousy – might have been just his illness. However, he *made* me understand. "You must believe me," Father Morini said. "In some regions the stories are everywhere. Behind every bush, every tree. Trace them, trace them! Quick, while they're still here!" He was angry that we couldn't stay to listen to Gugu stories for the whole week. Never mind that, because we had every intention of seeing them face to face for ourselves! So, off we scooted. As the good pastor directed, we boarded a wreck of a bus to Jambi. That's a province over the hills on the east side. We squeezed into the seats – they're designed for dwarfs, I warn you.'

'But I'm not go—'

'And we were off.' Theodore was out of his chair, waving his hands, hurling the words with them. Hoi, the bulldog, left the room. The goldfish swirled, making the water boil, as Theodore recalled the fateful ride in the Sumatran bus: out of baking, fumy Padang, grinding along the forest roads, zigzagging mountain peaks, up and around to Muarabungo. One day, then another, the journey went on. The twisty-turny, jungle-stifled road was no longer a joke for the two ancient men. The bus was moving like a storm-gripped coracle. 'My God, the noise! The mind-searing music – wild screechings from the wireless.' Theodore was roaring gloriously, in full, impassioned flow: axles bounding up and down, thumping into the base of the bus; women retching into their laps and over their screaming children, who were too frightened to notice. The radio switch broke off, and now the electronic music could not be silenced. And, none too soon, the end.

The bus gave an almighty lurch – forward, as if it too felt the need to be sick – and descended into a deep pit. Millet, a tall man, hit the roof. When the bus settled in the dust, there was, Theodore thought, a round dent in it.

Theodore dropped into his chair; an empty glass wrapped in one hand, a flint axe in the other, the fan driving a breeze over his damp forehead, behind him the little carrack in full sail.

'Millet was all right, as things turned out. Though he had to be evacuated in indecent haste. Caught "erysipelas" – don't ask me what it is. That was the end of the jaunt. And I fear it might be already over for the Gugu. The bulldozers have been in, the forests yanked apart. An international development project. Yes, the years have slipped by. I've even had the odd part exchanged – one of my hips is metal.'

'Do you think you'll ever get back there?'

'I just haven't got round to it. But, talking like this, I'm all stirred up again. I'll explode if I don't break my orbit, and get on out there with the evidence.'

'You really shouldn't go alone. I mean not into the forest.' Perhaps no one should, I thought. Forget the black-maned Gugu, didn't Sumatra have tigers?

'Well, if no one volunteers to come with me, I'll have to go alone.'

We could not have Theodore doing anything as rash as that. This man read his bedtime book using Zeiss binoculars. But I was not at all sure that trooping into the jungle with an octogenarian was my cup of tea. I said, into my gin, 'I'll have to think it through.'

'Of course!' said Theodore. 'Naturally.' But his fists were tightening. I worried for the glass in his right hand and the flint axe in his left. 'Well, I'll be going anyway. It's now or never.'

Back at the Low Tide Hotel the Australians' lights were on – a buttery shaft slipped out from under the door, on which hung their little swim-suits. The floorboards were absorbing a puddle and, in the slat of light, I could see cockroaches sniffing it. Reaching my room, I flung off my clothes and lay on the bedsheets. Soon, throaty discords vibrated to me through the wall panels. Poor girls – I pictured the two of them crouching side by side on the bed end, comforting each other, heads forward, hair wetted to the brim of the bowls on their laps, as they emptied themselves of all that morning's bad seawater.

'How about it?' I asked myself, turning on the light to diminish the snuffled breath of the waves, the groans of the girls, the clicking of a cricket trapped this side of the shutters. I rolled to the side of the bed and grabbed the smooth, photocopied sheets – the 'Introduction' to 'Hope at Large'. 'The implication of what I am saying is profound.' I heard Theodore's voice – ragged, controlled, vital. He was now talking about the future, not our human past, and his vision forward was as intense as, this afternoon, it had been backward through time.

'Let me put it like this, dear reader. The hypothesis currently enjoying pride of place in the academic world sees our history as a tale of the spreading of man from a common origin. A distancing of ourselves from our fellows. But the hypothesis that I am presenting to you instead is of creatures, from their separate geneses in similar environments, coming closer and closer as evolution forms each of them into a more and more human state – an ingrowing movement which one day will see a joining of all the world's races, in a magnificent consolidation and unification.'

I read this naked on my bed, the night air brushing the sea outside and rolling in through the window, quashing the hotel's lemon soap odour. Next door, the girls' groaning was less urgent – for them the worst was over.

'All we need is one creature – just one: one yeti, one Gugu, one leprechaun to examine – and then we will see our past and future as they are. That we are components of a huge and mysterious scheme for the bringing together of all our planet's higher thinking, of which we humans are but the vanguard.'

Theodore's vision was too wide for me to cope with. Perhaps I should just quietly leave it here. If it deserved it, some time in the future – a year? a decade? – the hypothesis would again reach the light of day, and then an Oxbridge don might take it in his soft, desktop hands, and examine it with interest.

I read to the end. I might as well. 'Once we have that creature, we will see the truth: that we are the most advanced form of higher thinking, and that we have the most obvious obligation to the humans behind us, those who've more recently appeared, to help them catch up. For they are the slower boats of the fleet that we call humanity. We must throw them a line. Haul them in. This is the responsibility of every single one of us, for only together do we have the strength to reach the horizon, a place where we will be one force that is united, strong and, at last, properly human.'

Humans who were lagging behind the fleet? Needing to be cast a line? What was this?

However, through the night the words 'obligation' and 'responsibility' were a bothersome itch. The irritation spread in a prickly heat, and finally settled on my conscience, an inflammation that just would not go away.

Ling, who had come to know Theodore through his own dabblings in the spice trade, borrowed heavily from Theodore's stock of English phrases, though he weeded out some of the pre-war ones. He called Theodore's Gugu 'little green men' and hissed just thinking about them, gritting his teeth and exposing nearly all of them in an extensive smile. He said, 'Who's for a spot of lunch?' The choice was a bowl of squid at one of the Chinese stalls or a picnic at a cheerful waterfall in the woods. 'You're the guest, Benedict,' said Theodore, 'you choose. Picnic in the countryside, or boiled squid?'

'The picnic,' I said quickly.

'Good-o. We'll have bags of time to make it up the slopes through the forest.' Theodore gamely picked out a sturdier walking-stick.

As Theodore drove, Hoi panted into my ear from the back seat. I raised my collar. For if Hoi had one fault it was his propensity to salivate excessively when excited.

We wound through terraces of nutmeg; all the while I was wondering whether or not chasing Gugu was right for me. Theodore was waiting to hear. Just looking at him, you could think of plenty of reasons for not going to Sumatra. He was a walking advertisement to stay away. It was where he had picked up his hobbling gait – I guessed it was as a railway-camp prisoner during his spell of minefield clearing. Following a quite different explosion, he had been obliged to readjust his damaged nose by hand. 'Wasn't going to have a boxer's hooter for the rest of my life, so squeezed it back up into place with my fingers. Just looks thoroughly drunken now.'

The trail to the waterfall was tremendously steep. Theodore took it at a charge. We followed the long way round, he tackling the thickets head on. The slope was creamy from a morning cloudburst, and we skidded and spun. Theodore heaved himself up through trees with the hook of his walking-stick. Leaves which disturbed his view ahead tended to get speared.

Once we were at the waterfall, Ling, Jo and I dabbled in the cold, smooth shallows. Theodore lobbed himself straight in, sliding through the water like a dolphin, digging his head into the beating cascade. The silver water was springing off him, erupting over him. He was fighting it, and the water was conceding!

I thought: Obligation ... The responsibility of every single one of us ...

We sat on the rocks and dried ourselves. The sun was leaf-filtered and scattered pleasantly over us as we unpacked the mobile drinks cabinet.

It was dusk now, but we had not started down the slope yet. We had all packed up, the ant crews had finished trundling away our crumbs, and the evening insects were ringing. But Theodore was preoccupied, standing alone with his stick, looking out over the island.

'All that was coconut once, with a little lonely track through it. Cattle wandered among the palms. Now they're going to build a colossal bridge to connect us to the mind-harrowing mainland.' He sighed, but was content. 'The world must move on . . .' One hand on his stick, another on his Zeiss binoculars, he breathed deeply, inhaling the last of the sun, the eternal band-saw racket of cicadas. He was gazing far away, perhaps as far as infinity, and all the while standing straighter than Nelson.

I really had to go. Go after his Gugu. I did not want him to fade out without a chance. Anyway, given enough Kubu guides to porter the gin, moments of the adventure might be quite fun.

'I'll sign up,' I said to Theodore.

'My dear boy!'

We agreed I would come back after my proper, imminent New Guinea expedition. The rains favoured mid-year and Theodore's orbit of South-east Asia would not bring him through Penang, which had the nearest airport to the island, until the June after next – 1986.

Ling said to me quietly, as Theodore sped off downhill, 'You can't take the old chap into the forest. He'd conk out – and just for the sake of some diminutive, hairy men.' He was pleading.

'Don't you worry about a thing,' I said, drumming my fingers on my chest, thinking back proudly through the better moments of my exploration career. 'No problem.'

Then Theodore tripped. He careered downhill, initiating a minor landslip. 'Hell!' I said, watching him go. 'What have I taken on?'

Ling shouted, as we chased Theodore. 'Remember what happened to Millet when *he* helped Theodore hunt little green men? Banged his head. He was about your height.'

We picked up Theodore. He was very heavy. Once he had caught his breath – his lungs creaked as they expanded and contracted – I said, 'What, by the way, is erysipelas?'

'Dunno, but Millet looked like the wrath of God when he had it.' Theodore plucked bark crumbs from his scuffed shirt. 'Only one thing saved him. Found a doctor in Bengkulu who gave us some advice.'

'And medicine?'

'No, advice.' He was rucking in the bushes for the walking-stick. 'Told us not to go anywhere near the hospitals! The treatment would be fatal.'

It's a joke, I thought. Only a joke. But I could not help myself. Seeing him wrestle with creepers, socking foliage with his binoculars, I felt faint. It was as if I had been sipping the Low Tide Hotel seawater.

But I was not stupid. Oh no. Immediately before launching out with Theodore in eighteen months, I would call on my cousin Henry, Alex's brother. He was defence attaché in Bangkok, and also a Gurkha colonel who was fond of Borneo. He combined military exercises with his passion for moth-collecting. He would give me a refresher course in this Asian forest! Yes, Cousin Henry would sort me out, all right . . .

Chapter Five

Thank heaven! That must have been Colonel Henry's thought. The last of the week's diplomatic-corps drinks parties was over. Mr Preecha, official driver, delivered the Colonel smoothly through the tall gates of the residences. The maid and cook, laying out the silver in the dining room, heard military footsteps clacking along the corridor tiles outside the flat – and stopped exactly where they were. Then they skipped to the door, drew their small brown feet level and bowed, hands shut tight together, like children in prayer. Colonel Henry returned the courtesy, but lowered his head even further. Then it became clear, as his white tunic strained, that he was reaching down to flick off his stiff black shoes. As they cracked to the lobby floor he was already tugging at the gilt buttons and emptying his pockets of assorted calling cards.

To accomplish his double life – defence attaché and moth-seeker – everything had to be done on the double. So even as the kit was peeled away one girl was padding off to brew his mug of tea and the other was ready to bear away the uniform as and when pieces of it came free. Bludgeoning the carpet pile with his quick Gurkha march, Colonel Henry plucked a rambutan from the fruitbowl with his right hand and tested the hilt of a ceremonial kukri for dust with his left. Definitely manoeuvring towards his bedroom now, he reached for the tea which was chasing him and clapped shut the door with his right heel. The shower hissed, the steam iron sped.

The Ambassador was keeping well out of the way, entertaining me with ambassadorial yarns. 'He was a big chap. Hairy – that's why we called him Boris. But that incident with the lipstick and the chauffeur was the final straw . . .' Such was the calibre of gossip that I had been hoping lay in store. So far, after two large gins, he had revealed only that his telex machine was on the blink.

I was there for my jungle practice. Eighteen months had been and gone. New Guinea's forest had been very interesting – kangaroos bounced through the lowlands, possums wrapped themselves around branches – but the Asian forest was going to be quite a different thing. We were the wrong side of the Wallace Line, ecologists will tell you. *Here*, you did not get possums, you got tigers. I was off with the old man in a fortnight, and I wanted all the practice I could get. However, it now appeared that the Ambassador, here on leave and a keen bird-spotter, was intent on coming along to the jungle too. And Henry had explained, taking me aside, that an ambassador's life was less expendable than ours. This meant that the 'jungle familiarisation' he had thought up for me could now be no more than a stroll.

A *stroll*? I had thought. How would I be able to fend off the Sumatran tigers if my jungle refamiliarisation was a stroll?

The Ambassador, in Thailand on well-earned leave from a neighbouring Asian post, eased back, drawing on his pipe. His forehead was a useful chart of his tension for any casual observer, and giving it a quick look over now I saw that his state was tending towards the neurotic. His eyebrows were squeezed up, snuggling together grimly. 'No telephones, no red tape. This is the life,' he said, trying to let himself go. 'And in the forest it will be just me and the birds.'

'And the moths, sir,' corrected Colonel Henry, running by in a towel, testing with his thumb the blade of a parang.

The Ambassador pulled his pipe-free hand over his chin, on which grew a scrubby copse of grey beard. He smiled graciously. 'And a moth or two, perhaps.' In December he would be retiring to his house in Essex, around which mist nets for unwary birds were craftily pitched – 'I like handling kingfishers best.' The project of the moment was the conversion of his lawn into a bird pond: 'Try and set myself twenty-five wheelbarrows of clay by nightfall.'

I was excited to be meeting a real live ambassador. The drainpipes and guttering of the official residence here in Bangkok were adorned with tangles of barbed wire to discourage assassins. So *this* diplomat almost certainly had a bullet-proof car.

Henry came by under a stack of specimen cases, formalin bottles, pin boxes, setting boards, collapsible swoop nets and whisky flasks – just some of the gear that every moth-man needs. 'Leaving at 05.30,' a muffled voice said. 'Prompt.'

'He means dawn, I suppose,' the Ambassador said. We had another sip or two, and I told him about Theodore and the bad time he had had in the war – about how he had developed a peace of mind, an understanding of the cosmos, and it had helped him pull through.

'Well, what is it?'

'What?'

'This understanding. Sounds like we should all know about it.'

'I never did get to the bottom of it. Quite slipped my mind in the end.'

'Hopeless. How could you forget to follow up something like that?'

'We got talking about his alternative evolutionary hypothesis. And his belief that ape-men inhabit Sumatra.'

'My God.' The Ambassador stared me in the eye for a little while, then went back to his bird book.

At 05.30 hours, prompt, the sky was ruffled in folds of cold mauve. We had cleared the worst of the city before the day's lorries began roaring in with charcoal from yesterday's forests. Buddhist monks, out for alms, floated swathed in saffron through the early blue fumes. The red road dust – 'Thai snow', Cousin Henry called it – began to boil up, and I saw nuns – shaven-headed ladies in what looked like white bedsheets – and a temple roof that burned brighter than the yellow sky. The ditch lilies had grown a toad's skin and were pitched right out of the water, which was a congealed broth of slimy leaves. The rains would come any time, and not a day too soon, to my mind.

The Land Rover rattled along, Mr Preecha at the wheel. The Ambassador sat beside him, occasionally lurching towards the dashboard. At first it looked as if it might be car-sickness, but he was shouting things like 'Plumed egret!', 'Tree-swift!' Then scanning the clouds – just a low-slung haze – 'Long-tailed shrike! See him?' The first bird names had come from him fiercely, but he had eased up and before long his eyebrows became completely unbuckled. 'Rufous-necked hornbill!' he cried.

The Colonel was tapping out a military tattoo on his combat trousers. 'A few Thais died recently from locusts,' he announced, as we sped by a wrinkled man who was picking cautiously at the marsh grass with a twig. 'Six victims? Seven? They were never sure.'

I imagined a shrieking black cloud descending on extended peasant families, the insects mechanically gnawing away the crops and then – the worst kind of nightmare – slowly beginning on the more tender children. Colonel Henry said, 'Locusts bought at the market, that is. They sell everything on the stalls, but these were juicy locusts. Only had to eat a dozen – fat with pesticide.'

Chains of ducks ambled along the roadside to manilla-brown ponds ruled over by a little boy whose head was shaven except for a plaited tail. The face of a giant simmering gold Buddha poked up through the trees. He looked especially meek and noble – the only head under the roaring sun without a hat on. The rice levels were being planted out by slush-splattered men who were putting more effort into the ploughing than the water buffaloes.

'Black-hooded oriole,' said the Ambassador.

Dead dogs lay around in the road. Usually, I learnt, you just drove over them, and tried not to hear the squelch of the meat, and the bones crumpling. We slowed for a dog which was bald, but still on its feet. Its radiator-grill ribs looked about to snap, the skin was so tight. 'That one's got only a few days in him,' said Colonel Henry.

'Fairy-bluebird,' said the Ambassador.

Just after we had dodged a mud-packed man driving a cow along the road with a branch, we took a left. The hills ahead had sheer faces which stared, white and pasty, from the jungle. They looked agonised, the way they were held there, captive, laced up so tight by the creepers. Along here, the far side of another cremated forest, was an undulating block of cooler swathes. The reserve, Huai Kha Khaeng, was up a track of scattering lizards, placid work-elephants, easygoing brooks, flighty jays, flashy bluebirds – 'Indian roller!' – and hurtling dragonflies. The forest dropped back a moment, and we were at the park headquarters – only a line of shacks with a flagpole, and a guest house dwarfed by an unstable tree with climbing pegs up the bottom hundred feet of it.

Next morning, at 05.30 hours, we were kitted out with waterbottles and mess tins. 'Don't want to get desiccation, sir,' Colonel Henry said. 'Victims of that one look nasty. Very nasty indeed.'

'Prunelike,' I explained.

The Ambassador put on his waterproofs to keep his sweat in.

Today our objective was to hike to the ridge – 'the one in the cloud', Henry said. Our two guides were to be Mr Odd and Mr Supakit.

Mr Odd went on ahead, into the greenhouse fug, his rifle held to his shoulder by a strip of frayed cotton with a flowery knot at the stock. The guns were not for rampant wild beasts, as I had been half hoping – for the practice – but for poachers. 'Caught a politician recently,' explained Henry. 'Said he was just out testing his gun sights.'

He stalked up the slope in his camouflage, swiping at small wildlife, terrorising the specimens into bottles, encouraging more of them out of bushes with his jungle-issue army boots. And always with the noblest of intentions. They were destined for museum archives. As well as the moths so dear to him, he was known to have a good eye for ichneumon wasps. 'Maybe new to science, that one,' he said, but before I could look it was locked in its drunken death throes in a bottle labelled '70% alcohol'.

Behind Henry, giving his parang plenty of room, came the Ambassador, hands clenched around his waterbottle, then myself, and Mr Supakit defending our rearguard, casting hopeful glances at his revolver.

As the forest pressed us with its musk odour, I made mental notes. The grove of wild bananas had been trampled by banteng, wild oxen, four or five days ago – as indicated by the black bruising on the shredded stumps. The football-sized dollops of excreta were not grassy enough to be a rhino's, so we knew elephants had been sauntering through.

Henry thwacked what looked like a loose power cable. 'See this liana? Cut it here and here and you can drink from it.'

'Good. Same type as in Brunei,' I said proudly. I was coming up to scratch.

'Some are poisonous,' Henry said, 'but of course, you'll know the difference by heart already.'

'With a bit of luck.'

Colonel Henry stopped what he was doing, wiping his blade on a foolscap-sized leaf. 'Bit of luck?' He seemed to be wondering whether to laugh at a joke.

'Which is the pretty one with a lovely reddish mane on it?'

'Pretty type? Lovely reddish mane?'

'It *has* been five years since my last Asian trip. And these survival tricks *are* so muddly.'

'God,' he said, breaking stiffly into a march. 'No wonder he didn't make it into the Battalion.'

This was meant to be 'managed forest' – opened up for the sake of the larger mammals – black leopard, bos, deer – but many tree crowns were lost to me in a knotted rigging of creepers; leaves of the different stratas bit greedily into the sunlight and by the time it had got all the way down to us, there was hardly any left. Vines were seized by different vines and the strangling figs were getting to grips with most of the trees in sight. The forest was busy. It had no time for us. We were shrouded not just by its immensity, but by its attitude – its impoliteness. Our thoughts were interrupted by its quirky shrieks. We were breathed on, and the forest's breath was thick and old, the essence of a wine that was fruity, mulled and corked.

'Blue magpie, I think.' Now the Ambassador's calls were weaker.

A loop of rubber hosepipe was drooping over the track. It might have been left by the forest workers, but on closer inspection it had red eyes. Most of the snake was milky emerald; it had a give-away smear of orange at the biting end. 'Some sort of adder, is it?' I said, giving its bush a tweak.

'Just a tree viper,' Henry said, pointing at it with his trigger finger. 'Will have a damn good go at you if you disturb it too much.' He lifted the snake's head with a stick and disturbed it too much. The neck, which a moment ago had been baggy, hinting at decadence, thickened out; the diamond head jerked.

'And what if the stick had been your finger?' I asked. The snake was going to do itself a mischief if it struck as hard as that again.

'Two aspirin and two Piriton, and hope for the best.' As Henry played with the snake Mr Supakit fingered his holster. His eyes were intent on the Colonel, not the viper, and he did not look at all sure which one he would aim at if the worst came to the worst.

'Blast!' cried the Ambassador further on, as he tried to focus on a clonking woodpecker. His glasses had steamed over. He was missing all the best wildlife and he spent a lot of useful energy polishing his specs on his wet sleeves.

It was not a good day for the well-thumbed bird bible. He had been hoping to tick off a few rarities, but the narrower the trail, and the higher we rose, the quicker his glasses fogged over. 'White-bellied woodpecker?' he asked weakly. 'Large cuckoo-shrike?' Leeches, as if sensing an easy kill, headed straight for him. 'It's my sweet blood,' the Ambassador said, slogging onward.

'Hold on, sir.' The good Colonel uncapped his specimen tubes and poured his preserving fluid down the Ambassador's creamy legs, leaving the prize wasps – each one a candidate for the museum archives – high and dry. Reluctantly, one by one, the leeches unplugged themselves and sloped off.

Our pauses for the Ambassador became more frequent. Sweat peeled from his red face. I said, coaxing him on, 'Isn't that a racket-tailed drongo?' I was carrying his waterbottle for him and kept it to hand, ready for if he had a seizure. 'Yes,' I said, 'I'm almost *sure* that's a racket-tailed drongo.'

Along the route were palm clusters with leaves that exploded in stars. *Exploded like stars* – I suddenly thought of Theodore: supposing the 'orange dwarf' explodes before time? Now, after eighteen months' wait and with only a week or so to go . . . ? I should have got him to map out the hottest sites for Gugu. The most he had ever told me was: 'All the action is between the mountains of Kerinci and Seblat.' When I had pressed him, he had said, 'No need to bother you with details now. I'll be there with you, after all, won't I, Giant?'

The Ambassador's wheezes were so loud now he was upsetting his birds. A pair of what looked like golden-furred martens stood on hind legs to watch our slow progress up. We cannot have seemed a threatening sight because they did not hide, but scuttled down to meet us halfway, puffing through their noses — 'Puft! Puft!'

Soon they bounded away, and somehow we reached our objective, the forested ridge. Henry, cornering a reluctant stick insect, suggested that the guides open a tin of tuna for lunch, and that I unfasten the Ambassador's leeches.

'Is this expedition of yours a joke?' asked Henry, his arm snaking towards his butterfly net. He was going for a skipper — to me, just another chip of fallen bark.

'Deadly serious, I gather.'

'You gather . . .' Henry whacked down the net, pulled it in and squeezed the skipper to death in his fingers, its thorax crackling loudly. He laid it to rest, reverently, in a casket. 'Sounds a shambles.'

'I've left all the planning to the old man. I'll be there only in a supporting role.'

Henry shook his head. If I had not been his cousin he might have given up on me long ago. 'I'm sure', he said doubtfully, 'he's *compos mentis*. If that's what you say. But even so, you must have a lot of confidence in him.'

'Yes,' I said. 'I suppose I must.'

How much faith did I have in Theodore? Bags of it. From the few details I knew from Alex, he had been through a lot more of life than most. And, having come through the war shining, guided by what I called his understanding, that gave him a right to be listened to by the world. For me that was enough. But had I extended my faith to his evolutionary hypothesis as well? To his Gugu — those lost, short almost-people?

If I had not really known the answer, I did now. I felt no surprise — I did not raise an eyebrow — when Henry pointed and said casually, 'And *those* are your ape-men.'

Two black furry legs were hanging out of the overhead foliage. More gibbons, a cavalcade of them, were up there, jiggling the branches. The body fur was intensely dark, the black shiny faces open, curious, childish. They looked amused by us. Their hands were loose, and drooped limply when not in use. The tail of one ape was caught by the sun, and was burnt by the light into a silhouette of frizzled rope. We stared back. Could they be Gugu? Not according to Theodore, but the gibbons did look very human; it was the way they were pulling sulky adolescent faces, or wiping their brows with their wrists, as if their hands were sticky from cooking in the kitchen.

Up until now I had tried not to think too closely. I had half wanted to believe in the Gugu – as in childhood, despite growing circumstantial evidence, I had clung to a belief in the tooth fairy. Now, before me, was all the evidence needed to shatter that hope. Suddenly I wanted to skip the rest of this nature ramble – inspecting a porcupine quill here, a freckled eggshell there – and go away to have an emergency think.

Colonel Henry said, 'Pity to take the old chap to his death for nothing – especially if he's been through so much already.'

The Ambassador was peering through his glasses. He exclaimed, pointing at a hunched-up gibbon in the far distance. 'I don't believe it!'

'What, sir?' asked Henry.

'Well I never. I never thought . . . In all my born days . . . Well, you know what that is, don't you?' Henry and I stared harder at the gibbon. The Ambassador said, 'It's a . . . it's a crested . . .' He squinted through his steamed-up lenses again. 'I wonder if I can give my book a tick?' He whirled the sodden bible out of his kagoule. 'A crested . . . You know, if that is what I think it is, then if I never see another bird in Thailand, my trip will have been worthwhile.'

He raised his pencil, as he gave the crested a final look over, lifting himself on to his toes. The gibbon pulled itself up for a clearer view of the Ambassador. For a moment both stared, apparently shocked by the moment of personal focus and at finding each other possessed of a sort of intelligence. Next thing, they both spun their heads away in disgust. The gibbon curled off through the branches. The Ambassador looked at his pencil. 'Perhaps I'll leave that one,' he said.

There was not much more to Colonel Henry's jungle-familiarisation course. It had lasted a week, and I felt less prepared than at the outset. And now we learnt from Bangkok that the British Embassy had had an urgent message for me from a Mr Theodore Hull. 'Just a few words of encouragement: Giant, you mad fellow! ATTABOY! Don't ring until arrival. Phoning costs the bloody EARTH. It'll be great to discuss plans; and best of all to put them into action.'

The orange dwarf, then, had not exploded. And, if he had lasted out this long, he would last a few more days. Nothing would stop him getting to inner Sumatra this time, it seemed. Only myself.

I required my emergency think. Henry dropped me off on the Bangkok road. I struck north, to the town of Chiang Mai, and dawdled in temple gardens. Then, the second morning, I received an offer from an ex-monk: a brief repose in the tribal hills.

Some temples had truths pinned to the trees – 'Time is the ultimate destroyer of everything' – but in this temple there were empty trees which shaded little boy novices with rumbling tummies. As well as having to learn to do without food until the evening alms – 'Sir, is diffy-cult' – they practised folding their robes, and slumped together, sleepily drawing ballpoint tattoos on each other's arms. Then ex-monk Simkiat sidled up, plucking his odd facial hairs out, one by one, between two coins.

Simkiat had been a teacher as well as a monk, and one of his schools had been in a Hmong village – 'Lots culture intrest, mister.' He always felt clear-headed after a return visit, and it was just the thing for me, he said. I liked the sound of this clear-headedness: the dreadful Gugu venture was just around the corner.

Now, thirty miles out of Chiang Mai, here we were. We had come by trail bike, but I was having to wait for ten minutes while Simkiat, somehow past his prime though only twenty-five years of age, had a lie-down.

Flies spun in the thin breeze that wound between these slopes, which had been freshly burnt – they smelt of firegrates – and were about to be planted out for the next maize crop. A little girl with pompoms like clover flowers in her earlobes shuffled up and extended a green peach to me in a hand that was old and gnarled. Though the fruit was tough on the teeth, the sourness freed the road dust from the back and sides of my mouth. A little boy was squatting nearby. He wore only a round black cap emblazoned with light metal discs and needlework, and, like the girl, he was smeared all over with old grime. The tribal lifestyle was ailing, succumbing to the tightening embrace of my world, the world of the consumer.[2]

But the score of huddled buildings retained a peace and strength that showed in the eyes of the weaving women and those plodding in with spinach, beans and cabbage, their cloth gaiters flinging up spouts of the water they had been using to wash off soil. The houses had wall slats that clicked together without nails. They were grass-thatched, and some had teak leaf fenders over their eaves. Here and there, corrugated-iron strips had been applied obliquely across the thatch, like Elastoplast.

Across the ochre mud to the right was a woman applying wax in geometric lines to a girl's skirt material, ready for the dye. Washing lines sagged with pleated Hmong skirts – bold tapestries, silver thread and coins arose from a midnight-blue appliqué and reverse appliqué. Small girls hoiked smaller children on their backs, drew pictures in the mist-wetted sand, and girls with almost a yard of hair – hoisted into a top bun

– crouched playing pebble-tossing games. Chickens pecked alongside the children, sweet sap smoke percolated through the thatch of the twenty houses.

The sun had broken on the horizon, and pieces lay scattered around that quarter of sky. That's enough of a snooze for Simkiat! I got up; the woman cooking poppy seeds in the doorway of Simkiat's hut leant forward to let me by.

Light came in through the vertical wall slats in low-angled yellow slices. The hut was divided in two, with a picture of the Thai royal family on the plank partition. I could not see much more of this, the better-lit half, than the smoke creeping over from a hearth, the sticky black beams and the dry earth floor. On a high shelf was a knife, a flute, a gong stick, candles. This was not a domestic altar, though every house had one, and I wondered if these were the bits and pieces of the village shaman. If Simkiat had got it right, a Hmong shaman went into a trance when called to consult with the spirits. He would ride off out of the physical world on a stool that for him, as he chanted and rocked, became a thundering steed on which to do battle with malign spirits, restoring harmony.

But Simkiat was a Buddhist and had come for a kip, not an alternative religion. The woman nodded at the partition, so I stepped further into the dark and bent around it.

Behind, in the midst of the dark space, was a candle, its flicker on a boy's face, which was intent on the flame. In his thin fingers he rolled a lump of resin. He rounded it into a pellet in the heat of the long wick, bringing it back and forth, controlling the temperature. Simkiat the ex-Buddhist monk, the former school teacher, was lying face to face with this youth on a bed of rolled-out bamboo, watching the resin cooking under his nose. His eyes were cloudy, overcast. The boy raised his head and brought out a pipe – just an old medicine bottle screwed into a bamboo tube – and jabbed the hot pellet over its hole. Simkiat had not moved. The resin crackled as it was played into the flame. Now the boy offered the pipe to Simkiat's mouth. Simkiat craned forward like a baby to the teat, and sucked long. The pipe was roaring; it seemed to me that the opium's sound was triumphant. After six of these gasps, Simkiat plucked the tube from his lips. He lay there, unresponsive to the world. Yet he registered my presence. He spoke at half speed. 'Good to be eating the smokes.'

'So I see.'

'Hmmmm. The boy is Tuang. Tuang is my very best pupil,' Simkiat said.

'So I see.'

'Now for you.' Blue smoke was still coming out of his mouth and nose. It must have been billowing inside him for a full minute.

'Not for me thanks.' I looked around the charcoal darkness for an addict or two who might be stupefied, propped against a post.

'No, no, is medicines. For the Hmongs is medicines. He smokes different moment every day – is no problem. After the smokes, he can get so much work done, and so.'

'You mean you think I can risk a little puff?'

'Yes, yes. Must. You can think wise. Help you body relax and relax.'

'What will I think wisely about?'

'Hah? All your thinkings and thinkings.'

'My thinkings?' Just the ticket! I would ponder on the Gugu and see what I could come up with to justify the risk of taking the old man into the jungle. Besides, Theodore had said that opium only 'shortens ya life a little maybe'. I took Simkiat's place. The things I was doing, just because of ape-men . . .

I smiled politely at Tuang, top boy of the class. He wore the Hmong blackish-blue voluminous trousers. His caramel chest and shoulders glistened with perspiration which looked as thick as motor oil. He had not noticed me come into the room, and now he did not notice that I was not Simkiat – a man who once used to wander shaven-headed and in saffron robes, but who nowadays wore a leather-look black jacket, his hair in long, limp curls, and, on his chinless face, stubble which he pruned with loose change.

The bamboos creaked as I got comfortable and as Simkiat collapsed, lost in Tuang's shadow. It was not an easy thing for me to relax with the breath of this boy in my face – it had a sour scent, as if he too had been persuaded to try the green peaches. His hairless chest rose and fell, rubbing heat and moisture over me.

I allowed myself twelve inhalations – one for each inch I was taller than Simkiat. I lay waiting for my muscles to soften, my mind to level, in point of fact to settle 'as low as shark's shit'. That was Theodore's phrase – the grimy heat, the slits of light, the earthy floor – this place reminded me of his POW cell.

I waited for the opium to do its work. I lay breathing deeply, awaiting an insight, a truth that would, after all, make it worth travelling to the heart of the Gugulands. The greatest truths, some old sage had said, could never be given, only received. That was the infuriating thing about them.

Outside the air was twittering, but I could not tell if it was little sky birds or children. Through a chink I saw a boy paw at the crotch of his tight new school shorts. Today was a special day: the officials had at last got the schoolchildren into Western dress, the national uniform. Sensing the alien in it, this boy had already yanked off his buttoned shirt. A girl beside him was changing hers for her Hmong jacket – deep, dark blue and with borders of stitchwork in sunshine colours.

What, then, opium, am I to make of the Gugu? What of the most famous account[3] – that of Mr Oostingh, a Dutch planter who got himself lost in 1917 in the eastern foothills of Mount Bukit Kaba? After hours of blind wandering, he sighted a man who was apparently in the act of constructing a fire. Oostingh went up, and was about to ask directions.

I saw that he had short hair – cut short, I thought; and I suddenly realised that his neck was oddly leathery and extremely filthy. 'That chap's got a very dirty and wrinkled neck!' I said to myself.

His body was as large as a medium-sized native's and he had thick, square shoulders – not sloping at all. The skin colour was not brown, but looked like black earth, a sort of dusty black.

He clearly noticed my presence. He did not so much as turn his head, but stood up on his feet; he seemed to be as tall as I (about 5 feet 9 inches). Then I saw that it was not a man, and I started back, for I was not armed. The creature calmly took several paces, without the least haste, and then, with his ludicrously long arm, grasped a sapling, which threatened to break under his weight, and quietly sprang into a tree, swinging in great leaps alternately to right and left. My chief impression was and still is: 'What an enormously large beast!' It was not an orang-utan; I had seen one of these large apes a short time before at Amsterdam Zoo. It was more like a monstrously large gibbon but a siamang has long hair, and there was no doubt that it had short hair. I did not see its face, for, indeed, it never once looked at me.

Opium poppy, was this another club-room yarn? Was the animal just one more balding sun bear? I asked the poppy the truth, and there was no answer.

'Simkiat? Hell-o?'

'Waaah?'

'Can I risk taking ten more breaths?'

'Is pure opium,' he said, his voice as light as a child's. 'The pure. But okay. You are a strong man.'

The boy, automated, you felt, was rolling the resin. His nails were sharp and long, stained from candle burns. His finger creases were clearly defined in black. He was revolving those fingers right in the flame. That was scary – the heat should be stinging him! But it was not. I had the feeling that even if his fingers had spat and blistered like unpricked sausages, he would not have registered. The opium was put in the pipe, and the pipe to the flame. The boy introduced the tube to my lips. The intensity of the burning crackle rose and fell with my breath. Rose, and fell; each time the sweet poppy resin roasted the mucus of my throat, and the heat of the smoke stopped scorching only when it reached the far end of my lungs. I imagined the opium cloud diffusing into my bloodstream.

Hearing of Oostingh's tale, other Dutch settlers came forward. Mr Coomans, manager of the State Railway, Padang, had observed little footprints in Bengkulu; others had drawn pictures of the tracks – Captain R. Maier, an official surveyor at Bengkulu, had an enviable collection.

But what of all this? I did not know. I had a curious sensation of a hand tightening on the back of my skull. The hand, I now knew, was the opium – suddenly a nursemaid who was wanting to be rid of that protective bone shell so that she could caress my mind. And to my surprise, though not horror, because my nurse was so loving, her hand discovered a zip fastener on my brow. She took a tight hold, and began to unzip my skull across the top, careful not to snag my hair. The bone casing fell away as the zip travelled, opening my head to a sequence of poppings. My brain was exposed, accessible; and it was suddenly cold. Very cold. And free.

But the revelation did not come. In the dark I could not see the apeman, only – not surprising in this stark dankness – the wartime cell, and that man lying back in it, breathing full and slow, at peace. Outside, in the daylight, the guards might well be loading a bullet for him, inspecting the edge of a blade. Yet, Theodore's mind was easy . . .

But regarding his Gugu, the opium had drawn a blank. However, while I was here in the cool snug of a hut I might as well take ten more drags. You never knew.

Even after another pipe load, my mind did not distil a thing. Or rather it distilled a hole – just a space, a big zero. And I took that as a sign. A confirmation. The Gugu were nothing – something dreamt up by the superstitious. I had no proof, but the opium nurse was of that opinion; she imparted it with a certainty that seeped right to my marrow. Also, it happened to be common sense. The Gugu were mythical.

Somehow I would have to break this to Theodore. And before we stamped off to Sumatra. But that was for later. I had a different problem here: my head was heating up. Soon it felt about to roar into flame. Hot sweat beads, whole chains of them, spun off my nose. I fought to get up and outside. I wanted fresh air. I had a blazing fever, and it was consuming me. My brain was expanded with the heat, and any second it was going to burst – splatter over the smoke-tarred rafters. I shook from the pressure of the imminent explosion. Help! I thought. Eeek!

The release came suddenly, as I vomited up the sour green peaches. After a while, I said, 'Phew! That's better.'

'It is *heavy*,' Simkiat said. 'So heavy.'

'It is rather,' I said, and bent to retch again, wishing I was two days away, on the train down from Bangkok to Penang, getting the breaking of the news to Theodore over with.

Chapter Six

Now, a couple of days on, my attention was on the far distance. I watched and waited. Women, doubled over, feet apart, were planting the rice out, their arms hanging loose from their shoulders, hands flapping with mud that was like a grey dough. It was as if nothing was about to happen; men were going to carry on chopping at the soil right up until the last moment.

The coconut palms seemed blackened by the sun. The hot air was as thick as car exhaust, the landscape, or that near part of it visible in the haze, was so parched it looked brittle.

But you could smell in the wind the change that was coming. The light monsoon was due, and the first deluge was whistling in this very second. Wide clouds from nowhere seemed to draw up and stop. The air sweetened. Motorcyclists stopped to put on plastic bath hats. Overhead, a higher cloud was as sharp and black as a mussel shell. It opened its valve halves. A sheet of water poured down through the slit and began to slap the land. Hens fled into bamboo-roofed shacks. Livestock careered into ditches and smacked against fences. The haystacks turned dark and limp. Children ran to cast fishing nets.

I watched, keyed up. We were the same distance north as Sumatra was south. In rain terms, the climate there was a mirror opposite. This afternoon the Gugu, had there been such things, would have been rejoicing at the outbreak of the dry spell.

I *would* go, I thought suddenly. Would go to the Gugulands. I was full with the drama of the moment, so buzzing with the energy of the changing seasons. Meteorologically – if in no other way – everything would be so perfect for our joint expedition . . . But there was to be no joint expedition. While in Thailand I had worried about Theodore's health, and the discovery that my fear had been justified, at least in part, was not far away.

It was 16 June. I was a day early, and had not had time to ring. The Low Tide Hotel, scene of the downfall of Australian air hostesses, had gone out of business, so I booked into the New Asia, a Chinese establishment – clean and, as the slogan said, 'AL-ways at your service'. One of their services was a telephone.

'You mad fellow!' Theodore's voice sounded vigorous enough. Neither did I suspect anything when he came along with Ling and Jo to George Town to take me out for a meal. The crunching grip of his hand was as normal. Only when we were catching up on news around the table, chewing our squid, could I see it in his face. He did not have the strength to hide it any more. His brow had a wetness, a glycerine shine, and it was not just a touch of 'flu. I did not suppose Theodore ever got 'a touch of 'flu'. I had been meaning to tackle him again about the war, his understanding; now it dropped from my mind. I handed over my gifts from home – a tin of British blackberries, a jar of Colman's mustard. 'Aha!' he said. 'What treasures do we have here?' But his rapture was forced. For the rest of the meal he was pale and slow. He shifted about in his seat and said he had gone off his dog soup.

Ling paid the bill – a little hurriedly, I thought. Theodore got to his feet with a sigh, releasing a gush of steam. He had a new stick: a yellow cudgel. 'The other fellow warped on me – but this is as good a weapon as any.' He tipped his head heavily towards me: 'If you don't mind, old chap, I'm going to have an early night. Tired – and perhaps a touch of indigestion.'

He dropped me off at the hotel. 'I'll ring you in the morning,' Theodore called from the Old Crate. 'Not too early: there's no hurry, is there? So have a good long snooze.' His voice was empty and like a distant echo of himself.

I had a lie-in, and not because I felt whacked. I was useless for anything else, waiting around for the call. Finally I went down to reception. 'Has anyone rung for me?'

'Rung, yeah?' said the old Chinese. He shuffled about, looking repeatedly into my pigeon-hole. 'No rung.'

'Can you bring me some breakfast?'

'Yeah, yeah, can do.'

I had a pot of tea and an egg, taking them out on to the balcony to sit among the old tiled roofs and floating street sounds – fruit-stall cries, car horns, bicycle bells, yells of ice-barrow men. Below, two motorcyclists carved each other up, meeting outside a lantern shop and spreading machine parts over the road. Penang had not changed.

I turned the overhead fan on and lay down under it. An hour later I rang Ling and Jo. No answer. At noon I took a shower. Then a nap. The fan – was it an obsolete aeroplane propeller? – dried out my lips, then

began working on my mouth and nose. I heard the receptionist's wad-
dling footsteps. He croaked down the corridor, 'Telafon, yeah?'

I followed him down. He took the steps one at a time; I was breathing
down his bald neck, eager to overtake and sprint to the desk, but his
elbows swung out, blocking any pass. I took the receiver and said,
'Theodore? Phew! I was beginning to get worried.'

'Benedict? It's Ling. You'd better come over.'

'What's wrong?'

'Sorry we didn't ring you earlier. Perhaps you could catch the bus up.
Number 93, isn't it, Jo?' I listened to Jo warbling in Hokien. Then Ling
said, 'Benedict, it's number 93. Theodore's not looking too good.'

There were signs of the changed season. The star fruit and mango
trees were clapped over with paper bags to frustrate the lesser pests.
Drains were topped up; the flow was swift, and the smell diluted;
bubbles came from greater, but lighter depths. Sugar-cane strippings,
banana-leaf wrappings, broken sandals and cardboard boxes went by
from the market at greater than usual speed.

I walked up from the bus stop. Theodore had moved to a new house
opposite a tree whose white hunting horn blossoms skated the road in
the breeze. In the garden was a durian tree, its unpicked fruits black and
splitting. The faithful retainer, Hoi, was on his lead in the shade of the
porch, his head laid heavily on his front paws, his teeth crinkling up his
muzzle, his eyes flitting between me and the minah birds on the lawn,
which were just out of reach. He was not salivating; he was not himself.
The house was silent.

I put my shoes among the others, beside Hoi, the orchids, the goldfish
and Theodore's range of walking-sticks. 'Hello there?' I called. 'Hello?' I
went indoors.

The sitting room was laid out just as the other had been: the stinkwood cabinet, Chinese vases, barrel table, Portuguese sail boat, Buddhist-monk lampstand – gilt, but with the shine taken off by faint wisps of
candle smoke. The yellow tiles were cold to my feet. There was the
formal black table where once had lain 'Hope at Large'. In its place was
a blue exercise book. On it was Theodore's swirling handwriting. One
word: 'Journey'.

'Hello? Ling? Jo? Theodore?'

'I'm in here, old fellow.' Theodore was laid out like a naked corpse on
the bed. He looked inflated and grey; a beached trout. 'Don't mind
telling you that I felt worse last night than in my entire life. Thought it
was the end. Unholy agony.'

'Shouldn't you go to a doctor?'

'Already been. Ling took me to a Chinese medicine man. Best doctor in Penang. Held my wrists for ten minutes. First the left, then the right. Or was it the other way round? Did nothing else! Just listened to my pulse. One kidney has packed up, he said. The second is close to it. He began rummaging, pulling stuff out of drawers – old sphagnum moss, nut shells, twigs, grass, straw, sponge. Never seen anything like it. By the time he'd finished he had a pile that was like the contents of a squirrel's nest.'

'What had he been looking for?'

'He'd found it. The squirrel's nest – that was his tonic. Ling brews up an infusion from it every now and then. Feel a little less poorly now.'

Theodore gasped, and swung his legs to the floor. 'Will this make you sick?' he said. Before I could say, 'It very well might do,' he had turned to reveal the eruptions on the left of his chest. They were dark, inflamed boils, the pool of them looking like spilt blackcurrant jelly. 'The medicine man said these were the outward signs of the body protesting.'

'I think he might be right there.'

Theodore fumbled as he did up his buttons, and said softly, 'I can't come with you.' His soul seemed muted. The words came out like a wind through marsh reeds, a lonely ghost of a cry.

'Perhaps in a few days . . .' I said. Theodore let out a moan.

In the sitting room I took a book of meditation from the shelves and spent the rest of the afternoon sneezing violently from its dust. All that evening, bellows came from Theodore's room. He ate nothing. 'Feels like me stomach lining is on fire.'

Next day there was a bark outside. But it was not Hoi's, it was Major Dick's. The old Gurkha soldier shouted from behind the gate, 'Come to see how the wandering oracle is doing.' With him was a Nepalese boy. He was particularly small – Pistol rather than Gun, I thought.

I called out, 'I'm afraid he's in bed. But I'll find out if he's up to seeing anyone.'

But Theodore shouted, 'For God's sake make him come in rather than hanging over the gate like a wet sock.'

'Heard you were off drink for a while,' cracked on the Major, staying put, the safe side of the gate. At the limit of his chain, Hoi leant lovingly towards him, his saliva spilling around the porch and into the shoes. 'A water diet, Hull . . .' Major Dick mused. 'Devastating.'

Theodore lay as if his malady was stone deafness. The Major went on regardless: bad news from the Honkers and Shankers, and his dopey financial adviser needed a hot chilli up his backside . . . Five minutes later, the Major rattled off a whimsical laugh, and when it could be heard no more, we knew he had gone.

'Dick read a book once, bless his heart,' said Theodore. 'Didn't like it.'

That night, as I rubbed our Gugu expedition ointment on his whale of a back, Theodore said, 'Better not to monkey about. Just go. Send telegrams with your progress. Whether the scent is good. I'll come running when you're on to them.'

'How can I go alone? I don't know the first thing about Sumatra, let alone where to look for the Gugu – if they *are* still around.' Which they aren't, I thought. Because they never were.

'I've written it all down. There's a blue exercise book next door. My list of contacts. Take it.' He turned back to the mattress, closed his eyes and muttered from the pillow, 'Take it, old Giant. Another couple of attacks like that and it'll sink the tub.'

'Hope at Large' must be given a full hearing. I would see the research through. He was offering hope to the world, even to the Hmong people, in the loss of their separate identity. 'If we don't continue rising from our animal state we're done for. We will squabble a final time and exterminate ourselves. Because we can't yet escape this small planet of ours. Our earth. This little dinghy in the eternal sea and space of time.' But I would not plunge off into Sumatra yet, leaving him in this state. Besides, when I snatched up the Blue Book, settled myself deep into a chair and opened it up, I found all but half a dozen pages were blank.

Though Theodore was well enough after two days to get up to read the papers, Penang, just now, smelt of death. The crop of motorcycle victims was higher than usual – 'Apparently squash 'em flat only one or two times a day normally,' sighed Theodore – and two Australians, caught smuggling heroin at the airport in 1983, were on death row, awaiting the decision of the Penang Pardons Board. They would be the first Westerners to hang.

Theodore, frustrated that he was not yet back to normal, went to a medicine man whose treatment started with the lighting of two joss-sticks. He pricked his own tongue with a pin, and, taking a notepad, wrote out something with the blood. Before Ling could see what the words were, he burnt the paper. The doctor put the ashes in a cup of water, told Theodore to drink the mixture, and wrote out something else – the bill.

Two more days on, Theodore was back on his feet and pining for something more refreshing than water. The *New Sunday Times* proclaimed loudly the result of the drug-traffickers' appeal for clemency: 'NO PARDON FOR AUSSIES'.

'I need more information,' I said to Theodore. 'Facts.' We were having a council of war.

'Giant, you must jump straight into the middle of the pond.' Theodore took his hand from his throbbing stomach and directed a finger at the centre of the map, the green mountain belt.

'But where exactly?' I said.

'Just jump.'

He hasn't a clue, I thought. He hasn't a clue, and I'm setting out there next week!

Several days later Theodore thought he could manage to take me on a drive to the club. But it was not what I wanted. I wanted something to go on: I was a man of expeditions not journeys. Where were the plans? 'Just jump,' he had said. But where?

'I feel a little like Moses . . .' he said, dreamy-eyed. 'Up that glorious mountain, looking down at Canaan, and not able to get to the promised land.'

Promised land – what was promising about it? The mosquitoes? The odd superstitious Kubu tribesman? I had no chance of seeing the Gugu in person, whatever Theodore thought. Even had they once existed it was becoming clear from my own enquiries that, such was the scale of deforestation, the ape-men would have disappeared long ago, along with the other no doubt intriguing specimens of fauna.

'Now, let's get some decent food down your gullet. Why not roast beef, washed down by a Gunner? That's certainly a good drink for going into battle with.'

'Why not.' I was not in a good mood.

'Cheer up, old thing! Listen, where you're going might be Canaan, but it won't be a land of milk and honey!'

'Really.'

We veered out of range of a wobbly trishaw. 'Where *you* are going, you'll get sparrow legs and cockroach eggs!' The joke was in poor taste. That was probably exactly what I would get.

Theodore was on a water diet, but water, he insisted, was bad for his system. 'I'll have tonic,' he said at the club bar. 'At least then I can pretend it's got gin in it.'

I told Theodore that it was time for me to get on with it. On with the expedition.

He suddenly frowned, seeming to clench his brows. 'Jumping the gun a bit, aren't you?' Then he snapped open the menu. 'Right, what are you ordering? I'm fed up to the gills with this "no fat" diet – all boiled fish, bloody, boiled potatoes. It's time for something altogether different.' As we waited to place our order, Theodore started shaking. First his hands, then the rest of him. I was reminded of the hawk moths on Cousin Henry's night traps. At dawn they quivered there, vibrating off the dew, taxiing across the white sheets which had lured them, and warming up for take-off. Theodore was vibrating like one of those expectant hawk moths, and it worried me – after all, he was a human, not a damp insect.

The manager came up and said, 'Mr Hull, what about fresh vegetable soup of the day, sir?'

'No more of that for me!'

'Fish with freshly boiled carrots?'

'How I hate bloody carrots!'

I ordered my drink. 'One Anchor, please.'

'Damn and blast it, I want one too!' Theodore roared. 'I've managed to get in almost eight decades of drinking. It's a terrible shock to the system to have stopped.' When his beer came, he swept the glass up, and in no time was itching for 'the other half'. Drinks always go in pairs, I remembered, like swans or bicycle clips. The colour surfaced in his cheeks. But on his third glass he said suddenly, 'If you don't mind, I must go homeward now.' In the car he undid his trousers; his tummy burst out thankfully. 'My stomach is swelling like a poisoned bullfrog's.'

He started issuing me with my final instructions. 'Make for Padang first. Find out what happened to Father Morini.' He spoke urgently – as if about to die before time. 'Ask for the Catholic cathedral. You'll locate him there – or his grave.'

'I'll save time. Fly.' I found myself also talking fast. 'What's Medan airport like?'

'Unless they've enlarged it, it's got a runway the length of a tennis court.'

'Do you know where I might get a ticket?'

'Surprise Tours. There's a girl I know there. Found her as a little child, sheltering behind a friend's stove. Took the dear thing into my arms. Was told I could have her if I liked. "Sugar Plum". I brought her back with me, found her a home. Now she's working for a travel agent. Surprise Tours. Don't suppose it's any good.'

He was right there, but before we could discover this Theodore had to have a little lie-down. Then he seized the 'phone. I watched him twist the dial, slumped at the desk beyond the Buddhist-monk lampstand, reading off Surprise Tours' number.

Theodore was not mechanically minded – you appreciated that if you ever took a ride in the Old Crate. It was the ferocity with which the gear box screamed resentment.

'Blast! How does this thing work. What does a bleep, bleep, blah signify?'

'Engaged? I don't know.'

'I'm damned if I do, either.'

We went there in person instead. Theodore parked at the shop's 'back-side'. It was not Sugar Plum's fault, but Surprise Tours issued us with a duff air ticket for the second leg – down through Sumatra, from Medan to Padang.

'Don't bother, I'll take the local bus,' I said, when two replacements had also proved invalid.

'That's as well, chum,' another English customer at Surprise Tours said. He spoke fraternally, as if we were both in the same boat, up against it. 'Because if the truth were told, you want to spend as little money as possible on Sumatrans.'

'Do you?'

''Course you do. Everyone knows that.'

'Oh.'

Theodore said it was stuff and nonsense. And anyway, he didn't like the cut of the man's jaw. But I did not want to go. This was not my expedition, it was *his*, and Sumatra – even in peacetime – sounded worse and worse every moment. Theodore said, 'Cheer up. We'll enlist the help of a spiritualist chappie I know.'

'Will we?'

'Chinese. He'll divine the whereabouts of the Gugu. Quick as a flash.'

Desperate measures were needed, but *this* desperate? Yes, I decided, and we drove to a man who lived up in the sky, on the top floor of a grey housing block. Aku the spiritualist seated us on the concrete balcony. He was Chinese, with shining bright, beautiful children who flitted silently to Theodore and clung to him. Aku was not ancient enough to have wise creases across his face, but his eyes were steady and unafraid, and he had long wayward hairs sprouting from his lower lip, and not too much business acumen, all of which was encouraging. He had a reputation in the better circles of Singapore. He addressed Theodore as 'old boy'.

'The good news is plenty, old boy.'

'Sounds encouraging, Giant,' said Theodore.

'Lucky star shining on your mummy,' the spiritualist said to me.

'What else?' I said.

'You sit under lucky star also. Later, always no worry with money. Later you have beautiful wife.'

Theodore interrupted. 'Yes, yes, we know all that. What about the Gugu?'

'Hold on, I'm interested in this. A beautiful wife? And you say money won't be a problem?'

'Money situation, no matter. Children very intelligent, but always wan dress up very beautiful.'

'Oh well, but if I'm going to be rich . . .'

'Only three children – all boy. If you wan more also, you no have.'

'Never mind, what will my wife be like?'

'Maybe Chinese. I have friend – you like to meet? She extremely—'

'What about the Gugu?' said Theodore. '*That's* what we've come to learn.'

'When you go to this island, not very luck. All looks very discouraging, but I got to tell you the truth, old boy.'

'Yes, and you are absolutely right, and I do appreciate that, of course. But dear, dear.'

'But you will find some luck.'

'Ah,' said Theodore.

I said, 'Point out where I should look. Here – on the map.'

The youth pulled on his dangling lip hairs, then waved my ballpoint pen in the air. He seemed to be trying to hold it and cross his fingers at the same time. He swirled his hand and rammed the tip down on to the map. The mark it made was not in the Gugu homelands, between Seblat and Kerinci. It was in some low-lying swamp – not habitable by Gugu, not habitable by anything very much, except perhaps the odd frog or lost crocodile.

Theodore looked at the map aghast.

'Useless,' I said, putting the right word into his mouth.

Theodore said to the spiritualist, 'Perhaps you'd better give it another couple of goes.'

I stayed up very late sorting through my rucksack, ready for an early start next morning. As I went to bed, everything was dark – all except for Theodore's bedroom. I listened for human sounds. There were the smacking geckos, and outside the insects fizzing and the dog choruses. In the sitting room, Hoi snapped at a fly. I needed a drink. I tiptoed through and thumped my knee against the barrel table. I looked in on Theodore; he was on his side, half under a sheet, around him trailing the thin blue smoke twists of the mosquito coil. The light from his door shone in a triangle towards the kitchen – enough for me to find a glass, and the tap. I opened the fridge and banged out some ice. Theodore was not disturbed by that, but he was awoken by the small crisp sound of my striking a match for my own mosquito coil. He rolled over to look, rolled back. Soon he was breathing soundly again. His head was cupped in his large right hand. As he slept, his feet and hands were trembling. He was like a hound dreaming of a long, wild chase.

'I'll do my best,' I murmured. 'But it really is a lost cause, you know.'

Chapter Seven

At 7.15, when I might have been catching up on sleep, I stood in the porch, waiting to leave on my doomed expedition. There were seven minah birds on the wire fence. They shuffled up and down, each with only one thing in mind: the chance to lunge for that top minah-bird position, the fence post.

The newspaper read, 'Same penalty for all.' Every sort of pleading had failed. Now the Aussies were to swing for sure.

I bundled my rucksack into the Old Crate. Jo and Ling had gone off on business, but they had left a note. 'To Benedict. Good luck and happy hunting.'

Happy hunting? As we drove, Theodore handed out last-minute advice. Each piece was worse than the last. 'Now, if the Indonesians sense that you have money, beware. They're just like flies. They'll sit on you.'

He was teasing; but I hardly heard. I said, 'I'll be careful, don't worry.' The morning sun was on the dome of the State Mosque as it thrust heavenward on its white stem, like a highly bred – possibly overbred – tulip.

'And, if you fall for a girl out there, make it a Chinese. They're all after your wallet, but the Chinese'll manage your money better than anyone; and they're dutiful. Best girls in the world. The rest you should avoid like the plague.'

'Like the plague,' I repeated vaguely. But I was beginning to wake up to the terrible reality: the expedition was only half an hour away now. '*Cousin Henry* said that a Thai girl will kiss her husband's feet every morning before he gets out of bed.'

'Yes, and kiss your neighbour's feet when you're away!'

'We had a chaplain at school with a Thai wife. She wasn't at all like that. Not at all.'

'Old fellow, cheer up. You know I'm only joking.' He took a hand off the wheel and slapped my knee. 'And I've been thinking. That spiritualist, Aku. Maybe he's right. Gugu might live in the swamp. There's a well-known aquatic type. The hair down their back is set so that, as they swim, it flows in accordance with the water currents.'

Drivel, I thought.

After a while, Theodore said quietly, 'It's for the best that I can't come. I'd only hold you up. I expect Sumatra's seen a fair amount of changes since my visit. Some for the better . . .'

As we drew near to the airport a blue-felt mist hung over the coconut groves. Fruit-catching nets had been slung under the durian trees and looked like spiders' webs spread out to trap stray children.

I wondered how it might be, over there. The constitution, as I knew from Indonesian New Guinea, told you that there was a God. He need not necessarily be Islamic. The government had formulated a basic sort of language to help weld together the different peoples of the archipelago. And rumour had it that in the Republic the custom was that you took life much as it came. You sloshed through the paddy-fields in obedience to the weather. You harvested the coffee and tea plantations to flexible yield targets. Factories and offices were run to stretchable schedules. In some regions, and the whole of Sumatra was one of them, this had been brought down to a fine art. In short, on the island I was heading for, each man and woman understood from birth that his or her life would be measured out by the unit known, fondly, as *jam karet* – rubber time.

We were at the airport. I said, 'Oh God. Are you sure you aren't ready to come?'

'No. I'm chicken. *You'll* be my arms and legs. Perhaps even the fulfiller of an old man's dreams!'

'Yes,' I said, catching sight of my pallid face in the rear-view mirror, 'perhaps.'

Theodore said, 'That's the spirit!' and leant over me to open the car door. 'Out ya get!'

Part 2

Rubber Time

Chapter One

As I have said, it is thorns that first come to mind whenever I think back to my involvement with the Gugu. Thorns – and then the ape-girl skipping through the midst of them. I always recall Pastaran's account with perfect clarity; yet, as I started out on the expedition, I viewed my objective with no focus whatsoever. Setting foot in Sumatra, tired, in a black mood, still unaware of Pastaran and the slip of a creature he blasted with his shotgun, I did not know my own mind – I was not even sure who was making the decisions, Theodore or myself.

Make for Padang first. Find out what happened to Father Morini. Theodore's instructions were still ringing in my ear, and in Medan I headed for the bus right away.

I hear that, given a certain low angle and yellow dusk light, Medan is a most lovely city to behold. But to me in my rage it was a city of rubbish-tip fragrances. The bus might in reality have been red and yellow and green, but through my eyes it was rust joined by body filler that might have been chewing gum. Holes in the rotted metal revealed hairy fanbelts and a spouting radiator. One headlamp worked; both of them had lost their glass. This must be Sumatra, I thought. A place of broken things.

I was travelling, which here, it seemed, meant I was waiting. I sat in a huff, painting the world black, as I absorbed, stack by stack, the wet heat.

The ticket collector said, 'You American?'

'No, English.'

'*Inggeris?*' The word brought a smile. 'In England and America,' he said with a wistful sigh, 'free sex.'

As the hours went by, market boys walked down the aisle, harrying us to buy newspapers, boiled eggs, coconut slithers, pineapple wedges. It was no use acting as if I were dead, as all other passengers did. They'll sit on you like flies, Theodore had said. And sure enough, seeing my white skin, they did. A boy of ten jabbed my knee so hard I thought it was a knife stabbing. I watched in shock for erupting blood. The boy beamed proudly to other travellers at my response. Soon he had taken the seat beside mine and was showing me his forearm, and in particular the tracks of blistered skin which looked like the result of a slave brand. He was trying to tell me the scars were worth financial compensation. He lounged, fondling my knee. 'You got money?'

They'll sit on you like flies, a voice said. I took the warning, and closed my eyes to shut the buzzing out.

'How much money? Mister, mister, how much money?'

'Very little,' I said. I wished I was back in downland Hampshire. There, acceptably far from the dull shadow of suburbia, reed buntings flipped in and out of pond willows.

'Is this money?' the little voice enquired. I felt fingers dabbing the wodge of soggy calling cards in my pocket. Without opening my eyes, I softly took his hand in mine, then crushed it. There was a yelp, and five minutes' peace.

We were off. I had been given seat number 47, the one behind the rear door, which would not close. Road dust billowed up my trousers and nose, and down my shirt and throat. The city's name, Medan, meant field. Just about the right word for its arterial roads, I thought. We wove through iron-clad houses, rubber-tree horizons, gangs of wild dogs. The road failed and rain smashed into my face. But this was better – the wild sway of the bus, the rock-thumping axles and the gritty taste of the dirty breeze were a distraction. I did not want to be here; I did not believe in the ape-men, only in Theodore's having a right to a chance. This was a task with no conviction, and therefore little hope. Even if they had ever been here, the Gugu were dead. And I was arriving too late for the funeral.

By daylight, dog-tired, I saw that we were up in the clouds. This was the Barisan Range; once (for the sake of argument) Gugu country, now only shelves of paddy, water pools that bounced back a lacklustre sky, and drooping power lines with wet cobwebs strung between.

No doubt, I moaned, I'll be back up here soon, scratching forlornly, a beachcomber waylaid in a desert. But first I had to find Morini, who was probably as dead as the Gugu. His grave would be in Padang, which, though a quite different blot on the map from Medan, *also* meant field.

Traffic had to share the road with peasants' spreads of coffee beans – sunbathing green and red pebbles that were kept from car tyres by sharp rock defence lines. Our bus thundered on, making short work of them. This was Theodore country. He knew this Malay race – knew if they could take a joke, if girls carried hankies up their sleeves, if boys made their beds. I knew a little of the language from Indonesian New Guinea, but what use were words?

'How did Theodore come to know Sumatra?' I was talking to myself. I was *often* talking to myself just lately. I never really got it out of him. He had been kicking around the region for years, of course. And history tells us of the Japanese swoop south in 1942 and the region's becoming embroiled fully in the war. Churchill had ordered, 'Singapore must be converted into a citadel and defended to the death. No surrender can be contemplated.'[4] But Fortress Singapore, swollen with refugees, did not last long.

The Japs closed in. Some of the last to get away – the docks blazing, boats tipping, oil flames on the water, dancing, roasting – made for the Allied base at Padang, West Sumatra. This island too was quickly overrun, many prisoners ending their war as slaves to the Manchurian Railway.[5]

From all I had heard of the camps it was a wonder Hull had ever left his alive. Precious few men did. They fell in droves – from dysentery, malaria or just the whip and starvation. It was not all that long before they were spending more time burying each other than laying railway sleepers. But Theodore had been strengthened by his little guiding light, the thing he had found while in solitary confinement.

The early light of the highlands was becoming less easy on the eyes now – no longer blunted by cloud wisps, but skimming cold and yellow off the irrigation ditches, off crinkle-sheeted mosque domes, even off the eyes of the trap ponies. Small boys swam naked in the wide brown river curves, or shivered in the higher brooks. Men tried to plug spirting channels, girls sung on verandahs, women were up to their hocks in field sludge; they all stared to see the white man go by.

We were beginning the winding descent; I knew because everyone was getting out plastic bags. As the first child was sick into hers I saw, far out, the mist belt of the coast. Padang would be down there somewhere. In its centre would be the Catholic cathedral and Pastor Morini, or his remains.

Yes, I thought, you should be here to help, Theodore. Really you should.

Now the air had a tropical hum. Forests arose and sang to us. They lifted me from my sulk. In gorges, water spun in virgin cords of crystal. This was a scrap of old Sumatra, the unmolested remnants of what, to humour Theodore, we are calling Guguland. A common kingfisher snatched a fish. Watching it, I felt elated: I could not help it. This was not such a bad place. And if only the Ambassador had been here to see that flung ball of slick emerald.

Padang – too grown up nowadays to be overawed by the mountains alongside – was already cooking. The heat sprang into my face off the greasy bus-station concourse. My rucksack was lobbed down from the roof. I wrung the worst of the night rain from it, inspected the break-ages, and looked around. One bus was being pushed by a score of hands, another was spitting oil, another puking black fumes. The remainder were just hotting up the passengers inside. A casket of dried fish was being wheeled up a bus side with two ropes. This was sheer cunning. For the second time I could not help but enthuse. The cool skill of the team was a wonder. Then the rattan split. The fish scattered, skidding away to trip up market boys and lodge themselves under the coaches' balding tyres.

'Hello, John. What your name?'

I had best be going; hawking boys were closing in from all sides, food trays on their heads.

'Hey, mister, where you go?'

'John, where you from?'

I softened – it was their fingertips tapping me softly and their mis-chievous, crooked-teeth smiles.

'My name's Benedict, though, not John,' I said in English. 'You must have mistaken me for someone else – I expect we all look alike. I come from Hampshire. That's near the London area.'

'Ah John . . . London Bridge is falling down.' The trays jived. The boys patted me all over with laughter. Their smiles of sweetness would make you forgive them anything. Then I noticed that one of my trouser pockets was empty.

Among the long line of pony-trap taxis I spotted a man who looked honest. His horse turned its head round to give my heavy gear a good look over. As I boarded the trap the bells between the animal's ears tinkled uneasily. 'What's his name?' I asked.

'*Kuda*,' the man said. 'Horse.'

'Horse?'

'Horse, John.' The driver flicked a green switch to Horse, who began delivering fat balls of manure on to the spread of sacking beneath his hindquarters. Then we tipped forward, and into a jerky trot towards the Grand Hotel. Our route took us into the hot throat of Padang. Painted wall sheets which were weighted with rocks on twine advertised films showing in town. Certain colours cropped up again and again – the grey of the gun steel that reared from the hero's loins, the seering oranges of dynamited bridges and jeeps; the blood reds; the pinks of Euro-American women's flesh. '*The Iron Mercenary*', cried one poster, '*Bloody Magnum*', another, and '*Midnight Woman*', '*Eliminators*.'

We had stopped at the foot of some eroding steps. A tailless cat sat on the bottom one, and Horse the horse licked it. The exterior walls of the Grand Hotel had been newly fronted with crazy paving. The first slab had come away. There was a fresh cockroach corpse in the dent where it had landed.

A boy led me into a narrow yard of cheese plants. I stepped over a great many bobtailed cats, all of which were ignoring heaps of rejected hotel food. Beyond a corrugated-iron corridor was my room. Theodore had warned that this hotel was not grand, and he was absolutely right. The door was three pieces of hardboard. Mosquitoes wafted lazily back and forth through the gaps. The vibration of my key turning in the lock was enough to make the lights flicker. On one wall was written in English, weakly, 'OH MY GOD!'

Ask for the Catholic cathedral. You'll locate him there, or his grave. After forty winks, I pulled myself together. I headed through the grainy early evening light to the cathedral. According to Theodore's Blue Book, it was run by an Italian mob, the Xaverian Mission. I got directions from the men who were blocking the pavement. These were not beggars, but craftsmen, skilled in the use of bicycle wheels, which they pedalled by hand to grind stones. The stones were hammered on to brass rings, and you took your pick from whole trays of them.

'The cathedral? Over there.' One man was pointing to a cul-de-sac, the other up to the right where pony-trap lanterns were being lit. In the dusk the streets had a scent of stables rather than exhaust fumes and the ponies were heavy-footed, eying the juicier grass verges.

Beyond the military police building, with its pretty black cannon, stood the cathedral, yellowing in the last sun. It was modern – a chocolate-coloured roof, if I remember. The most striking aspect of the building was its lack of extras. All its outside surfaces and angles were plain. This promised sincerity. I listened: a service was in progress. I could hear the low grinding of prayer. I slipped through the iron gates and inside to a back pew. Nearly all the supplicating heads were female, hair pressed down by arching fans. The only white participants in all the hundreds were myself and the ancient priest. He was in vestments, tottering about dangerously at the foot of the stone altar. He had a stoop, and even from here I saw that he had hairy tufts on his chin, which was half lost in his throat. He looked malaria-riddled enough – but Father Morini? No such luck, surely.

The congregation cleared. The Chinese girl on the organ turned to check that everyone had gone, and clicked the switch off. Outside the sky was blackish, a red-marbled wool that hung close over the city. I waited for the priest to come out. Through the rippled glass of a side window·came a fractured glow from the prayer candles. Across the garden was an illuminated rockery with a grotto in cement, the Virgin enshrined in it.

The priest emerged wearing the white gown that Theodore had mentioned – buttons from neck to ankle hem. I wondered if he had to do them up every day, or whether there was a zip at the back.

'Good evening. Is Father Morini in?' I said, in Indonesian.

'Morini?' The priest took on a lonely-eyed look.

'He's dead, is he?' It struck me that I might just make the next flight home. Yes, I thought, if I packed my bags tonight, I could probably make it.

The priest was pinching at his chin, his eyes concentrated on the bugs and slim-winged fliers which were fidgeting up and down his garment, excited by its moon whiteness. But it was not the creepy-crawlies that made him uncomfortable. It was me. Was my Indonesian that bad? He began to back off, waning into the darkness, gibbering a little. Whether Morini was·dead or alive, he did not want to talk about it.

An Indonesian in a heavily ironed shirt closed the cathedral doors, swivelled the key. He reached for a switch. The lights around the grotto cut dead. 'You leaving?' he said.

I was leaving. But a scooter was looming from the back of the garden. It idled right up. The driver was another European – bulky arms from too tight short sleeves. I guessed that by daylight he had a jovial, russet-apple face with a good shine to it. He nodded as he looked at me, as if I had just said something of no mean significance. I had said nothing.

'Father Sandro,' he said in English.

'How do you do. I've just been talking to the older Father.'

He blinked, understandingly. 'Was Spinabelli. Me? Am Sandro. You want?'

'Morini.'

'Ah. But is taken from us.'

Dead. That was that. Home! I thought, picturing a cool Pimms in the garden in June. Home! Delphinium borders, pond-skimming house martins, fat earthworms working luscious lawns.

'Pasaman,' Father Sandro added. He waved a hand, reining in my attention. I had gone closer to him to hear above the engine; now I had to step back to allow his arm room. His face lengthened. He was a defeated man, suddenly.

'Is no telephone,' he said. 'Is no shop, hotel. When we, er . . .' As he searched for the English word, he pushed up his mouth, and the beard that had been perched on his chin slid up his face. 'When we have the letter from him, is good.' You did not get letters from dead men. You just didn't. I was stuck here for a bit longer. 'Is not in the contact. Lots, lots trees, jungles. But Pastor Morini, he is not so alone. Two priests is buried with him. All is difficult to find.'

I reconciled myself. When all was said and done, it was only fair on Theodore that I should stay to exhaust all possibilities. I had said I would try my best. After all, I would only have to stick it out for a week. Ten days at the outside.

Father Sandro was tutting. 'Morini can be far from the home. Away three weeks? More?'

Lawks! 'Can you tell me, have you heard stories of him believing in, well, you know' – I braced myself – 'ape-like people? *Orang pendek*? Er, from the forest?'

As the Father laughed he rocked his scooter seat. He had to lift his hand from the throttle for balance and the engine died. 'Over breakfast many times he talks only of this. Is an amusement for us.'

'But for him?'

'For him, not so much amusement.' The Father kicked the engine over. 'And now, I leave for urgent business. If Pastor Morini comes, who is asking for?'

'Benedict.'

'*Benedictus benedicat.*' He enjoyed his joke for a while, lavishly crossing himself. He was away, leaving me there in the rising scooter smoke. Fading with the sound of the engine was his laugh. 'Pastor Morini, oh Pastor Morini . . . hee hee!'

It was rather sad, actually. I had let myself go. In the good old days, a month ago, I used to be able to do a hundred press-ups before bed. Now I could hardly lift a finger.

I thought I would get on as best I could without Pastor Morini for the time being. There were nine contacts in the Blue Book, all told, each one a man who had had some sympathy with Theodore seven years ago. Contacts two and three were here in Padang, and I would try them first thing next morning. I must get cracking. *You are my arms and my legs.* I would pull myself together and do my best for him. I got down on the floor and did thirty press-ups. I might yet be that 'fulfiller of an old man's dreams', I thought, and went to the bar for a stiff drink.

*   *   *

Contact number two was the head of the museum, which was an archi-
tectural showpiece and worth a detour anyway. Its multiple roofs –
stacked like the weightless horse saddles – were wings spread protec-
tively over the paint-dappled body. The museum dominated its sparsely
vegetated garden, which was the setting for an outdated military plane.
Inside, the museum chief showed me his pride and joy: the Malay
regional costumes – shimmering loose jackets, cummerbunds, sarongs,
dance hats like mitres. But when I made enquiries about the Kubu and
the ape-men, he replied with nervous, sharp laughter. You really could
not blame him.

Contact number three was Mr Sukid, a regional planner who had
been posted in the interior, with the Kubu. He was recovering in Padang.

'Excuse me,' I said, reaching his house. 'Is Mr Sukid in?'

The woman who had been sitting up on the high, wooden porch took
up her broom and began making rapid, vicious strokes with it, like a
canoeist in trouble.

I repeated the question. So you're a friend of his, are you?' she asked.
She lowered her broom handle towards me, as if it might have to serve as
a weapon. 'He didn't have many.'

She was expecting me to go away. I waited, squeezing the Blue Book.

The wind had picked up a scrap of street litter, and was harrying it. I
watched it dodge and spar, then made out its kicking tail – a kite.

The woman muttered, 'Well, he's been taken away. Back to his
family.'

'Why, if you don't mind me asking?'

'*Why?* His trouble.' She was looking me over, wondering at me.

'Trouble?'

'Very bad this time. Talking to himself, playing in the trees. Thought
his wife was St Elizabeth.'

'*Who?*'

'St Elizabeth. Then he woke up one morning – he said he was a tree.
That was the day before they took him away. Told him they had a
special garden for him. Dug him up, replanted him at his family's.
Prapat, near Lake Toba.' She was walking off indoors, but slowed to
turn back to me; the light caught a crucifix around her neck. 'Are you
sure he's a friend of yours?'

'No,' I said. 'No, I'm not so sure now.'

Up and down Padang the Republic's flags crackled in the gathering
breeze. A schoolgirl fished in a ditch, and seemed glad to have caught a

polythene bag. It was white from the sun. She walked off, blowing it into a balloon. The rain came; soon the streets were slicks of black water. I could not deny it any more: Sumatra was somehow growing on me. I was becoming attached to its lost sense of urgency. Rubber time was good for the soul. And if I complained again at the climate I could thank my lucky stars I was not being brewed here with a war on.

In the bar, I decided I would head for Bengkulu the next day. All the remaining contacts lived there. I put my ballpoint through a block of Theodore's writing. Three down, six to go. And who the hell was St Elizabeth?

'Say,' a North American voice said, 'can you get this boy to fix me a drink?' He looked uncomfortable in his seat, and his tie was limp. 'I can't speak the language,' he explained.

The only white people I had seen so far had been the Italian priests and those who had come in off the streets for alcohol. There had been a luminescent-skinned Californian, just discharged from the local jail. It was a smuggling charge – Swiss watches, made in Singapore. There had also been a Swedish girl who had run in after being cautioned by the police for not wearing a bra under her blouse. And now there was this man wanting a drink. I had seen his name in the register – it was Mr Swartz.

'Don't you speak *any* Indonesian?' I asked.

'Not a word. And they keep calling me "backpack".'

'That's *bapak*. It means "sir".'

'And my beard scares the hell out of them. They run from me in the streets. And I don't mean only the kids. Office clerks, the newspaper guys – you name it, they get up and run.'

It was an Anchor beer that he was after. 'Better make that two,' he said.

'Oh, thank you very much,' I said.

Swartz looked up at me. 'You want one as well? Sure, make it four then.' He let me in on a 'useful tip': always order twice as much as you need. 'Saves on your patience. Discovered that one in Jakarta, first day in Indonesia.'

'I must remember,' I said. We chose a table. Swartz pressed in his sizeable stomach – as he bent to sit down. He kept his briefcase between his knees. He was being sponsored by an international bank, he told me, forearms on the table, rocking urgently in the chair. 'I'm on a grand tour, looking into the human angle of development projects in six countries – Thailand, Singapore, Brunei, Malaysia, Indonesia and I'm so screwed up I can't remember what the shit is the other one.' He plucked at his front teeth with a thumbnail. A peanut seemed to have got lodged there. 'Burma, is it?'

'I can't help, I'm afraid.'

'Yep, that's the one. Burma.' He swept a forefinger round the inside of his collar. 'Or is it?'

Soon he was ripping open a packet of nuts. His pockets appeared to be lined with them. He could lob a nut into his mouth from the hand on the table and seemed to obtain his nourishment from the act itself, from being a certain cliché of America. His eyes were darting, hunting.

I said, 'How long have you got for each country?'

'Ten days.' He crunched the peanuts madly. He had developed, through over-use, particularly strong muscles on his brow; they formed a thick Y as he churned his schedules over.

'You must be a busy man,' I said. 'How long have you been here?'

'Five.'

'So how many projects have you see—'

'And don't ask me how many projects I've seen.'

'I won't, then.'

But in the end, he just had to let it all out. 'Shit!' It was more of a gasp than cry. 'Two days in Padang, and I've done what? I've got two schemes to check out here. My job is to report if sponsoring them is a good deal, right? So far, neither project manager has even let me on the site. Forget welcome parties – I haven't even shaken a gofer boy's hand. The clerks say, "Sorry, backpack, he's got a meeting." Two days! Some meeting, eh?' Swartz karate-chopped the table. ' "Look," I tell the lady. "I'm the guy who decides if the project goes into the trash can or not, get me?" The clerk gives me a cup of tea – too much sugar, and in a glass – God only knows where they get it from.'

'Well, it's grown locally.'

'I wait an hour, then she says, "Sorry, backpack. Come back tomorrow. *Pagi pagi* – "morning morning" – what sort of language is that?'

'One *pagi* means morning, two *pagis* mean early in the morning. It's beautifully simple.'

Swartz churned and churned. His eyes came at me from time to time, but they were never on me. 'What do three "paggies" mean?'

'I think they only go up to two.'

'Are they hiding something?' Swartz said to the bar boy, who was listening in from a safe distance. 'I don't know. But they're gonna regret this.' He reached into his briefcase. 'Boy, what a work problem.' He did not bring out papers, he brought out pills – a selection, three bottle-loads. The first lot were dull white tablets, the other two were capsules decorated with the warning colours that insects use: fluorescent orange, and yellow and black stripes. He went for the white tablets, and placed one at the front end of his tongue. He emptied his beer down, and the pill was washed away out of sight. 'And what are you here for?'

'I'm trying to investigate the old stories – about ape-men in Sumatra.'

'Boy! Are you serious?'

I did not mind all that much: I was well aware that I would have to face ridicule throughout my journey. I expected Swartz to say that the Gugu were around all right – least his steak last night had sure as hell tasted like one. But he just rapped the table twice. I understood the rapping was shorthand for expressing encouragement, a less time-consuming way of saying 'Go for it!' He said, 'Met a guy who collected these stories. A kind of hobby. Know what I mean by "hobby"?'

'Yes, it's an English word, actually.'

He tapped the table again – 'Go for it!' – but his eyes continued to flick around the room. 'Well,' he went on, 'I know something that'll grab you. We – and maybe you British were in on it – built a road up through the highlands – the Trans-Sumatran Highway. Some parts were dirt up until just a few years back.'

I thought: That was when, aboard the rocking, whirling bus, Millet hit the roof. And where Theodore's own expedition bit the dust.

'Well, the road lay unfinished for years. They'd forgotten to budget for thirty-five per cent of the funds being salted away. So they ended up with only road lamps up. They led in a beautiful line through the jungle. Picture it? Electricity all wired, but not a sign of paving!' Swartz took a swig. 'Can you beat that? The road got started again, and then the stories came in. Heard this through a colleague working on the site – the experience almost killed him.' Swartz pitched forward, confiding. 'See, these tales going round among the Indonesian roadmen, they were concerning little people – little men scatting off into the forest. Kubu? Hell no! These were genuine monkey-men – weeping, throwing sticks at the machinery, raising hell. Most just kind of ran though.'

Extraordinary, I thought. People even now really tell Gugu stories! 'Can you give a better description of them?'

'No, can't rightly say I can. Who knows what they were? Just another mystery, I guess. Except now you can bet the region is clear of them. Those construction vehicles drove straight through that place.' He began picking at his peanut-littered teeth, starting with the upper-left molars.

'It's much as I thought,' I said. 'Theodore wouldn't listen.'

'Pardon me?'

I explained, 'Theodore's a free thinker. A philosopher, really.

Theodore Hull – like the lower portion of a ship. I'm here looking for
evidence on his behalf. He has an understanding of life . . .'

Swartz's fingers rapped. 'That's hot!' he shouted. 'What's the
understanding?'

'I never got an answer. He came to it while he was a prisoner-of-war,
on death row.'

'I get it. The understanding helped him escape.'

'Oh no. That was probably because the war ended early.' I tried to get
something of the seriousness of this over. 'In at least one railway camp
they made prisoners dig their own graves, Mr Swartz. They were only
saved because, before the Japanese got around to shooting them, the
atom bombs were dropped: it meant an unexpected surrender.'

'So if the understanding didn't help him escape, what's the big deal?'

'Well, it's extraordinary, isn't it? Peace, despite looming death . . .'

'And now you're here looking for monkey-men for the guy . . .'
Swartz had lifted his empty glass and was waving it at the bar boy.
'Well, you can tell Theo that—'

'Theodore,' I said. 'It's Theodore.'

'— that he won't even find the Kubu tribespersons. Least not living in
traditional style. They just skulk and beg.'

'Is it really that bad?'

'I believe. And everyone's getting irate because they won't come out of
the forest and accept modernity.' I sensed the hardness in Swartz. It
vibrated from his hands through the table. 'As regards your monkey-
men. Whether they were there or not, there's no sense in you worrying
over the creatures. Now you won't even find their firesticks.'

Swartz was only confirming what I had thought. But we would see.

As I got up to go, I asked, 'Don't suppose you know who St Elizabeth
was, do you? One of my contacts thinks his wife is St Elizabeth.'

Swartz shook his head, not at all surprised. 'Here,' he sighed. 'You'd
better take one of these for when you reach desperation point.' He
tossed me a white tablet. From his tone, it might have been a cyanide
pill. 'It's the best way.'

'What are they?'

'Valium.'

'Oh, I don't think . . .'

'It's okay. The United States – that's where I come from – it's run on them.'

'Well, I'm finished with Padang. Tomorrow I'm going by bus to
Bengkulu, to the south.'

'Jesus. That's a one-and-a-half-day ride,' he said. 'You'd best take two
more.'

* * *

Every half-hour or so came the sad tunes of a child leading a blind man through the crowd, fingers around the dry, veined hand, steering it to where it might best reach out and waggle imploringly.

We had been crumpled in the sun for a couple of hours, waiting for Friday prayers to end. Water was flicked around the road to kill the dust; dresses were opened for bouts of breast-feeding, goats butted in the road. Fruit, eggs, corn-cobs were paraded by emaciated boys; two girls with snuffles kept white handkerchiefs over their faces. An infant every now and then self-consciously touched the rings in her newly spiked earlobes.

The sound from the mosque was a sacrificial one. This was time given up from money-earning, and, after Swartz, it was a relief. These people were released from that monied numbness. They devoted space to a thing outside themselves, gave up a part of their existence to a higher being. I warmed to that, to the deskboy at the Grand Hotel who had made floorspace by the bar five times a day to roll out his mat and pray. I warmed to having to wait in the sun. In Sumatra, Theodore had joked, flies would pounce on my wallet. I had been constantly on the look-out for money-licking proboscises. But without a doubt Sumatra was shaping up well. These people left themselves breathing space, seizing opportunities as and when they came along. Sumatra, post-Swartz, was a joy.

The driver rose, blinking into the sunlight. Babies were flung into shoulder slings and we clambered aboard. The ticket collector swung up and began dishing out sickbags.

We trundled along the coastal belt and up into the wringing forests until, uncertain of time, we reeled down again to the sea, and Bengkulu.

Bengkulu used to be horrible. I did not have Theodore to tell me that, but an obscure hardback which he had told me would do instead.[6] The lifespan of a man was two monsoon seasons, the Bombay proverb went, and it applied even more accurately in Bengkulu, when the British began to settle there. 'All our Servants are Sick & Dead,' they reported in 1685, '& at this Minute [there is] not a cook to gett victualls ready for those that Sett at the Compas table. Ye Sick lyes Neglected, some cry for remedies but none [are] to bee had. . . . Wee now have not liveing to bury ye dead.'

The stockade, Fort York, was the 'most irregular' piece of defensive work that Dampier, a gunner for a short time there, had ever seen. But the English manning it were, if anything, even more irregular. And all because the provincial rulers of Bengkulu had invited the English East

India Company to build a pepper factory in Sumatra. They came, and slowly extended their territory, but malaria and dysentery reaped a rich harvest, at one time dissipating the force to eleven British soldiers. However, when Joseph Collet arrived in 1712 as Deputy Governor, he refused to be downcast, writing home, 'All the People that have dyed here since my arrivall which are but few, have apparently been destroy'd by Drinking or Women.' What is more, 'Severall Kings profess themselves to be our Subjects. I always receive them with the forms and air of a Superiour. They tell me I am a good Man and they pray for my life daily. I treat them as a Wise man shou'd his wife, am very complaisant in trifles, but immovable in matters of importance.'

There were only four white women. Two of them were leaving Bengkulu on the ship which carried his letter. Of the leftovers, 'One of them is now actually kept Dark, Blouded etc. and the other is a Woman of the most indifferent personage but yet of consummate virtue. The rest are all blacks and a man that ventures on them seldom fails to gett the Bencoolen feaver.'

Two years on, the handsome Fort Marlborough was constructed right on the bay. The pepper crops were gathered in, troublesome neighbours were quietened. The settlement survived a further century, by which time profit from the spice trade was uncertain. In 1824 the British handed over the plantations to the Dutch, obtaining in return control of the Malacca Strait. It was probably a bargain.[6]

When I turned up, most of the tombs of the old European graveyard had been used as building material. Cows rubbed the loose skin of their necks on the remainder, splashing the black whisk ends to their tails between weeds and cowpat flies. The original stockade, Fort York, was a forgotten mound, unexcavated and unloved; last year an abattoir had been built on it.

Erman, the hotel errand boy, showed me these relics. For a bony urchin, he had a good grounding in archaeology. He had a frog tattooed on his wrist, and the hotelier said it was because he was like the squashed frogs that lay desiccated on the road, with thin bones and stretched, translucent skin.

'Where do you come from?' I asked.

'From nowhere,' he said proudly, as if it was a big place, faraway. 'I work in the hotel. Sleep on the verandah outside.'

'Have you ever heard of the Kubu tribe? From Jambi Province?'

'No, sir. I never went to school.'

'And no stories about ape-men?'

'Ape-men? People like monkeys?' He spoke simply and seriously, through gaps in his uneven teeth. 'They're stories – just stories.'

'Yes, I'm rather afraid they are. But you'll ask around for me?'

He would.

'But, Theodore,' I said in the night, 'it's not looking so good for your Gugu. You've only got six contacts left. Seven, if you count Pastor Morini – but I shouldn't bother.'

Contact number four was Roger Witters. 'Drunken Aussie, very nice fellow,' the Blue Book said. 'Tough as boots. Out in Sumatra looking for radioactive dirt.' But Roger Witters had decided to go home early. Number five – Mr Simplat. 'A simpleton,' the Blue Book observed, 'but basically sound. Held government post at Arga Makmur, don't ask me where it is.' I looked Mr Simplat up, but too late. Simplat, like number three, was a changed man. Now the authorities had despatched him to New Guinea, a thousand miles away – an office-bound post in the provincial capital handling the visa applications of evangelical missionaries. Number six was a secretary to the Governor. He lived on the far side of the European graveyard, the better side. Before I paid him a call, I would have to give my road-spoiled shirt a good work over.

Contact number seven was lost without trace. Number eight, an ethnologist – 'a great big, Jewish-faced, pleasant sort of chappie', according to the good book – had retired home to attend to a domestic crisis. Number nine denied all knowledge of having met Theodore Hull.

My shirt still damp from Erman's scrubbings, I set out for the Governor's secretary. This was Theodore's last man. His house crouched behind hyacinths and bugle-flowered creepers that scrambled out of control along unnaturally luxuriant shrubs. It was a bungalow: spick and span, grilles on the windows, two waxed cars beneath a lean-to. Very nice too. I stalked up the short cement drive. The lawn sprinkler coughed as I stepped on the hose. The garden was as lush as a river glade; leaves looked fat with juice, about to spirt open.

There was no bell at the door, so I knocked. 'Cross your fingers, Theodore.'

Just then, unaccountably, a door panel gave way. It thumped on to the carpet behind. The pile must have been very springy, because the panel bounced right up and deftly somersaulted. A large dog, with a coat matching the beige carpet, leapt for cover. I never set eyes on the animal again. Through the hole I saw a girl of about sixteen blinking at me. She lay curled on the sofa like another dog. Her mouth was open, and she was about to scream.

'Sorry,' I said. She gaped for a little while, and a little while more.

Then she began to stretch out, cautiously extending her bare feet to the floor.

I knocked again – a statement of business. She opened the door and stood side on, holding it tight. She was slim, too slim for her build. 'Hello,' I said. 'Is backpack – I mean Bapak Roistani in?'

'Away.'

She was still pressed against the door – a touch scared, I thought.

'When's he coming back, please?'

'Two weeks? He's in Jakarta. Is it important?'

'He might be able to help me with my research.'

'If you like you may come in, and write down a message.' She spoke formally, her tension showing in the trembling of her lips. She was probably alone in the house.

I took my shoes off, left them with all the others in the porch, and the carpet pile sucked in my tired feet, pampering the sore, damp skin. The room was sparsely furnished; pieces slightly tacky – French polish everywhere – but probably worth a mint in Sumatra.

'Please,' she said in English, 'sitting?' Her voice was easier. She was softening, opening up, warming. She gestured to the second sofa, a spreading movement with a long, loose arm. I took a seat and she lazily dropped back into hers, tucking her legs up. The feet were very small indeed. I liked the neatness with which they folded away. Over her shoulder she called, '*Satu kopi!* One coffee!' A pair of women's shoes clacked on a hard floor close by, next door.

I saw no point in leaving a message – I could not call back in two weeks. Heaven only knew where I would be by then. I put my calling card on a table carved with a forest scene – Lake Toba, up in the north, a Batak warrior with a narrow, boy's chest, thrusting a lance through the rib cage of a second, plump warrior. A maid brought in a silver pot of coffee, and a tiny cup – only one. Then the girl whispered, looking at the coffee pot. 'Name is?'

'Benedict.'

'Bendit, you are pretty.'

I jolted. I looked at her, unsure of her intention. Her eyes were glued to the coffee pot. 'Thanks,' I said lightly, 'and so are you.'

'I will entertain you.' She rose and went over to an electric organ, spreading her hands on the plastic keys. She clicked her nails on them as she thought out some cords. 'John Lenhan – you like?'

As she played, her gold ornaments jingled. The organ cheerfully released music that was a far cry from anything resembling John Lennon. Suddenly she jumped up and spun around to me. Her name was

Segma, she announced. 'You like?' She was hot — I could smell the perfume lifting from her.

She amused herself showing me the photos around the room. 'This is me,' she said, her hand running along the shelf to a gilded frame.

'Really?' I saw a spoilt little girl bound firmly in a sarong, like a tight-petalled bud.

On a frail mahogany cabinet was a photo of Bapak Roistani, the secretary. A fatherly face; a decent, likeable man shaking hands with the President, trunk bent forward in a half-bow, the photographer cutting him off at the knees and almost missing his proud smile.

I noticed an oil painting of Fort Marlborough. 'That used to be British,' I said to Segma. She thought I was joking, and laughed all the way back to her sofa. 'You are fun to talk, Bendit.'

I took a seat, because I was going to have to wait a long time before she thought to offer me one.

'Tell, Bendit. What do you doing in Bengkulu?' Segma slipped her fingers around her ankles. She wore a ring with a ruby block on it. As I told her about the ape-men, a smile crept quietly around her face. But afterwards she said, 'I know of stories, also.'

'You do?'

'You are — ah, I do not speaking English good — excited?'

'Surprised, yes. Most people think that the ape-men stories are a load of nonsense, just silly.'

'Silly. Yes. This is a correct word. Silly. No thinking. Peasant think-ings. Crazy-man thinkings.'

Crazy-man thinkings. I wanted to stand up for Theodore. I couldn't. I asked Segma what her story was.

'My story? I remember later.' Obviously she was stringing me along. She had been bored; I was a playmate for her. She asked me how much a house cost in England. And a camera? And was I married? Why not? The sun went down.

From outside, a man's voice called out to Segma. I did not understand the slang, but he had the assertive cadence of the courting male crickets. She replied quickly and crossly, with hardened lips. Her hands were trembling. She said to me in English, 'I have sent him away. He is not important.'

'Who is he?'

'A boy.'

In the garden, the frogs were belching louder than all the night's insects could scratch. The lawn sprinkler had upset the local ecology.

'Please, I have you for supper?'

The meal was ready on the glossy white melamine table next door. I washed my hands in the finger bowl. She watched from behind. The knife and fork were the first I had seen used in Sumatra; in the class of restaurants I frequented you ate only with your right hand.

'Aren't you eating?' I asked.

'Finished already.'

But she hadn't. I was eating her supper – her peppered chicken, fried mackerel, rice. Was it against her upbringing to eat with a male stranger? I did not know. I wondered if I was being assertive enough. She was what Theodore would have called a smartipuss; I might do well to adopt the arrogant tone of the crickets, like the man outside.

Afterwards it was coffee again. 'You wait,' she said, all at once springing up. 'Do not go.' She left the room. The thin rattle of the air conditioning joined with the insect noise, but the frogs were still louder. It made me uncomfortable; the natural order of things was upset here.

Segma returned wearing a dancing dress. It confined and steered her movements, heavy cloth with its gold and silver interstitchings in tight rectangles, a black jacket with gold flowers studded unsparingly across it, a swathe of fiddly plum embroidery which began around the back and crossed her chest to drop over both shoulders. But the garment was supposed to be worn with eyeliner, port-coloured lipstick, and nail varnish, perhaps a necklace of chain-linked sheets of pressed gold. Segma, without these, looked outdone.

But then she moved; she was different when she moved. She revolved herself, carried lightly on her toes, her lifted hands helping her float.

'Golly,' I said, with sincerity.

'I want to dancing. But ... no music.' I thought she was doing well enough without. She tapped her toes on the carpet, humming, elbows tight in against her hips, and I imagined a gamelan orchestra of gongs accompanying her. I could not get over my luck: a beautiful maiden performing just for me. Yes, all in all, I was taking quite a fancy to Sumatra.

Each dance told a story. In the first she was a dipping bird. She preened, picking at her sleeve, her fingers parting, closing, parting.

'And now, a dance of Java.' She put an imaginary pitcher on her head, then bent at the knees, balancing it there on a make-believe whorl of cloth. She raised her arms, made them wings, and flew. High up, she swayed, circled, gyrated. She was a bird savouring each quiver of this courtship dance, and I had forgotten it was an act. I was mystified by her, by this image. This *mirage*: these hands had never shifted clods of paddy, nor closed round a hoe, nor sluiced a pail – the fingers with nails which made her fingers splay so finely, so like flight feathers. Her scent was exotic to me and I breathed her in, this creature that was attending to my senses. She put the pitcher down with care and revolved her hands by her chest, winding wool: coiling up a strand that was between us, binding it in, binding me in. I was pulled to the edge of my seat, gazing at the supple fingers as they fluttered about her, over her long narrow waist, then her willowy, pale neck, the blossom-soft skin which had been kept so carefully from the sun.

She sat down, her body taut, suddenly afraid of my eyes on her, but also quivering, inflamed. 'Are you interested in me?'

I thought before I spoke. *If you fall for a girl out there, make it a Chinese. The rest you should avoid like the plague.*

'In what way interested?'

'In the American way.'

She means what that bus conductor in Padang called 'free sex', I thought. But of course she'll never say it. After all, she hasn't even dared eat with me.

'In what way is that?' I said.

'Free sex.'

Then – I did not know if it was good or bad luck – the poor old youth yelled from outside again. I watched Segma's burning, clear black eyes closely. Would she be embarrassed to be found alone with a Westerner, dressed up, her skin darker from its hot glow? She looked disdainfully at the door, drawing her nails along her jacket. They made a reedy noise as they travelled the cloth. No. She would not be coming out to play.

'Tomorrow,' she called. 'See you tomorrow.' The youth walked off, scuffing. The lawn sprinkler let out a grunt and a pained hiss – he had tripped on the hose.

Segma slouched back. Her eyes dropped to the carpet and stayed locked there. She said, 'You can *mentjium* with me?'

'I don't know what that word means,' I said. But I could guess. This was an adventure for her. I was beyond her knowledge, foreign to her world. She touched her lips with her fingers, showing me what a *mentjium* was. But her eyes were held tightly to the carpet. I looked at those long fingernails, paraded along her lips in a rank – inflexible, even, buffed.

'I'd better not,' I told her, after a short think. 'Besides, what will your maid say?'

She said, as if it was a complete answer, 'You won't touch me. Except on the mouth.' Segma was speaking in Indonesian now, maintaining control, strongly aware of any movement I made. She was feeling me, watchful, thrilled, half glimpsing the unknown.

'Who said I wanted to touch you?'

'I've seen you in films.'

'Not me, in actual fact. American actors.'

'*Sama, sama.* The same. I've seen it.' She nodded, sure of this. And her gaze loosened from the carpet.

It was just about time to leave. Supposing her daddy came back home early? And what about her mum? No. I would kiss Segma goodnight. That was all. On my way out.

She was not even going to get up, so I bowed down over her, stiff-legged, my hands cupped behind me, like a flightless bird. She straightened her back, and tilted her head to receive the kiss. This was an easier posture for Segma – slouching had been an affectation. I was now poised above her. This was ridiculous, but she seemed to think our act the most natural one in the world, for the modern generation. My face was tipped deep within her rising, perfumed cloud. I lowered my lips to hers. As they were about to join, she closed her eyes quickly. Her lips were pressed towards me as an offering. She was a flower fully opened out, petals unfurled, trembling. Her mouth softened into mine. Our teeth tapped together. At that she suddenly pushed my head away. She was in fright: her nails were extended, ready, set on my cheeks.

I went to the netted, inner door, the last-ditch defence against the insects which had been gushing into the porch all evening through the panel hole. The girl was cooing to herself, alone in her thoughts. For all Segma knew, I might have left already. Then she spoke up – in my language again. 'I have not had this done before.'

I thought, That, my dear Segma, is obvious.

The maid came in to clear up our coffee. She hadn't missed much.

The maid's brief presence had cooled Segma, fetched her back to her world, her reality. Now she said, 'Tomorrow. Six o'clock. You can eat here.'

I hesitated. Little wings clicked and clattered on the netting. 'And you'll tell me about these ape-people?'

'Of course,' she said. Her colour had gone. She did mean it.

I tramped back to the hotel. The stars were sparse and the road utterly black. By the graveyard I walked into a cow. It must have been cogitating in the road. We jumped from each other, and the cow cantered off in the direction of the beach, as if to drown itself.

The hotel had been locked up. I knocked and knocked. Erman hopped out from under a bench. He lit a paraffin lamp. In the glow I saw he had a swollen face – a dark puff where there should have been an eye socket.

'What happened?'

He unlocked the door for me. 'Nothing. Family trouble.'

'I thought you didn't have a family.'

Erman shrugged, and moved off heavily along the corridor. 'No one wants to talk about your stories. They gave me a lot of trouble.' A shadow sprang up the wall boards as he raised a hand to his face.

'I'm very sorry, really I am. I'll make it up to you.' I patted his shoulder. 'But you're not going to be put off, are you? You'll keep asking, won't you?'

'You'll pay . . . ?'

'Yes,' I said, 'I'll pay.'

'No,' he decided.

'But why not?'

'I don't like being hit. I just don't *like* it.'

The expedition had claimed its first, but probably not its last, casualty. By way of compensation I promised Erman a fat fee if he could get a Baptist or Catholic priest to scribble down who St Elizabeth was. As for Segma, I thought, lying in bed, she was not as unsubtle as her fractured English forced her to be. And she was certainly attractive – not as a woman, but as a piece of design: the shallow curves, the subtle mouldings, the additional gold fixtures. Her physical form gave aesthetic pleasure. My God, she's beautiful, I thought. It was what Theodore would have said.

Chapter Two

In the morning Erman made me a gritty coffee, then galloped off to find a Catholic church.

The sun came from out of a fog, which told you that it was going to be an even cleaner, whiter heat than yesterday's. I walked off towards the harbour, by way of the beachside shacks. Women were rooting about at the tideline, pawing at the surf suds, flopping with the seagulls on shellfish, while goats wandered among rolling coconuts – worn as smooth as bowling balls – leaving behind neat pellets of orange excreta. Would the women care to miss the tide and chat with me about ape-men? No, I decided, they would not.

Fort Marlborough sat fair and square on its hillock above the harbour. It was restored, and looked like a wedding cake – chunky and whitewashed, with cannon-ball stacks and a propped-up old gate of nail-dotted wood.

Below the Fort, in the reek of salt and fish and stewed seaweed, were the cannon. They lined the wharf, encased in concrete, like anti-tank blocks. Perhaps they *were* anti-tank blocks. Fishing boats were being sucked and slapped by the harbour water; naked boys were paddling a log out. Nets were being spread on the wharf by fishermen in plaited-leaf hats. The men's shadowed faces in the raging sun looked black and melted, like blobs of tar. Would they like to stand around being roasted, as I enquired about Gugu? I would rather not find out.

The boys had splashed ashore from their log, and were whooping at me on the breakwater, one-legged, pulling shorts on, silver riverlets twisting off them. I walked up the coast, taking a track along the red cliffs, and the children ran, twittering, after. Soon the sea was forty feet below us, smashing on black rocks, wiping them in spilt cream. A dead chicken rolled in the wash. Far out, fishermen were swaying in small boats, handling sails. The shacks here had palm-mat walls and fluted posts. I would have stopped to ask in the porches, but the boys made that impossible. 'Hey mister!' 'John!' I must lose them. A child was playing his kite off the cliff edge. He hauled the line in and joined the gang.

This was hopeless. I doubled back. But there, by a mosque domed with lichenous rust, was Erman. His face looked worse. The bruising was crimson and he had an insect's expressionless, bulbous eye.

'I thought I'd come and collect you,' he shouted. 'The boys said you'd be coming in from the sun about now.'

'I can't chat to anyone with *them* here' – I jabbed a finger at the nearest child. 'They're a nuisance.'

'You don't want them?'

'Can you do anything about it?'

'Of course. But are you sure?'

'Why shouldn't I be?'

He showed me, swinging a punch at a boy who had square, irregular yellow teeth. He fell flat on his back with a thump and began screaming at the sky.

I closed my eyes. 'I didn't mean . . .'

Too late now. The crowd was not filtering away, it was growing. Girls masked with white skin-paste came out from the shadows, risking the sun. Grown-ups pushed through the banana gardens or hurdled balustrades. They were shouting at me. Nearer at hand, bigger boys were working through the crowd. I said, 'It's lunch. Time we were going.'

As we trotted, Erman told me that, looking for a Catholic church, he had found an ape-man story. We must go to a house with a bamboo pole.

Bamboo poles are nothing out of the ordinary, but this was taller than the house and was erected so that it pitched out over the road like a fishing rod. Woven foliage pendants, lanterns and yellow ribbons hung down from the end, a palm-leaf sign that announced a wedding.

'Come in! Come in!' screamed an old dear, suddenly there in a black dress. 'Come and see the wedding preparations. Come and hear about the ape-girl.'

'Ape-*girl*?' We chased her up an unweeded alleyway between two wood houses, where men of all ages were milling around, doing nothing constructive. 'Ape-*girl*,' I repeated over my shoulder, but Erman was dropping back. He would rather leave me to it.

The old woman hacked through the crowd with her elbows. Men were hugging me, wrapping me in their warmth. A wedding invitation was squeezed into my pocket – a white card, tagged with red ribbon.

'The bride!' I called, in party mood but waving both arms to defend my breathing space. 'Where's the bride?' She was already being pushed forward by the old woman, who steered from behind with the bride's little arms. The girl walked looking straight ahead, shaking under the weight of all the eyes on her, and seeing nothing – apparently conscious only of herself, the burning of her cheeks, the brightness that she was spreading. She had on a long ruby dress cross-splashed with gold, and no shoes. The woman hoisted the bride's hair to her head, and held it there. This was only one day in a week's preparation: today was teeth-grinding day. The girl's smile was bright and wide, but the family's standards were high – they were going to smooth out every corrugation. After the seven days she would be near-perfect: her cuticles smooth, her hair a black satin, her eyebrows two slender crescents. I was jerked off to see the bridal bed – a four-poster which sagged under the weight of its smooth drapery, in a little broken box of a room which hitherto had slept five.

'A story!' a treble voice sang. 'He's going to tell us a story.'

An old boy in a sarong doddered up the alleyway. He had been weeding – the only man doing any work around here – but he looked dug up from a local sandpit. His black skin was doubled over in parts, and his elbows were rough from wear and were stained a ferrous colour. He had a parang, which he swung loosely in his fingers, and he smelt sweet from the cut grass; he was flaked out, so breathless from the work that his handshake was like the clawing of a drowning man. A fisherman, I was informed. A storyteller whose skin had been burnt by sea air. I looked at the fingers now on my arm, and then at the wedding party. Wait for it, I thought, drawing my pen out. 'The Rime of the Ancient Mariner' . . .

'The thorns', began the old soul, conjuring a pin from his collar, and holding it up in his fingertips for everyone to see, 'should have ripped the creature's bare skin but instead they skidded lightly over it, accommodating themselves to the animal's curves.'

The men were gathered round in a tight circle, and leant over the bannisters, fencing out the light. The old sea salt did not have to demand silence.

'Birds which should have shrieked and clattered through the branches merely hunched down a little. The animal parted the saplings and spiralling creepers as if to avoid creasing the leaves. The only obvious disturbance to the jungle was in its wake: leaves lifted in the gust; gnat clouds were momentarily unbalanced.'

Children were squeezed through to watch the old man, and my chasing pen. I heard the story of Pastaran the peasant and his ape-girl –

delivered to him by Allah for his adultery. Happily for Pastaran, the tale of the encounter never did permeate the outside world. And there was at least one very good reason why not.

The peasants seem to have been oblivious of the outbreak of war, the Japanese pincer strategy, the Allied troops making a dash for it, the prisoners on the railways or locked in cells as spies. Before the fighting was over, Pastaran was killed. Not gloriously, in action defending his daughters' honours against overexcited Japanese footsoldiers, but in a minor traffic accident in Kota Baru. He was standing a little too near the kerb. As he was swapping market gossip, a Japanese armoured car, out on manoeuvres, backed towards him. It applied its brakes too late. Even in the manner of his death, Pastaran's incompetence had manifested itself.

The burial took place without fuss. Most of his twelve children turned up: Radamun, who had a minor place in a pickpocket team at Bukittinggi fruit market; Ahmad, who had attached himself to the Lutheran missionaries in Padang, had been renamed Paul and for small coins ran errands to and from the church; the other sons who took over the farm and maintained the land's progressive impoverishment; and the four married daughters, all of whom were pregnant.

Pastaran's wife had told the tale to the mariner back in 1945, the year that the Dutch East Indies was declared the Independent Republic of Indonesia. Since then the account had accumulated some thirty years' dust. And how much had it warped? How much detail had been added over the decades? The secret liaison? The twelve children? The brass ring shattering? And wasn't Pastaran just a suburban neurotic anyway? Quite possibly. But Gugu stories *were* told in Sumatra. That had been confirmed. And my blood was up. *All we need is one such creature – just one.*

I always try to be punctual, and it was dead on six o'clock as I walked up to the house, through a plague of frogs. The frogs were congregated around the water sprinkler, but they spread right up the drive, where they were happily licking up insects drawn by all the house lights left on.

Segma called me in. She was leaning back on the sofa, in a pose I thought I had seen in a Hollywood movie somewhere. I was walking on to a film set.

'Can I play you music?' she said. Her eyes were as evasive as before, but smouldering. Something strong was working inside her. She wanted to go further with me; she was again absorbed in this venture; she enjoyed the danger of it.

'Tell me about yourself,' I said. 'You went to school in Bengkulu?'

'Pa! This is not interesting. You tell me about yourself.'

That was not interesting either, but she listened, discreetly looking me over, until supper time. As I ate, she stood behind me, hovering, waiting and watching. The finger bowl, the peppered chicken, the fish, the rice, the finger bowl again . . .

We returned to the sitting room. I said, 'Why don't you ever turn the water sprinkler off?'

'Why should I?'

'It seems a waste of water to me.'

'Of no importance. It can flow.' She sat down. Her sofa was distinctly nearer than last night. 'You are satisfied with the food?'

'Thank you. It was very good. A little hot for me.'

'Am I a little hot for you?'

'What?'

For a moment she was quiet, silenced by what she had said. She pressed on, afraid, but wanting: 'This is a phrase, isn't this? Am I a hot girl. Like American. But here the girls are frigid girls. This means they are like the re-frig-er-er-erator to the boy. They don't even kiss. I kiss — you try my lips last evening — and therefore I am a hot thing.' She nodded to herself, checking she had got the words right. 'You see, my English is good.'

'Your vocabulary seems to have advanced a lot since yesterday.' I bet she had been picking her girlfriends' brains all day for smutty words.

'But you are more interested in the monkey-men than me.'

'Well . . .' Well, she was right. She was a spoilt child. She needed a good, fatherly slap. No devout Muslim would tolerate this. 'I'm afraid it's the job I'm here to do.'

'All work and no play makes Jim a bad boy.'

'How true,' I said. But my aloof manner was crushing. I had lost interest, and she had lost her power and was now unsure. She folded in, looking suddenly younger and vulnerable through her innocence.

'What do you want me to tell?'

'You said you had a story?' I felt for her — so pale and soft, the unknowing child.

'There is a ship to the island of Siberut from Padang. You hear of the Mentawai islands?' She paused, then suddenly she reared backwards, cringing from a repulsive sight at the bottom of my sofa. A cockroach?

'You have hairs on your legs,' she gasped.

'What were you going to say about the islands? My colleague mentioned them.' Theodore had mentioned these islands — beyond a clutch of smaller ones which were like cowpats – 'Green cowpats. Forested – or some such green tangle.'

'I do not like hairs.' I had rejected the girl; a sourness had come over her.

'That's a pity, then.'

'They are unclean. Like the primitives of Siberut island. *They* like hairs. They like hairy monkeys. They like them too much. They pull the monkeys from the trees and make hot love with them. They kiss hard and sex. The boys do this to girl monkeys. Siberut girls are taken and sexed in trees by boy monkeys. They are animals together. Here, at Sumatra, you can find nothing. No more of the monkey-men. Is finished. But at Siberut, you find this.'

'You believe this?'

'My father tells me this. He is the Governor.'

'A *secretary* to the Governor.'

'My father says the primitive men's brains make them close friends to monkeys. That is why they cannot believe in Allah. And they eat roots and worms.'

'This is just market chatter, obviously.'

'I have seen a book with photos. Men with not enough clothes dance for the pleasure of the monkey.' She lifted her chin victoriously. So there.

'Well, this sounds most interesting . . .'

Segma talked as if the 'monkeys' were part human. As if they were Gugu. 'And you think I should go to Siberut instead of tracking down a Kubu to talk to?'

She took time to answer; her thoughts were not with me. 'Asking the priests in Padang for full information. Then you visit to Siberut. The Kubu primitives are worst. They are dirtier than the monkeys. And most Kubu is finished. You will not find many of these. Even the government officers can't find these people – and they try very hard.'

'I've heard it said.'

'So you go to Siberut, not the Kubu.' A man's footsteps interrupted us. There was a rap at the door. Segma shouted at him to go away. He kicked the shoes about the porch. Segma yelled that she would be half an hour. The man shouted three words contemptuously. The last of the three was 'John'.

The footsteps receded. The lawn sprinkler burped.

'One of your boyfriends?'

'He will be my husband,' she said.

'Ah.'

I saw her satisfaction. She belonged here; this was her home ground.

She was reassured, now that I was isolated. 'So, we say goodbye . . .' I was as I had begun, alien to her, a foreign land in which she should not trespass.

'Right. I'd better go.' Quick-smart, I thought, using a Theodore phrase. 'Nice to meet you . . .' She stayed put, lodged in her sofa. I walked briskly to the door, wondering where the fiancé was. Crouching with a blunt instrument in the water-sprinkled shrubbery? Or loitering for me in the graveyard?

'Wait!' Segma jumped up. Something in her had cracked. The former longing had broken out. She came pattering after me on her toes. 'I will kiss you goodbye. Like the film. You are the hero.'

'Which film?'

But she did not want me to question. She wanted the thrill of abandonment. I said, backing towards the net door, 'I don't think this is a very good idea.' But her lips were already reaching to mine. What film was this – *Bloody Magnum*? Her mind had left the room; it was no longer with me. She was playing the female lead, burying herself in a role which at a guess was thankfully only Hollywood passion, circa 1939 – *Gone With the Wind*.

She took her face away, drawing breath like a poor swimmer, and saying, 'Remember I loved you, my darling,' and again settled against me. Fine for a movie, but this was real life! Her hands were tearing through my hair like those of Vivien Leigh – or Bette Davis, or Dorothy Lamour. She did not know herself; she was out of her own world, and in some imagined modern land of liberation. In the final sequence her lips were bolder, pressing and seeking; and, as the shot faded, on cue, out of shot, the jealous fiancé knocked at the door.

Chapter Three

That was how I ended up trailing to the offshore, lozenge-shaped island of Siberut. I was looking for monkeys who hopped down from the trees to make hot love with maidens. These, tales belonging to the ignorant and superstitious, were the origin of the Gugu. I was certain. It was just as the opium had said. But I was meant to be Theodore's arms and legs, his ambassador, the fulfiller of an old man's dreams.

It was back to Padang first thing next morning. The ship was leaving for Siberut in three days. No time to wait for the wedding – neither that of the family which had invited me, nor Segma's.

As she had advised, I went along to the Xaverian mission. Father Sandro said that actually Stefano was my man – he knew all about the Siberuts. He left his scooter and whisked me indoors and along a bare corridor with a sky-high ceiling, telling me about St Elizabeth.

In the history of the Church, as we all know, there are those individuals who have been given a sign by God. You might get stigmata, or you might get angels – then again it might be Odours of Sanctity, a musky smell of roses. But for Elizabeth it was the full works. She was given real roses, a whole bunch. In Sandro's eyes, it had happened like this: Elizabeth was a good woman, but, if the truth were told, her confessor, Conrad, he thought, was not so good. Conrad beat her for giving away scraps to the poor. And the day came when Conrad caught her red-handed – she was definitely handing out crumbs.

'What do you have there, Elizabeth?' Conrad enquired, as she hid them in her apron. He ordered her to show him. But – miracle! – when she did, there was not a single crust. Instead, heaps of lovely roses.

'What a sweet story,' I said. We were outside Stefano's door.

Father Stefano was a thinking man with heavy spectacles. He spoke in Indonesian from low behind his desk, muffled by paperwork. He had a hermit's face with a groove in his chin. There was an unapologetic certainty about his quietness, which gave him a subtle charisma.

But about Siberut – oh dear, Father Stefano *was* a bit of a misery-guts.

When I asked him had he heard the word going round that monkeys were given gifts, and *special* favours, he did not laugh one bit. He said, 'These people are balanced with nature.[7] *We*, Benedict, are not. Why do we not want to learn from them? That is what you are asking.'

That was not what I was asking. I was steering towards whether, for example, market women really said that Siberut girls hung around in the monkeys' favourite courting trees.

He was still talking. 'And you are asking, why do we, in the "developed world", think of ourselves as the only civilised ones? You want to know the answer?'

Not just now, no, I thought.

'Why do we count these people as uncivilised? Because they are lovers of nature? No. The answer is this: fear.' He humped his shoulders and whined like a boy. 'Oh Benedict, the prejudice towards these primitive people has not yet been wiped out of the popular mind.' He laid his hands suddenly but noiselessly on a leaning tower of paper. 'We have identified civilisation with technical progress. This is wrong.' Stefano lowered his head, as if he was now going to dip into a book. 'And so, Benedict, now you know why I am sad.'

What use, Theodore, could Stefano be as a religious missionary? Normally they came to say that their creed was at least one peg up.

'I think I'm a little too pessimistic,' he was saying. 'Are the Italians known for this in England?'

'Not really. Mainly spaghetti, stylish cars and men's handbags.'

He was peeling open a tome that was almost as big as 'Hope at Large'. He sank into it, muttering that, pessimistic or not, it did not seem fair that the island was promised to loggers.

'I'd best get there right away then,' I said.

We were about to cast off. I propped myself on the ship rails, looking out at the quayside smiles and tears, and at the sprinkling of dark glasses – the Italian mob. In the midst of the crowd was a freckled-faced woman with blonde hair tied up securely in plaits. She was Sister Heike, the Lutheran nurse. Her cheeks were sunken, their colour lost, as if she worried too much for others. She tutted at the breeze, and waved her handkerchief to test it; the cotton flew high and slapped on her thin, bluish wrist. A wind was getting up – this was going to be just Theodore's sort of escapade. I should have thought to bring sea-sickness tablets.

The gangplank was dragged clear, the hawsers slashed the green water. The engines rumbled the deck under us. Passengers began clonking back down the metal steps to the middle deck, where the rust roof was dropping away in sheets. Down there, wires which were the communication between the ship's organs trailed whimsically around your feet. The plastic insulation had nibble marks in it – either rats' or children's. I had seen all this on the way up and had decided I was better off on the deck, out of the simmering human fug and with the lifeboats.

When the middle deck was packed with humans, the lower deck was filled. The families down there shrieked less and less as they stewed. Banana peels whirled into the sea from the little port-holes. Fish bickered over them.

I had staked my claim at the stern, at a spot that now appeared·to be directly in the sooty billow of the engine. By the railings were a flock of Batak Christians with guitars and pirate headscarves.[8] Minah birds, above me in three wooden cages, said 'Ooop! Ooop!' every time someone tripped over the stray ropes or the winding gear. My neighbour was a lanky black monkey who sat tweaking his waist collar, which was attached by a chain to a loose structural post.

Now the harbourside oil tanks were as small as food cans. I pinned my map of Siberut out on the deck with my jungle boots, and had a good peer at the island's convoluted river. veins. Apparently, on arrival tomorrow, a Father Fernando might offer me advice.

'Hi!' a voice said. I groaned, and tried to hide under my redundant Guguland map sheets.

'I'm John-o. And you?'

'Me? No, I'm Benedict.' John-o was shifting my rucksack, making a space on the oily boards between myself and the monkey.

He was an Indonesian, from Jakarta. 'I teach English. And I'm a kinda student. I hang out in the downtown precinct.'

'How interesting,' I said, and sighed, folding my maps up. The ship cut its engines, and less blue smoke came up from through the planks. Broken down already? I wondered. We were not fully out of the bay yet. Around us were spindly craft with striped outriggers; John-o said they were *perahu*, but from up here the leggy boats were lame, pond-skating flies.

'It's okay. We'll wait here. It's the storm.'

'Storm?'

'The storm out there.' He waved out to the dusk, which was going black just where the sun was meant to be setting. From the hood of the cloud jumped an electric spark, a buckled white prong.

'It's okay,' said John-o. 'It's all part of the experience.'

'What experience?'

'Sure,' he said, but he was frowning, baffled. Then: 'Hey! You like my pants?' He was smoothing spread hands over his Levi jeans, just like the advertisement.

'Very fetching,' I said.

'And the sneakers?'

'Oh yes. Very nice indeed.'

'How come you're not wearing yours today?'

'I haven't got any, actually.'

'Say, you have to be real poor. You also a student?'

'Normally you could say I was an explorer. But now I've somehow become an ambassador for—'

'Hey!' He snatched my hand and shook it hard, as you would to make a Coke can spurt. Next he showed me his amethyst earring.

A man in a creased white uniform came round with a notepad. First he fell over the Batak singers; then he thumped his head on a birdcage. 'Ooop! Ooop!' the minah birds said.

'Oh hell,' I groaned. 'Here's the chef taking orders. And right now even the thought of food makes me queasy.'

But, looking at the chef, John-o said, 'Here comes the captain.' Seeing us, the captain veered away sharply. He had met John-o before. 'He don't like my earring. He isn't very cool.'

'No, he certainly isn't that.' Around this first bit of his circuit, the captain had already oil-stained both cuffs and collected the lump on his forehead.

'He probably makes out I'm a hippy.'

'But you're not?' I did not know. Did Indonesian hippies have drug-needle tattoos, like the British one Theodore came across in India?

'How can I be a hippy?' John-o said, as if I was stupid. 'If I was, I'd be in the jailhouse.'

'I hadn't thought of that.'

John-o began to clap his hands to 'Jailhouse Rock'. After two verses he remarked, 'I'm a progressive.'

'Ah.'

He offered me a stick of gum. It was stiff and dry with age – as if normally left unused in his top pocket, kept by the heart as a talisman. After a while I said, 'A progressive what?'

'A liberal. Most of my friends are. My earring is a demonstration.'

'Of what?'

'No, man. A *demonstration*.'

'Oh, I see. Against something.' He nodded, sighing, trying hard to be patient. After another while, I said, 'Against anything in particular?'

'The system. The rigidity of the ball game.'

'The rigidity of the ball game?'

'Yep.'

'Why don't you demonstrate on the streets?'

'Are you kidding?'

The Bataks were now hymn-singing in English. 'Seen-g pra-ees, seen-g pra-ees, see-ging pra-ees to the Lo-ard.'

John-o said, 'I'm vacationing. I'll stay on the ship while it tours the whole Mentawai island group. Then Nias — that's where the primitives jump over stones to prove their manhood. What are you doing? Also just checking the islands out?'

'Yeah,' I said, 'just checking the islands out.' Then I reconsidered. This progressive liberal might have an original thought on the Gugu. Being an affluent urbanite, he might be less embarrassed by folklore; part of him, the modern, Westernised part, might be yearning for the mystery of legend again.

'I'm studying the old tales of Sumatra,' I told him. 'Some of them are about people who are half ape, half human. There are even people — well, there's one person — who says that here in Sumatra there are creatures who are still descending from apes.'

'Holy shit! Who told you that crap?'

'A friend.'

'Looks like you've been mixing with the wrong kinda people.' With a cautious eye on the Batak Christians, he whispered, 'That's communist talk.'

The ship coughed. There was a rattling of chains and much grinding of metal, and we were shifting again, cutting out of the bay into the unprotected water. The sky was black, except when it was being shattered by lightning. The minah birds began to cry, and the monkey buried itself under my rucksack. The wind was cold, hostile. It came in spasms, tugging at us, hacking at the water, whitening it, pitching the ship up on to the sea hillocks, and twisting us sideways back down again. The Christians stopped their strumming. They wiped sea spit off their guitars. All but one of them packed up and went below. The remaining boy came away from the railings and rolled his New Testament up in a blanket. Then he snuggled in with it.

It was now dark, but in the brief silver of the lightning I saw that John-o was laughing. 'This is it,' he cried.

'What is?' I said, the wind sucking oil-fume spews over us.

'The experience.'

As the experience got worse I said, 'I hope the crew know how to undo the lifeboats. They're all wired in. A blow-torch is what's going to be needed to tackle that stuff.'

'Stay cool. I spoke to the captain before he left Padang. He said this is the finest ship he has captained. So we have nothing to worry about.'

'How many ships has he been in charge of?'

'Only the one.'

'Ha!'

'Relax. He's been on the ship for thirty years.'

'Thirty years? How long do ships last?'

But the student was hunched over, trying not to retch. I tasted the water coming down, and it was salty. Saline rain?

The Batak Christian crawled off, as if to find a slightly quieter place to die. We were alone on the deck – alone but for the monkey and minah birds. I cloaked myself in my jungle tarpaulin, glad to be left space in which to think about St Elizabeth's roses and other encouraging miracles.

Through the black, with the cross-slashing rain stinging my eyes, I could make out clouds like up-ended bolsters. Below them were the crinkling banks of sea, and across the hedges of waves the veering grey smear, our ship's reflection.

The minah birds' cages clunked and clunked together, as I thought of a tale the quiet Father Stefano had told me. He had heard Sandro yacking outside his room about the miracle of St Elizabeth and had called out that he knew a rose story of his own, though it was more in the Eastern tradition.

The more I recalled Stefano's story, the more I had to tell it to somebody. It crystallised Theodore's nebulous 'understanding'. John-o was looking as if he needed cheering up. I said, 'Talking of experiences, there's a story I've heard.'

'Yeah?'

'Yeah. This man, a European prisoner-of-war, is thrown into an ancient dungeon, built by the British during their time here centuries ago. He's alone, maybe going to die, but he's calm. And the calmness of his solitude develops to such a degree over the months that he finds the interruption of the daily shower an annoyance. In fact – you'll like this – he has begun to feel that "Time is something of our own making – as insubstantial as matter itself. 'We' do not exist, as consciousness, in time or matter at all."[9] And what the heck, you might say, does *that* mean?

'Your guess is as good as mine. You see, the prisoner, lately of the Malayan Civil Service, had met a wise old man out in India while among the Telegu, who were labour for the rubber plantations. Now, as a prisoner, he recalled his words – about the nature of time and so on. He'd also said, "We are greater than matter and can even create a shadow of it ourselves." So he pictured a rose there before him in the dim light. He thought and thought, and soon could actually see it suspended in front of him. By concentrating, he could revolve the rose at will. He studied it – the velvet of its petals, the serrated edge to the leaves, the red of the smooth and brittle thorns. The rose stayed beside him, a companion; he left it in the cell when he went to the bath house; he came back; it was waiting for him, lighting the cell. And the day came when he could even smell its perfume.

'The daily trip to the bath house is obviously what most prisoners live for – the brief caring hug of fellow prisoners, the whiff of cleaner air, the bickering of sparrows. Each one of these things is beautiful to them, and tells them that it probably is worth living. *This* man has to be cajoled from his cell. He wanted only to be back in the dungeon with his rose. He felt, and this is the nub of it, John-o, "I had escaped from prison, from time and from matter, and was free for ever." '[10]

'So, that's it,' John-o said. 'He doesn't get liquidated or anything?'

'That's the sum of it, yes. But—'

'Cheese! That's great!'

'There's more. You see, with time, imperceptibly the image of the rose grows stronger, as it hangs suspended right in front of his eyes, till one day—'

John-o said, weakly, 'I'm going downstairs. Coming?'

'But I haven't finished. And what about your "experience"?' But John-o was too busy looking for a bag to vomit into.

I preferred to brave it out there, with the waves washing the deck clear of the Christians' banana-skin refuse. The sky was shot through with lightning, but the thunder was lost in the beating of the chains and the smacking water. The monkey was shivering, its head under its hands. Its hair was stuck down with water, its arms like frayed ropes. The minah birds rocked in their cages, sleepy heads deep inside their shoulders. The monkey was alone, I was alone. He looked at me through the wind, as if waiting for the end to the bedtime story. I told him: finally the day came when the rose image was so strong that when the prisoner came out of his cell friends noticed that he wore a scent of roses! It happened again and again. *We are greater than matter and can even create a shadow of it ourselves!*

The ship slanted to left and right, keeled forward, was hoisted back. The ropes uncoiled and writhed. The waves and the rain swept through in a pelting brine, and there was no telling them apart. I thought of

Theodore, and more especially now about the second prisoner – what he had put into words about their peace, about that rising out of self. It was an escape from our bounds of matter and time. 'Time is the ultimate destroyer of everything,' the Thai Buddhist temple had said. And the understanding both prisoners shared seemed to be that, even discounting heavenly intervention, you could bend our earthly rules a little and feel free of them.

Some time in the night a wave must have caught the monkey, washed him from my side. As the ship rolled he must have juggled at the end of the leash, his small head being thumped against the hull as we pitched and yawed – thumping, thumping like a gong stick. I woke in the morning to discover the chain leading beyond the railings. I tugged, and it came up quite easily. The collar was empty, gnawed apart – as if the little chap had not been able to stand the bashing any longer and had decided to do away with himself.

Poor, miserable animal. So human, so unhuman. A chimp, a learned gentleman had once told me, has maybe ninety-five per cent of a human's genes. What, then, makes the five per cent difference? Perhaps the people of Siberut, if they had any understanding of monkeys whatsoever, could explain this to me, along with the other outstanding matters.

Chapter Four

The elements had rearranged themselves by dawn. The rain was well clear, and out there below a sky of pallid cream ribbons was a thin spread of palm trees. 'Siberut,' John-o said.

'There don't seem to be many houses on it.'

'No problem. The ship stops at Muarasiberut. That's the biggest kinda habitation. So obviously we ain't there. Not until we stop.'

We stopped. A flotilla was coming out to meet us. The canoes – splinters of wood sliding on a polished tray – gave me a clue where to spot houses. I traced a short rank of them. They were squeezed between the yellow palm trees, draped in mist sheets.

Passengers were being shuffled off. I picked up my rucksack, and said goodbye to John-o.

'Stay cool,' he said.

I told him I would try to.

In the rising heat, as I watched from the canoe, the rank of houses thickened. It was a white line that replicated and replicated until, at the harbour side, I saw sandy lanes with the occasional shrub protected in a bamboo cage, and a main lane of cement. Some of the huts were shops; by the look of it they sold only inessentials – cigarettes, sweets. The sound in the morning air was the clonking of wooden rice pestles.

I stepped ashore and watched the ship easing into the distance. It had looked like an unsalvageable wreck back in Padang, a menace to proper shipping. But on the edge of this coconut isle its solid metal hulk was imposing, scientific – predictable and therefore secure. I was sorry to see it go.

Ship arrival was an event, a market day. Along the path men were squatting and women kneeling. But they tended nothing; they were already sold out. These people did not talk Indonesian. They did not seem to be Indonesians at all. The *Indonesians* were over there, in their yards, their fingers getting dusty as they sorted through rice grains spread on mats, their chickens picking up the rejects. The other, nearby,

people were older. They did not do their Western shirts up, did not
bother with bras. Bluey-green tattoos curled around them in symmetrical lines. Designs emerged from under the clothes, boldly ascending the
throat, climbing the jaw, winding up on to the cheek. The designs came
forth unabashed: stripes, hoops and garter bands scattered out from
under the frayed shirt, skirt and trouser hems to the end of every limb.
The Siberuts were quieter than the Sumatrans, but they were more
forward. As they smiled I could not help noticing their teeth: they had
been deftly sharpened into points.

I had been heading for the town centre, but now I realised I had
already passed right through it – a minute's stroll. The church was
bound by a patch of short, clean grass. It had a roof the colour of
brimstone, and stone walls that looked as if they were here until Kingdom come. In the porch was a display case offering charms at rock-
bottom prices: a St Christopher medallion at five rupiah, a crucifix for
little more.

The door was ajar, letting through a smell of grass clippings. I
glimpsed a pampered lawn and cosseted shrubs. This might have been
suburban Surrey – a transported block of Millet country. But from out
of the cloister shadow came a swarthy European in a Paisley dressing-
gown. His breath smelt of mint toothpaste, and water droplets hung in
his beard. He had a newspaper folded under his arm – *Corriere della
Sera*. The issue was five years old.

'Father Fernando?' I said.

'*Momento*.' He about-turned and walked off, scuffing his slippers and
sticking to the shade.

Father Fernando was already dressed. He strode up with tobacco
smoke jetting from his nostrils. His hair was combed back, dark and
shiny with water or grease. He was a short man. His black-framed
spectacles looked big on his face. Sideburns fanned out to his earlobes,
and the two yellow-stained fingers of his right hand were fixed in a
victory sign, awaiting another cigarette. I gave him some post from
Stefano and told him about the Gugu stories. I asked if he knew contact
number one, Father Morini. He laughed. 'Morini! Oh so very funny
man.'

'Quite,' I said sadly. 'Now, I've heard stories of there being a close
relationship between monkeys and humans here, even now. I'm sure
there's no truth in it, is there?'

'They are friends,' said the Father, pride decorating his face. 'Is nice.
Good.'

'Closer than friends?' I said. I was determined to get further than I had with Father 'These–People–Are–Balanced–With–Nature' Stefano.

'Closer than friendships? And-a, how much closer?' Fernando asked. His eyes were narrowing.

'How much closer?' I braced myself; I might get a Latin slap for this. I said, 'As close as you can get.'

Fernando hissed. He did not redden and he did not flex his jaw. He clapped his hands, and he laughed. 'These stories! Interesting thing! Where you hear?'

'Just a town girl.'

'Oh.' His face lost vitality. He told me what he knew. It was not as good. The island had four endemic species of primate, and none of them sounded to him like lovers: not the joja, which was the Mentawai langur, a creature with a black back, white face-ring and throat, and a fine dark tail; nor the bilou, or Kloss gibbon, thought to be the most primitive of all gibbons; not the simakobu, a close relative of the proboscis monkey; and not the bokkoi, or Mentawai macaque, unique for his calls – a harsh bark from the male, whinnying, screeching and coughing from the other troop members.

'What form does their friendship take, then?' I wanted to know.

'You ask them. You ask them everythings. The Siberuts know the apes and the monkeys more than any peoples.' Fernando drew a cigarette out of his top pocket. It took its place in his hand as naturally as another finger. 'But sex?' He tutted gravely. 'I think no.' He coughed behind his hand. 'Please, you can-a ... inform me when you know? For the sciences?'

Quite. But this was the first really bad blow for the evolutionary hypothesis. Fernando was helping to confirm that any monkey- or apemen tales were plain silly. 'Well, I've got a week before the ship comes back,' I mused. 'And the Siberuts know the primates better than anyone, you say ...'

Fernando said, 'Three weeks. You have three weeks before the ship to Padang.'

'Three weeks? But the timetable says—'

'The timetable!' He snorted in the way he had done once already when I mentioned Father Morini. 'If you have the emergency, maybe you take the chance with the little cargo boats.'

'Take the chance?'

'You know, normally is safe.'

'I suppose I'll have to risk it.'

Fernando took two almighty drags of the cigarette. 'Have you the full medicine?'

'Flagyl, tetramycine, a few other broad-spectrum antibiotics . . .' I laughed, 'Why, is there some deadly disease I don't know about?' Millet's disease! Erysipelas! I had looked it up in the old medical dictionary, a family heirloom kept in my bedroom: very soon sharp red patches appear, spreading in all directions with 'superficial blebs'. In chronic alcoholics the prognosis is less favourable.

'There was a Dutch boy, two weeks past. He was-a studying at the south. He wanted the Siberut music for his recorder machine. He had *so much* equipment. Except-a the medicine. The fevers came for him. A medicine man was brought to the assistance – the magics, the spells. The boy – he is almost dead when he is carried here. Sister Heike was at his bed all the days and all the nights. Doctors on the mainland, they refuse to come. She gave the Dutch boy much relief. He is-a buried last week.'

'What was it?'

'Malaria? Typhoid? The both, you know?'

'Poor boy.'

'He is your age. And much-a like you – the tall, the gold hairs.'

Father Fernando said that before I did anything else I should register my arrival with a local administrator. 'But your clothes. I think you change them. Before the police see – you understand?' I did. My hair was salt-caked and smelt like seaweed. In the midday heat it would probably attract beach flies. Fernando conducted me to-a bathroom off the quadrangle – he clapped sharply to wake a gardener in the bushes – and gave me a sample of his home-made orange juice.

The administrative office should not have been difficult to find in such a small town, but it was. Finally, I adjusted my shirt, shuffled through my calling cards for a cleaner selection, and knocked on the unlabelled door of a prefabricated office. There was no one in. I perched myself on the verandah beneath the coat hooks. From these hung two warped black truncheons. After five minutes a little boy happened by. He stopped, scraped his navel, then whistled across the track at what might have been a potting shed. A man groaned from inside. The boy ran off. The man ambled out and then round to the back of the building, tugging a flat cap on. Through the thin office door I heard the scrape of his chair. I knocked again.

'Come in!'

There was an old filing cabinet, a desk with a typewriter and files, curtains of spider webs, and a chair, which the man pointed at, taking his cap off again. 'You are a Dutch student, I remember.'

'No, actually. I don't believe we've met before.'

He looked at me as if searching for something mislaid. 'You have come back to see the beautiful wildlife now?' He gestured at a poster which featured some jungle fowl. Next to it on the wall was a calendar, and it was set on March. The outside world was on to July.

'Come back? I haven't been here before.' Indented in the floor cement were the tracks of a chicken. I followed the prints round to where they looped under the desk.

He was still prodding me over with his eyes. 'Whereabouts do you come from. Hampersterdamp, isn't it?'

Hampshire, he means. I said yes, and told him about my village, its hill, church and duckpond.

'You have come back to listen to more primitive music?'

'I think there's been a misunderstanding.'

He said, 'Yes, I am very confused. Now you are saying you are not Dutch.'

'I never said I was.'

The man got out a large register, and showed an entry. It was the Dutch boy's – the date of his arrival, no date for his departure; the word *Mati* pencilled in for the moment instead. 'Dead'.

The clerk said, 'And you are not dead, either.'

I looked to the wood ceiling, and the fauna thriving there. 'No. Not dead,' I said. 'Not yet.'

The administrator filled in the columns, shrugging miserably as he confronted each: 'Name', Address', 'Occupation' . . .

I had not eaten since the previous day's lunch and felt ready to drop, but Fernando, seeing me coming, finished the last mouthful of a pasta feast and said I must now register with the authorities.

'It's okay. I've done that.'

'You already go to the local man – just the Siberut man. Now you go to the different. The true police. The chief.'

These were proper policemen, who had truncheons that were straight and glazed instead of warped, and they had uniforms that glittered with metallic trappings. I was sat down in front of the chief's desk. The officers gathered in a semicircle behind me, allowing the chief a three-pace space. This lent his words an extra authority, but he was friendly enough, after I had signed saying I was not a subversive or a journalist. He locked away my passport for safekeeping and told me I was free to go where I liked.

Back to Fernando.

'Come,' he signalled me off down the path again. The sand was wet from the storm, and crunched loudly under the priest's sandals. He said we were making for a village headman who was staying here – he preferred the town life. 'His son goes away tomorrow to his village. He takes you. There you start to ask all about the monkeys. Is simple.'

'Bet you it won't be,' I said.

A man selling yesterday's newspapers was whistling loudly; boys rolled tin cans with sticks ahead of us along the path. But no one stopped to watch us walk by, our shoes turning up coral tubes, the sun beginning to dry the damp from the white tacky houses. We turned off to the right, up wood steps to a building of planks with a tin roof which banged as it buckled under the heat. A girl wearing a dress of curtain material was pedalling on a sewing machine; an even smaller one hacked at chillis. Above them was a biblical quotation from Rome. I smelt fish frying. My mouth began to water.

'Benedict, this is my friend Michael,' Fernando said in Indonesian. The headman, with his shirt uncreased and his buttons all done up, was a disappointment. He did not have any obvious tattoos. His teeth had not been sharpened. The newest tooth was metal, and this stood out, looking ostentatiously blunt. 'It is a modern village,' Fernando explained.

I put out my hand to shake his. But Michael was in a state of shock. He stared at my blue eyes, my fair hair. His jaw trembled as if he were going to cry. He said, '*Orang Belanda?* Dutchman?'

'No,' I said.

He got out a photo and held it up to my face. 'Yes.'

While he was muttering to himself, Fernando said to me, 'The Dutch boy's family come here to thank – the funeral. They leave the photograph – the remembrance.'

It was in black and white, a portrait of a likeable chap with an unformed but well-meaning face leaning against a set of tidy bookshelves, arms folded loosely, an angle-poise lamp on his desk; this was a campus bedsit perhaps. He was almost my height, and pale-skinned. Otherwise he did not look like me at all – his hair was discernibly curled, for a start, and he looked an indoor sort.

Michael had gone the grey colour of bad meat. 'He stand where you stand,' he said slowly. He brought up a chair for me. 'Do you like chillis on your rice?'

Food at last! 'Brilliant,' I said. 'I'm famished. But not *too* many chillis.'

But he was not offering. He looked to Fernando. 'He said "not too many chillis"! The same with the *orang Belanda!*'

Michael's son Carlo would be leaving by tradeboat tomorrow, and he would act as a guide. The modern, official, village would serve as a launching pad for my forest trips to the left-over, traditional people. They would be the ones to clue me up on what sparked Segma's story off.

Carlo was thin – all except his cheeks, whose deep flesh was pitted as if by a hundred hot pins. As he was introduced he hummed a pop song, jiggling the gold chain around his neck. Fernando said, 'This is your guide, your father, your son, your friend.'

But he's only a boy, I mumbled. 'Father Fernando . . .' I bent to his ear, and said softly in English, 'this isn't going to work.'

'He is strong at the sea,' he replied.

'What if I catch the mysterious disease?'

'Then, is no problem.' He slapped me across the back, heartily, like a drinking mate. 'Because to die is always so much the same!'

Even before we departed next morning the little cargo boat with its passengers and crew of ten – only three bunks – was rolling like a drunk. There was one lifebelt. It had been half eaten through and the seasick captain used the loose remains as a pillow. No one saw us off. We rode away into the sunrise – passengers, the poorly crew and the chicken livestock all doing their best to lean against the roll. On the oily deck, just in front of the telephone-box-sized bridge, was a tattooed old man who lay like a spare piece of timber across the hold, being doused with spray. A girl with a baby in a sling was retching over the right-hand side; two scraggy boys and their dog were doing the same over the other.

Half a mile out, the sea jade, we turned south and followed the coast down: the complicated dark mangrove branches, the scooped-out coves of beach palms, the dipping backdrop of forest hills like a saturated green sponge, behind. In the heat of the day the cool water spray was drowsy bliss – as long as the salt did not dry on your lips. Flying fish skidded over the waters. Dolphins swerved and skewered our waves, reeling and melting in the foam. But to watch them turn and pitch – grey rubber skin half unwrapped from the water – showed up our boat's incompetence in the waves. They were having to wait around for us to speed up. Soon they got bored and split off.

Carlo spent most of the time at the wheel, putting on scarlet nail varnish. He had a monogram tattooed high on his shoulder.

'What about the traditional tattoos?' I asked. 'They're rather attractive.'

'My father says it is not modern,' he said, plucking out the single hair from his chest, then walking his fingers over to my packet of biscuits, Golden Honey Crunches, a farewell present from Fernando. 'Also it's illegal. Like the forest houses.' He bit into the plastic wrapper and shook the pack, like a dog killing a rat. 'And, as the saying goes, "There's nothing can halt the Vision of Rulek." '

The Vision of Rulek. I had not heard the proverb before. We all know about the Sword of Damocles; I had recently got wind of the Roses of Elizabeth. Now there was the Vision of Rulek. Watching the first of my Golden Honey Crunches disappear forever, I asked Carlo what it meant.

'Don't you know? That the future will be one of order. When we talk about Rulek's Vision, we mean his vision of a modern future. It's a common enough saying.' He helped himself to a second biscuit. 'My father told me that Rulek was a saint.'

I would have to check this. Father Stefano was a bookworm. He would know.

I watched one of my jungle boots tumble overboard. Now if I ever got into the forest it would have to be in bare feet.

To take my mind off that, I told Carlo some British proverbs – a rolling stone gathers no moss, a stitch in time saves nine, time and tide wait for no man. By the time I had explained them Carlo was half way through the Golden Honey Crunches, and succumbing to requests to pass them round. The captain, hearing the crackle of the wrapper, squeezed out from his bunk and wormed into the bridge. Suddenly he had a healthy appetite. Carlo said that the Vision of Rulek was so strongly adhered to in the village I would be lucky to get away into the forests *at all*. The modern villagers did not like people digging up the past.

'I wish you'd told me this earlier.'

'Yes, and we'll anchor for the night at the bottom of the island, opposite Taileleo.' It was the village where the Dutch boy had caught his death. 'It would have been interesting for you. But the medicine man who did healing spells on the Dutchman isn't here today.'

'Let's be thankful for that, at least.'

The spare length of timber arose from the deck and inched hopefully into the bridge. The captain cursed and handed the biscuits over. There were only two left. Carlo was on the floor, shuffling backwards into the captain's bunk, saying the words – neither happy nor sad, but with the unshakeable conviction of a seer – 'There's nothing can halt the Vision of Rulek.'

Before dawn we were heading round to the west coast. We watched the Indian Ocean hit the shore in thick, jagged folds. The island was hazy with the beaten-up water. Here, there were none of the mangrove trees of the eastern, silty waters, just bent palms. Some trees had given in to the smacking waves, and were lying horizontal. The chickens were put away in their baskets. Everyone else on board had to cling on as best they could.

In the mid-afternoon we swung right, and rolled up into a bay. Through the veil of surf spray the beach looked like a long smudge of gold watercolour on a blue and green wash. The anchor was man-handled overboard. The chesty coughing of the engine ended and the sound of the bay hit us – the searing of waves on the beach and the hiss of the percolating surf.

The crew paddled us ashore in turn, two by two. The passengers did not look excited to be home, not even expectant. It was their duty to return here, I thought; they had come back only for the sake of loved ones. It was the done thing.

I settled in the dugout, heavy enough by myself to make up the full boatload. Carlo would be along next.

The rollers sucked us to the beach. I stepped out into the shallows and trudged up the sand shelf, enjoying the solid ground, the grit between my toes. The dugout was cutting back, splitting the breakers. I looked around and about but I was alone on the sand. Seeing that the others had gone on, I felt happier – there was somewhere to go to.

I pottered about, waiting for Carlo. The shore was barren – it was just me, the worn, sunburnt log stumps, and the square crabs, high on their white legs, poised ready to dash for the sea's next wave of edibles. Hermit crabs were dragging themselves over a stony bank to a log of sago, their shells on the pebbles sounding like someone picking through broken porcelain. A little ringed plover ran by, stabbing at the brief mirror sheen left as waves slipped back. In a minute, Carlo would be here to tell me more of the bird's habits.

But Carlo, like Theodore before him, was indisposed. He would not be joining the quest. I discovered this after a half-hour wait for him under the sun, when I heard the low guzzle of the boat engine. I looked up and the sea was like a rope of crinkled tin foil, and the boat like a toy being parcelled up into it, as it left me. So much for Carlo, my guide, my father, my son, my friend.

I humped my rucksack on to my back and tracked the fresh human prints up the storm beach to a divide in the palms, and a sandy path. The salt breeze was replaced by a fug of rottenness. The whistling thump of waves was only a muffled echo.

A bridge of machine-cut planks took me on inland, through a band of sago marsh and crimson dragonflies. I could hear the wings of the flies. The path was now bordered by a ramshackle forest which gave out a low buzzing. From close up ahead, a cockerel sang out, and I could make out the chatter of a flock of small birds. Coconut meat lay in curls to either side on bamboo sheets, making the air sickly sweet. I passed a leaning thatched storehouse, black with damp. Little flies rose from the copra in rusty clouds. The sand under my feet was brick-hard now, and had no weeds. I suddenly knew that the bickering sparrow sound was actually children – a playground. I broke into a trot for the first glimpse beyond the palms.

The village was a single unswerving line, locked in a blue haze. So this was the Vision of Rulek, patron saint of modernism. It was not a holiday-poster view. The houses had walls of white board, and their roofs were bolted metal plates. They had windows of netting and glass, and looked as if they had been designed against an inevitable vandal problem of the future.

However, the further you went away from the front, and the nearer to the forest, up the straight, straight path, the softer the lines of the buildings became and the friendlier, more honest and open their faces. They had no doors and were thatched with palm leaves, notched logs leading up to verandahs which looked out over the path's monotonous gardens of weed.

The sound of the children was getting nearer, but the first inhabitant I saw was a middle-aged man who needed his shirt seeing to. He was coming right by. I did not want to stare, but he was wearing a stiff crown of fine white, red and orange beads. Burning red leaves were tucked into it. He also had a yellow bud behind his ear. He balanced a pole on his shoulder, steadying its slung-on knots of coconuts with a tattooed hand, using the other to tap his lips, asking for a cigarette. I had brought some with me for such occasions – it was a hot tip from Father Fernando.

I paused again beside a flagpole which had no flag, and a sign of bent tin that said 'Sagulubbe'. To the right, in front of a white building that must be the school house, were the children – sixty or more, facing the building and the tree tops splashed across the sky behind. In five higgledy-piggledy lines they waited for parade. The boys rolled up their shirts to prove their bravery under elastic-band fire, while the girls slouched or giggled, pretending not to be impressed by the boys. The children were in Western-style clothes, the state primary school uniform of white tops and crimson bottoms. Maybe it was the distant presence of the forest, or maybe it was the fault of the children themselves – their crusty bare toes, the flower petals and leaves that they had hooked through their blackish silk hair; whatever the reason, just here, the uniforms looked ridiculous, like fancy dress.

'Attention!' A boy had stepped out in front to address the assembly. The children wagged their heads to rid themselves of their flowers. I moved backwards into the banana-palm shadows, out of his view.

Before classes, it was exercise time. The pupils began arching hands and pulling their limbs to a routine that bored them. There was no challenge in this. These children's muscles were supple, their skin was firm and their feet were tough pads. This physical training had been dreamt up far away. It was designed to tighten up townsmen's shivering, fatty flesh, to get air into the lungs. But the physical jerks had been completed, here on the jungle coast, and no one was out of breath.

The senior boy sang a single, quavering note and began to conduct an anthem. Here, in the forest's shadow, was a parade of children being taught to shout defiance at it. The tender voices scared the life out of the trees, upsetting the natural world. Finch clouds rose and flipped out towards the beach, and a purple heron, en route inland, had to do a detour.

Once it was all over, a man crossed from the white box houses opposite, on the left side of the path. Coins jiggled in his trouser pockets; he was dressed as if for a town outing. He stopped at the front and addressed the parade ground in Indonesian. The younger children started nattering among themselves. Some turned to friends and spluttered with laughter, rolling their shoulders hopelessly. They could not understand a word.

Parade was dismissed. The children trooped into the classrooms. I walked up the path. Seeing me, the teacher checked his shirt was done up, and flicked his sleeves for dust.

'Welcoming you to the city of Sagulubbe,' he said. 'I am speaking Engliss.'

'Hello. You're the teacher?'

'I am Head Teacher.'

I was waiting for more, but he had finished. His face was thin and eyes quick – judging, mathematical. 'I am Benedict.'

'Good. *I* am too. And I am happy you see the school attendance. Also I am glad you are not a hippy. We have had Americans come here with short trousers on. Too bad.'

'But *every* man here except you has short trousers on.'

'It is necessary, for now. Fishing, making the sago, hunting. It makes this necessary for them. But you do not do these things. You must dress properly. You must get your shoes and put them on.'

'What about the traditional loincloths?'

'*Apa?* What?'

'The skirts and loincloths worn in the forest. I read about the customs at the Catholic mission – Father Fernando very kindly let me browse through his books.'

'Traditional clothes?' The voice was alarmed. 'Where? The grass skirts and bark cloth?'

'Well, there aren't any here. Not that I can see.'

'Good.' His eyes slowly closed, and he leant back on his heels. 'Yes, none here.'

I glanced at the school; from the sound of things a riot was under way. 'I won't be staying here. I'll be going into the forest.'

'*Apa?*'

'I'll be leaving for more traditional houses.'

'*Apa?*'

'I want to know more about their customs – how stories of monkey-men might have accidentally got about.'

I thought he might titter, but the teacher nodded earnestly and led me off. He thought he had mistranslated.

Across from the school block, by the house from where the teacher had strutted out, was a square white office which was being eaten up by ants. Inside was a desk and wall posters of rules signed by Headman Michael, care of his town address. Nothing else. The teacher pored over my travel papers. Outside there was a sudden roar – either an extra large wave thumping the beach, or a louder chapter in the school riot. The teacher said, 'Where is your guide?'

'I've got Carlo, but he hasn't come ashore yet.' I looked out through the crack in a warped plank and down the track towards the sea. 'I hope his canoe didn't capsize. Mine jolly nearly did.'

'Carlo will not come ashore now. The wind is too high. The boat is gone to hide.'

'But he can't just leave me here!'

'The boat can be back later. Two days? Three? Four?'

'Five? Six?' I said, catching on. Damn.

'For now, I can be your guide.'

'I see.' I could not face it. I am not usually quick to judge, but I did not take to his bossy tone. And he *would* keep staring rudely at my bare feet.

'Now, during your visit, you live in the room with key. Follow.'

'But I'll be leaving tomorrow.'

'*Apa?*'

'I want to get away from here. To talk to remoter people.' I reminded myself, proudly, 'I'm an ambassador for Theodore.'

'You stay in Sagulubbe. And when the boat travels away, you go with him. Today I give you a guided tour for the village. That can be sufficient.'

'No, it won't.'

'*Apa?*' The teacher's English had yet again suddenly let him down. Then he said, brightly, 'But first I give you hospital.'

His idea of hospitality was ditchwater tea with biscuits, which he got from the only village store. He was also Head Storeman. We sat at either end of his kitchen table. Every now and again the teacher poured more tea and asked me why I was not married.

After ten minutes, I said, 'Aren't I interrupting? I mean, shouldn't you be teaching?'

'Please. Do not be afraid.' He was nudging a packet of biscuits along the formica. 'Self-service.'

Thankfully he left me alone twice. Once he went behind the house to finger the chickens and test their meat content. Later he went to try and restore order in the school. He hoiked out a boy and brought him back with him, leaving the other pupils yacking on in their own language. Once the teacher had seated himself comfortably, the captive sadly took his arm and began to squeeze it up and down. Having to give Head Teacher a massage seemed to be a routine punishment.

'I'll leave you both to it, then,' I said, as the boy started on the teacher's fingers, pulling the knuckle joints one by one.

'You wait for me in your room,' the teacher murmured. His eyes were closed, and he was in ecstasy.

I lay in my stuffy quarters, and once, when I thought the coast was clear, tried to sneak out to look round the village by myself. I got beyond the white box houses and to the first of the thatched buildings, but as I reached the unfinished mosque, so far only a rickety skeleton, there was a shout from behind.

'You! Wait.'

'Me?'

'*Kemana?*' It was the Indonesian. 'Where are you off to?'

'*Jalan-jalan.* Just walking.'

He said in English, 'I walk with you.'

Curses, I thought. But I would not put my foot down, not yet. Theodore had not survived the war by putting his foot down. I thought of him now, sitting at the serious black table in Penang, wondering how far I had got and tapping his fingers on an opened page of 'Hope at Large'. Waiting, waiting.

The teacher marched me between the path fences, along the garden fronts, where coconuts hung from racks while they went about sprouting shoots for planting. 'The church,' he said. 'You see the church?'

'Difficult to miss it, actually.'

The church did not back on to the path, it ran along it, but otherwise, though it was cumbersome, it blended with the thatched, gabled houses. Strangely, it was siding with Siberut, not with the tight, low white boxes of its own St Rulek.

We crossed a channel on a plank bridge – slimy underfoot and cold on the toes. The water had a red tinge, as if someone had washed a bad wound there. These houses were a vestige of Siberut, not of modernism and elsewhere. They were on stilts, were airy and breathed easily; their thatch was steaming in sleepy tongues.

'Just houses,' the teacher was saying. But I had not asked about the buildings, I had asked about the twisted leaf tassles sprouting from the eaves. And what about the simplistic wooden birds which spun on strings along the house fronts, suspended ten feet up? They were not for children, they were for everyone.

'I am sorry you see this,' the teacher said, waving a bony arm at a tub of sago left in the path. It was dripping, deposited in a hurry. Someone had run off to avoid us. I had grasped this much about everyday life in Sagulubbe: the teacher's presence blew away the population. They scattered along with the red path ants. The gardens, the verandahs, cleared before us. The babies stayed where they were, swinging from rafters in bamboo cots, but everyone else – those not on the scrounge for a cigarette – got up and left.

'Sago is primitive,' the teacher told me, 'only from the jungle.'

'Actually I think you might have got it muddled up,' I said, 'because funnily enough, sago is the most efficient source of carbohydrate in the world.'

The teacher was startled. No one seemed to have remembered to tell him. '*Apa?*'

'Yes, it's a fact.' He would concur, once he had thought it through. I had lived off sago for seven months in New Guinea, and should know. 'It takes less man hours to grow than anything else. Corn, rice, manioc – you name it. If you think about it, the sago palm grows by itself. The swamps where it lives are self-perpetuating. All you have to do is chop it down, mash up the pith, stamp it through a filter of sacking, and let the starch settle out. Nothing to it.'

The teacher's face was a sad and disillusioned one. 'You talk like a communist. A hippy.'

'No, I don't.'

'You are against rice. You are anti-civilisation. But rice *will* be theirs one day.' His hands closed into white marble fists.

We walked on. 'And rice is less wholesome,' I said, remembering.

Soon there was more trouble. The women on the verandahs kept their breasts covered, according to the teacher's master-plan, but there was little that could be done about the working men. They drew the line at going around in clammy cloth all day. They simply would not. This meant that their tattoos were visible for all to see – the hoops stacked up their ankles; the circuits of petals scaling calves and shins; the cross-hatchings on thighs; the glorious spiders astride navels; plain lines shooting up and over nipples, spanning shoulders, only coming to a halt once they had reached the fingertips or curled to the rise of the cheeks. Father Fernando had said the tattoos varied according to clan and individual taste. You accumulated the designs as you grew up.

'Please! Do not look at the patternings.'

'They're beautiful,' I said, not able to help myself.

'*Apa?*'

'Look, every time I say something you disagree with, you pretend you don't understand. I'm getting sick of it.'

'The patternings are *un*beautiful.'

'Perhaps it's just a matter of taste.'

'No, it isn't.' He had switched to Indonesian.

'Oh dear. I hope we're not going to keep on disagreeing.'

'No, we won't,' he said. We were walking very fast. I was missing the details of the notched gabling, of a snake carved on a post, of squared-off lizards and hornbills in relief. In the darker shadows, up in the porch rafters, the Siberuts had turtle-shell displays – showpiece antlers, prize-sized gaping skulls. There must be galleries of them up in those rafters. They were set on boards, painted and braided, laid out as neatly as Cousin Henry's moths, though linked by folds of cobweb. They looked like hunting trophies – pigs, deer, monkeys. *Monkeys!*

Three men stopped in our path. They had bows and arrow quivers – a roll of bark with bamboo endplugs. Their skin smelt clean and sweet – I felt dirty beside them in my sticky shirt. They crossed themselves.

'Catholics?' I said.

'You are very stupid,' the teacher informed me. 'They asking for a cigarette.'

I took out a packet. The teacher swiped the first two for himself. We started walking, and he gave me a long speech in Indonesian, the last paragraph ending, 'You'll understand how bad the old times were before long. For instance, do you know how much pain the men went through to get those disfigurements? The pattern they're to have is put on the banana leaf and then it's pressed to their skin. They get an arrow, dip it in ink, and then they cut them – just as if they're carving wood.'

'The pain probably makes the designs even more precious to the wearer. I bet you that these men and women were once proud of what they'd gone through.'

He changed back to English – confiding, fraternal: 'There was a terrible time, mister. The American came. He was a hippy – short trousers, bare feet. He spoke the same like you. He went into the forests. To the old houses.'

'Oh yes? How far away are they?'

'*Apa?*'

'Never mind.'

'And, when he left, the people made a jumping tiger mark under his arm.' The teacher patted the space below his right armpit. I got a hot waft of perfumed deodorant. 'You see, he is too ashamed of the picture. He wants to hide it.'

But all the tattoo patterns that I had seen here were straight-line designs, or flower petals and buds, and symmetrical ambiguous insect and arachnid shapes. Fernando had said there was an ecologist called Tony Whitten who had been done during a gibbon research project,[11] but that had been only a dithering circumnavigation of his navel. He had taken his doctorate at Cambridge, was on the United Nations Development Programme and did not sound like the hippy that Theodore had salvaged in India, not one little bit.

I had seen enough of the village in the teacher's company. I made my apologies and skipped off through the garden plots to talk to the old, sharp-teethed men. They did not understand a word of Indonesian; the teacher smiled tolerantly, waiting for me to give up. The men were trying to be friendly. They put my hand between theirs and showed their jagged teeth, smiling right into my face. But that was always before they spotted the extra shadow on the path. The sight made them twiddle with the coral discs on their earrings. They sucked on their fingertips, putting in orders for cigarettes, or took nipa palm leaves from their earlobe holes, and busily rolled their own. And the teacher never had to leave the smooth of the path.

'You know,' I told him, walking back, vanquished, 'I'm sure some of these kind people would be very happy to let me sleep in their houses.'

'You can sleep where I tell you. I am Rulek, Head Teacher.'

'Rulek?' I hesitated, off balance. 'You mean ... as in the maxim, *There's nothing can halt the Vision of Rulek?*' Rulek blushed with pride.

I winced at my mistake. Apparently you did not have to pray to Rulek, patron saint of modernism. He was down here on earth among us, in flesh and blood. And there was nothing you could do about it.

I braved another day of this – never getting much off the path. Life went on here as usual – in a half-baked way. No one was ever very excited, no one was ever very sad. Everyone went about their chores, unimpressed by their visitor, just keeping half an eye out for free cigarettes and aspirins. The older boys ate apart from their families, clubbing together to pool their stashes of rice, which they cooked up with cassava leaves. They did wear tattoos, but the designs were squiggly love hearts and initials that were like worms caught out in the sun and shrivelled crisp. Agga was the oldest of the new generation; children worshipped him. Boys winged around him making nervous, hammering laughs from the backs of their throats. They tossed marbles around his feet when he idled on the smooth, straight path. Whereas Rulek walked with small shuffling steps, as if in slippers, Agga, heavy boned, walked with his pelvis forward. He did not disperse crowds, he drew them, pointing out the neat, closed box houses, and telling youngsters that I had one just the same on the far side of the world. While I sat on my bed he led parties of underlings around my room, pointing to the clean cement floor, the mechanical action of the lock in the door, the bugs having to fight to get outside again, some dying in the attempt and stacking up on the window sill, no ants to carry them off.

When it came down to it, Sagulubbe was a manifestation of outside, urban thinking. It looked as if an amiable compromise had been negotiated with nature: water was collected by directing the rain dribbles down the palms; coconut shells were their ladles; fresh produce – cassava, taro, banana, sugar cane – came in every afternoon from the forest gardens; women went out at night to scoop for river fish and shrimps with hockey-goal-sized V-framed nets. But by the way the settlement was fencing out nature, the houses clinging to the straight, weed-free path, it was expressing a fear of it. It was holding out, waiting for reinforcements to arrive.

That evening there was a blood-orange sunset. Under the cloak of the dusk, the villagers were clustered on their house fronts, the blossoms in their hair on the wilt, and I, Rulek's new neighbour, was slumped in my doorway, knowing that for Theodore's sake I must abandon rubber time for a short while. Time and tide wait for no man, my culture said. And it was high time to plan an escape from here.

Chapter Five

Escape. I hitched up my mosquito net, and lay within it, thinking of capture, of being a jailbird. The ticky-tacky house was a prison – a trap of silent, closed air. It excluded most outside sounds, even the hen cries. This cell of a room insulated me, enhanced my loneliness. I thought of the words: *I had escaped from prison, from time and from matter, and was free for ever . . .*

Later, rain began pummelling the village. I got up, opened the door and let the night in. It was a gale – a proper one with rolling trees, skies of leaves spinning like bats. Taro plants were snapped-back umbrellas, and the banana palms flapped and slapped like old macs. Any moment I thought the sea was going to boil over and immerse the village. Whoever thought of putting the modern settlement on the doorstep to the sea? Not anyone who lived here.

But the sea did not come, only the wind. The sound of it thrashing the metal roofs with rain was worse than thunder. The porch cement – already shattered and loose – was being picked apart by the gutter overflow and opening up into what looked like a beachscape of crab holes. A spider was flapping overhead, suspended upside-down from the eaves – arms out, bracing it like bicycle spokes. I might have been tempted to give up this ape-man jaunt, go back to bed and take Mr Swartz's Valium. But no. Theodore was waiting for me to report back – sitting up tonight, maybe, 'Hope at Large' spread out under the light of the Buddhist-monk lampstand, and dipping into favourite passages. *All we need is one creature – just one.*

If I was any good I would leave for the forest, here and now. After all, I had felt my way through rainforest creeper strings, bark shards and moss hanks before at night, knew how to live off the land. So why not? What was I scared of?

A gas lamp, Rulek's latest investment, was blazing into the night from just next door, on the left. I stepped out into the wind. The rain in my face smelt of sap. I looked into Rulek's kitchen – the lamp in its net of prancing insects, Rulek drinking coffee, eyes fixed on a typed report. Far off up the track to the left gleamed the orange light of a coconut-husk torch. The flame jiggered on its bamboo handle, glowing on the underside of a bark-shield umbrella, and off a hand held up against the glare. Suddenly the night blotted the flame out. A baby began to cry.

I thought it over, tickled by the wet and the flying leaf chips on my bare back. Leave now: if I lost the depressed centre of the settlement path, with its dim stars of coral, I could inch along the keeled-over fences. I would have to make it across the slippery planks that bridged the gully. It would not be much further from there. Easy.

But not for me, thanks. I was not going to miss a night's sleep to tiptoe hopefully through the night snakes. Not with the rain scything down my back. I thought of leaf fragments like stewed tea-leaves getting between my toes, of maimed scorpions and a smack in the eye from wet palm leaves. Let alone the predatory dogs. No, I would wait for dawn. Rulek would busy himself awhile with the school parade. I would wait for him to commence his speeching. Then I would make my bid for freedom.

The sky was a wash of yellow, which gathered, folded over on itself and thickened. I was ready, biding my time. I had my parang, my shorts and a shirt, and a bundle containing my camera, the Blue Book and my malaria pills and mosquito net – no sense in ending up like the Dutch boy.

Siberut boys were coming to school with their fingers entwined, flowers threaded through their hair. Girls were holding hopping races – cat-collar bells rang from their ankles. The children spoke a fluty sing-song language of long prosaic sighs, older girls quietest, squatting in circles and hugging each other and occasionally kicking bottoms.

'Attention!'

Silence. For a second the only apparent noise was the sea, far off, and the shuffling of the children's hard feet as they got into line. Tight buds, glossy-tissued petals, flame-rashed leaves – they were all flung away, pattering on the sand. Hair was combed out, parted, bunched. 'Good morning, children.' It could have been any school assembly in the Western world. After Exercise Time, the children were filing off into their classes at a trot. The oldest set the pace, the newest pupils copied. This urgency was a thing that had to be learnt – this discontent, this desire to change, to progress.

No time to waste for me either. Rulek was in the senior classroom, ranting happily. I slipped away.

Chapter Six

Where was I going? I was not sure. But the path out of the settlement was a well-trampled one, and it led to somewhere that was in better touch with the forest, and its primates.

But first you had to cross a puddle of tannin-brown water which this morning was hip-high. It was warmer than the settlement puddles – trapped here for a day or two at least, but not yet oil-sheened from rotting plants. The pieces floating on it from last night's storm were like potato crisps. These were rafts for wounded creatures – stick insects, and black bugs with antennae like oiled feathers. There was also an unripe fig, the wing of a butterfly, bark rubble, angry wasps spinning in circles as they drowned, and scum around the margins which was made out of kicking gnats.

I waded the ditch – swatting the wasps as and when they went for me – but the path the far side was just a continuation of the water, an accidental canal with more marooned wildlife that took you under the awning of the forest, and then inside the muffled green shadows. I would have preferred a dry track, so that my feet could harden, but I had not yet been punctured by a single thorn.

A sound drifted as light as a new scent around me. Like a child's placid singing. Yes, it *was* a song. I twisted about for a clear view. She – not a child at all – was in a pool of sun on the open front of a garden tending hut, swinging her feet, her nose pressed against the thinly furred head of the baby at her breast. This mother's voice was a high cooing that fanned the open air, hardly reaching out of the clearing. Her dove calls dropped gently about her – she laid them like a mantle over herself and over her child. I walked on quietly. I did not want to disturb her, or the energy that she focused only there, her home, a human nest in a space of dry white light, scorched leaves, static lizards, wood-shaving peels and contented, mud-bathing pigs.

Lizards with rainbow skins rattled away from the splashes of sunlight. Grey alluvial mud squirmed out from under my feet, slugs of it jetting up between my toes. The morning air bore the long, whistling notes of faraway gibbon calls – misty and thin and with a hint of loneliness.

I had been forced by the calls to stop and take notice – they were like a weak cry for sympathy. Now they were fading, drifting loosely, but, standing so still, I distinguished another noise – a methodic booming, a double heart beat that must be seeping here from the swamp forests, the sound of men thwacking the grated pith of the sago palm down to snowflake size.

Then I jumped. A boy in a tee-shirt was standing only ten feet away, just off the path. He was the colour of the scrambling tree roots, though clearer skinned, and he looked as strong and almost as hungry. His hands were thick and dry, and he held them heavily by his sides. I was relieved that I recognised him: Agga, the youth who had led children's guided tours around my box room. He said, tipping his chin over in the direction of the gibbons, 'Old mans say it make heart lonely. It make heart cry. Like death music.'

'And what do you say?'

He stepped on to the path mud. His hair was wet from being wiped by leaves. 'I don't say. It's old times.' Without asking, he took my parang out of my hand. 'I will be your guide?'

'How much?'

'Ten thousand rupiahs?' He slapped his thigh with the flat of the parang. A black ant with a pea head rolled off him, leaving a smear.

'Five thousand.' I took my parang back.

We agreed the deal. It was simply a business transaction – cash for all services rendered. He recovered my parang and strode off, clipping back vines, pointing out tripping roots. Around us, the sago pounding was sometimes a plucked cello resonance, other times a tempered throbbing, a muffled noise from underground – the effect of the differing stands of leaves that sliced and spliced the boiler-house air. We would reach a Siberut priest's house in a couple of hours. We would find out how forest men looked upon monkeys. We would walk on to another house if need be and we would keep on doing this for as long as necessary. A day, a week? Before I knew it I would know what was behind Segma's monkey-men tale. Then the way would be open for me to move back to the mainland and demolish the greater myth, that of the Gugu.

Now we were in a place of dark cellar smells – the wet musk odour of boxed apples and pears in winter storage. It was raining, but only the fattest of drips slipped all the way down here through the leaf nets. Agga crouched to point out four branches that had been propped together and tiled with leaves like a child's playtime teepee. 'This is the rare thing. Prayer to gods.'

'Oh yes?'

Agga was fascinated by me – you could see it in his eyes, hear it in the long, reflective silences. Why my interest in the forest, my confidence that it was going to produce an answer useful to the modern world?

'The priest of the Siberut talks to the god of the forest. And to his dead fathers, and mothers. But he cannot talk easy. Therefore, he uses the leaves to help talk to ghosts and spirits – even all the stones have spirits, they say. He is called the *sikerei*.'

'Interesting. He uses leaves as go-betweens with spirits. Does that include monkey-spirits?'

Agga was lopping down banana leaves for rain capes. Well, you know, he said, these people did so many peculiar things.

The Siberuts were his family, his blood, but to Agga they were of only sentimental value. They were something left over – things he had grown out of, slightly embarrassing relicts from childhood. He distanced himself by speaking objectively, as if they were an exotic species of fauna he had read up on.

The priests, he told me, killed pigs and chickens and waved the leaves and fell sort of asleep while singing; that was how they talked with the spirits. For, in order that the balance of the forest might be preserved, every spirit must feel content. The animal skulls inside the *uma* clan houses were not trophies, they were homes for the souls of animals whose bodies had been lunch or supper.

The fizzing of rain on the canopy leaves was as soft now as slow breathing, and almost lost under the thump, thump, sago-bashing lifebeat of Siberut. Ahead, the forest was broken open by a river some twenty yards wide. Its reflected light brightened the underside of tree overhangs and lit spiders' webs. Bird chirrups from the wild sugar cane rattled along the banks of ooze. A spider with legs like a dwarf kitten's was dabbing at the wraps of shoreline weed.

Agga slid a dugout canoe from out of the water grasses; we paddled across and climbed the far slope. We were in the backyard of another field house. Three women were on the verandah, shaded by its low thatch, tightening black bark fibre into a broom head, picking at a nylon fishing net, cradling a baby.

The first woman to see me had tattooed skin that was slack even around the tighter corners. She said a single word to the others and pointed to me with her chin. The word made them scramble to cover their breasts. The old woman stretched for a cotton wipe, a second yanked a blouse out from under a dog, the third was slower and held the material between her fingers as if it was infected. She covered herself quickly, as if to get it over with, and then got on with what she was doing — using her knee to wipe a little rust off a safety-pin, then lifting the baby to clamp her firmly between her knees. Something in the woman's precise grip on the infant and on the pin stopped the baby's contented bubbling. She kicked a little, jiggling the metal coils around her ankles, then she drew air and bellowed. It was ear-piercing time.

The woman drove the pin, which was so rusted it was like a wood splinter, through the baby's right earlobe. The cries were very loud, but the job must be done and it was straight on to the second ear, as casually as if she was sock-darning. Soon that lobe also had a ferrous stain. The tears were kissed away. The second woman plastered a finger-load of taro and banana over the baby's mouth. The safety-pins jigged prettily in her ears.

'These are old times,' Agga said, humping himself backwards up on to the verandah to sit on the pole floor. 'These people still eat sago!'

Food! I had not had any breakfast. I sat down beside him and our legs swung in time off the edge, disturbing the flies from the dog below. 'Is there any sago to spare?'

The three women straightened their backs and looked at me more closely. They had understood, and they looked as if I had handed them an unexpected present.

'You *want* some sago?' Agga let out a short, controlled laugh. 'There is no need! They have eggs.' He got up on to his knees and with his head against the verandah ceiling groped about in the baskets up there. The beams issued a desperate squawk, then a lot of clucking. Agga sat down. Sorry: eggs were off. 'Later we can find rice for you.'

'Don't worry. Sago would be fine,' I said.

Agga was muddled. 'Question, please.' He sat up and lifted a finger, as if he was back at a school desk. 'You are very hungry?'

I explained that I had not eaten since lunch yesterday — one of Rulek's ropy chicken-and-burnt-rice specials, biscuits with indiscernible soft centres for pudding. Agga sighed. 'Too bad.' It had been, I said.

The old woman ducked inside and slid out a platter. On it were two sticks of sago in charred leaves. Agga unwrapped them. 'I eat sago too,' he whispered. 'When I am very hungry.' He was being kind, trying to save my embarrassment: I must be desperate, he said. As it happened, I was.

But soon I was rocking forwards and back, happily breathing in the smell of old smoke from the thatch, and chomping into the sago — bland, gelatinous, pink and grey, but it grew on you. The river glade was looking settled and soft in the young daylight, and I had gathered from the women that a man called Uhu had a priest, a *sikerei*, staying. Just now he was in the forest washing sago out, the next stage after whacking the pith from the tree trunk. I was on my way. Everything was going according to plan.

After five minutes we were not so much walking as wading. The sago forest was a darkly roofed space of water pools and round tree columns and fallen palm leaves as brittle and sharp as autumn bracken. In the midst of the beer swill was a frame of poles about shoulder high with a lanky boy dancing on top of it, a man behind lifting a wooden tub of water up to him, and an infant with black paint stripes on his cheeks steering a boat of twigs. Seeing us the older boy hunched himself over, as if suddenly naked, though he had a bark loincloth on. The man dropped his bucket and waved to us, using his face more than his hands, because he was miming having a good smoke. Agga lobbed a tobacco wodge over and he tucked it into a waist pouch without saying thank-you and got on with his job. This was Uhu, Agga said, the man who had the priest staying.

We watched while they finished off, the sludge of discarded pith around my sore feet as soft as steeped Weetabix. The solution from the pith spluttered through the tray's bark filter, down on to a leaf comb to settle in a canoe trough. Uhu wore only his loincloth, but seemed to be fully dressed. His tattoos wrapped him up, converging in complicated junctions on the shoulder – scattered wheels, crossroads, flower heads, a leggy insect with pitched antennae crawling up around his navel. He had a gentle woman's eyes, and earrings carrying nuggets of mother of pearl. His hair was uncut, centre-parted. The tail of it was bound around in red cotton and laid in a rope down his neck, which was loosely collared with bead loops. He wore flowers in his hair and armbands, and dropping from his crown – a chequered tapestry of little beads – were two yellow hanks of fibre. No wonder Rulek did not like this culture: this was flower power; the men looked like hippies.

Uhu scooped up the toddler, held him out to drip off, then we all set off down a path that led to a modest but dignified square house that had a palm-leaf-tile face and shredded leaf swathes from the eaves. In its shade, beside a little enclosure with a trap door, was a mob of bristly black sows with eyes hidden beneath earflaps. They waved their fat heads at the flies, and scratched their chins with their trotters, nuzzling the earth and sucking on fruit stones.

Uhu put the child down and spoke to the building as if it was a person.

He inclined his head good-naturedly and waited for an answer. The house grunted. Agga signalled me to follow him up the log steps. Uhu had other business to attend to. As we ducked indoors he was laying banana bait behind the trap door of the enclosure and, with an axe, beginning a stalk in the direction of the dozing pigs.

The small through room was decorated with animal relicts – squirrel tails, antlers which forked towards the ceiling like white flame tongues. The main room, behind, which was even darker and had musky loft smells and a central space floored with boards instead of poles. A man squatted in the slanted rectangle of doorway light. He was not praying, he was cogitating, shuffling leaves as if they were playing cards. His eyes seemed to soak up the darkness of the room.

I went in. Behind the man a dog was sniffing at a pig jaw on a rack above a fireplace, and a woman and a small girl were hunched scratching meat from bones below turtle shells hanging on the wall like kitchen saucepans. The roof was too low for me. My head was up between the beams, and my hair snagged on the black stickiness of the ceiling thatch. Up here was stored a metal-bladed spear and bunches of sticks for future arrow tips, and yet more animal skulls. The jaws of the primates were delicately but firmly bound up – cobwebs fleshed out the bone, beetles had set up home in the eye holes. Tomorrow morning, when the sunlight was low enough to slip in through the wall cracks, I would be able to make out the four species. I might have asked the priest about them right away, but his mind was clearly elsewhere.

Uhu came in, dragging a pig by its rear trotters. I had not heard its death scream. The body clattered over the pole floor – the sack of black, flaky skin, the stumpy feet, the dazed eye. 'The religions,' said Agga. 'If you watch.'

The old priest jerked a parang into the pig's stomach. The insides flowed out of the rip. He hoisted up the intestines and sploshed them into a metal bowl. I reeled from the smell, but he was already yanking out a steaming jelly of livers and kidneys, and grinning with the look of someone unwrapping a present.

Agga said, 'Pig helps these peoples understand futures.' The priest gave the heart – a soggy lump that fitted well in his hand – a thorough look over. 'Now he is reading the futures,' Agga said, as the tattooed fingers stroked and stroked the heart veins. The *sikerei* squatted there, not much company, and pondered. Flies were already fighting on the carcass, but he was not going to snap out of this for hours.

I could do with a bit of fresh air. We went out on to the verandah, where Uhu was down on his haunches beside a set of wooden slit gongs, crushing up several plants with crackers that resembled wooden mixing spoons. He looked affectionately at the juice, but Agga said it was *o-mai*, arrow poison.

The pink sky was thinly clouded. If this had been dusk at home, wood pigeons would be flying over to their beechwood roosts. Instead fruit bats were cruising across the last sunlight. Two little boys hunted around the camp with toy bows and knob-ended arrows designed to knock out sunbathing lizards.

'Why don't you cut back the bushes more?' I said. 'Let in some more air. It would dry up the mud.'

Agga looked apologetically towards Uhu, who had carved a feather into a paintbrush and was painting the poison, now a greeny-brown gravy, on the arrow blades. 'If these people cut the bush too much, they believe they make the forest cry!' He was going to laugh, but he looked at me and changed his mind.

'It's thoughtful of them,' I said, 'worrying about what the forest thinks.'

Agga played the air with his parang. 'You have tobacco for me?'

The little girl slogged into the clearing with a dripping log and rolled it up the steps. Then she lifted an axe and split the wood in one clean blow. Out sprang handfuls of wet, white fingers – worms which grappled with each other and after a while shrank from the sun. The girl jumped down the steps, captured the two boys and deposited them beside the log halves. The boys gawped at the worms twisting in their slime. They were handed a twig each, and shown how to tease the wrigglers from the holes. She mimed sucking them up. 'Mmmmmmm!' she said. Delicious! The boys dabbed the worms. They dropped their fishing twigs. 'Mmmmmmm!' Uhu said, waving his paintbrush. The boys picked up their sticks and together excitedly prised the first worm out of its home.

'So what do these people do when they want to cut down a tree for a canoe?'

Agga brought his knees up to his chest, and hugged them. He looked smaller than he had done this morning. He had wider eyes, and a child's puzzled face. 'I think he says to the tree "please".' He cringed.

But what was wrong with that? It was a thoughtful thing to do. I recalled Father Stefano's words: 'We have identified civilisation with technical progress and have excluded the primitive people from it.'

Agga looked at me from behind the shield of his huge knees – pent up, his eyes fixed and critical. I had come here, to the forest, for an answer; he and his modern generation were leaving. I was a threat to his every aspiration. Uhu, however, was gazing fondly at my face, sadly and sentimentally. To him my interest in the forest was poignant, an enthusiasm that should be shown by *his* young. It made him feel fatherly towards me.

'I'm beginning to see what Father Stefano meant,' I said. 'Everything must be kept in balance. The philosophy of harmony.'

Agga began fidgeting, notching a floor pole with the parang. 'If you want to know, when they kill a monkey or pig or deer they are sad too.' All of a sudden he biffed the verandah and a wood chip sprang up like a cricket. It was not a hard blow, but it was delivered unthinkingly, an act of vandalism, the only violence I had seen here. The sudden frustration released from him was a shock.

Uhu had finished. He wiped his hands on his string supply, a ball of grassy strands wedged in a beam nook, then he settled down at my side. He smoothed his fingers down my back and, while ironing me like this, named the objects around us, beginning with *soo-loo*, the sun, which was melting on the trees, then *sak-ok-ok* the pigs, *carai*, the bark sheets of the walls. Having had more than enough of that, Agga said that if I wanted to see how the Siberuts perceived the monkeys, I should go on a hunting trip. But Uhu would not want to arrange a hunting party for no reason. Hunting was work.

All evening Agga kept his face in a post shadow and scrutinised me from the dark, trying to see what made me tick. And he wanted something of me, my confidence to come here. He crossed his legs if I crossed mine, hummed if I hummed. I thanked the girl for bringing us a taro, banana and coconut mix, and it turned into a duet.

We slept where we were on the verandah. During my dreams the hens cried out, splitting the utter darkness open. Agga was kicking to get out of our mosquito net, Uhu stringing his bow. Then both were dancing in the lamp light, a snake flexing in the mud around their feet. Then, during the late chill, fingers were prodding me. I opened my eyes again and a grainy light was hanging thickly from the leaves. Agga was saying that we were off, Uhu wanted to take me hunting.

As we left, two dogs were arguing over the dead snake, a reticulated python, the largest predator on the island, a ten-foot length of black, blue and yellow with four ticks like squashed red peas clinging to its neck, and three arrows sticking from its hide.

Uhu walked ahead of us, his quiver slung inside his elbow, the bow undrawn, tobacco smoke spinning in a twisted plume over his shoulder. Away from the gardens and the marginal thickets, the forest had a high, fan-vaulted ceiling and fluted root struts. It was spacious and linear, with not so many hairy ropes, knotted grapplers or huge, pale parchment leaves.

Uhu's tattoo lines broke up the plains of smooth flesh; he blended well with the broken shadows. But it was not just the artwork that camouflaged him. Agga swayed along without having to concentrate, angling his limbs efficiently through the sleeves of wet bark, sidestepping ants which hoisted their pincers at his feet, but Uhu made his way as if each branch and leaf and beetle had an aura, a presence, to which he responded fully – you had the impression that he was being buffeted by minute fluctuations of energy. Agga and I were moving *between* the trees, and he was moving *within* them. His was a quite different forest from ours.

We were winding uphill and the forest was tightening. Before, the trees had easy trunk folds which hung like curtains; now they were closing ranks, and the way they caged the air, the way their dampness thickened up the green light, I could not help but be reminded of captivity, of prison cells and dungeons.

Uhu stopped. He crouched, leaning on the bow with his knee to string it. Agga whispered to me, '*Ky-la-ba*. Hornbill.' It was the local language. He had forgotten school and slipped back in years. But Uhu was not interested in the hornbill. He slid out a flightless arrow which was sharpened like a pencil, but given an additional spiral cut to encourage the poison well in.

We had spotted it: up in the canopy the silhouette of a solid, tidily rounded form; from it hung a silky tail. As monkeys go, he was heavy. He had the sagging shoulders of a desk-bound man, and a black coat that was glossy even against the light. I could make out the white facering and pale throat. This was a joja, the Mentawai langur. He was alone, and so quiet – there were no agitated chuckles, no nervous highjinks or wrenching of leaves. He had not noticed us, and was a very easy target.

Without warning Uhu shouted out to the monkey. 'Whay-a!' Where was the sense in that? It was like a warning – a last chance. 'Whay-a!'

The air was suddenly very still, as if the whole forest was scared by his yell – all the stingbugs crouching in their bark holes, the cicadas tucked close into the lichen-tinted barks, the ants demobilised. Then the monkey bounced on his branch. He yelled back at Uhu, bundled himself off along the tree, spun on his feet, rolled away, then back.

The first arrow clipped a stem, and skidded and jiggled, just off target. The monkey did not see it, but picked his teeth and listened for another. Uhu crept as near as he would want to go – much closer and the poisoned arrows would come back down on us. The joja peeped down, behaving like a naughty child. He even drew the branches apart to get a better look – not at Agga and myself, but at the man with the weapon, the man drawing the string back, a wince of concentration on his face as he released the next arrow.

The monkey looked down, curious and excited. He wanted to play. I wondered what he thought. That this playmate was a higher version of himself – a human? That he was just another monkey? That the playmate was a monkey-man? The expression on the monkey's juvenile face turned from curiosity to surprise. The arrow was embedded in him. He turned away as if ashamed to let us see his fear. He moved off a couple of strides. Another arrow came up – this one only parted his fur. The monkey began to scream: first in fast, chaotic screeches, then in slower, faltering spasms that sounded like retchings. He toppled – recovered. He reached up to a branch. I wanted the monkey to make that grab, escape.

Without taking his eyes off the creature, Uhu was feeling for another arrow, drawing it out of the quiver with his fingertips. The monkey was stuck there, arching for the branch. He was transfixed, as if he had jarred his back. Uhu loosed the arrow. But there was no need. The joja, who had been so stiff, slackened his grip, then tumbled. I hoped he was dead already. Before he hit the floor, his head cracked on a low branch – the noise of a falling coconut. And then he was lying in the leaves on his back, a creature of mostly arms and legs. Steaming blood seeped from the base of two arrows which protruded untidily from his waist.

Agga rushed forward to yank them out. I came forward softly – the monkey had been a naive, expressive little creature; but Uhu was not mourning. He strode up, and his eyes were resolute. I waited for his face to snap open and spill tears – Agga had said that the dawn calls of the gibbons made the hearts of Siberuts cry. But no. He looked fresh and relaxed, as if he had just had a good long soak in a hot bath. And, imperceptibly, as we walked back downslope, the loudest sound in our world the water squelching up from the leaves underfoot, his fullness and calm reached into me. I felt humbled and exalted in having taken part in the natural cycle of death and life. It was a cleansing peace, as if a great burden of guilt had been discarded and I had owned up to a transgression; all that remained of me was free, natural, with no concept of sin; I was honest, just a soul.

Then, coming to the first garden, this sense gave way. We were leaving the virgin forest, shifting from the natural to the human. After the ocean of leaves the man-made clearing was like a landfall. We were back home, our points of reference more of the rational. Suddenly questions needed answering. Why not take part in the natural cycle of life and death using lizards and hens? Why kill primates at all? And in particular, why gibbons, whose calls could make grown men cry?

The sun was weak, as we reached Uhu's doorstep. The clearing was filled with dust and quiet, just the birds bickering over night roosts, the quick rustle of lizards on the sun-fried leaves, the pigs slumped in their mud from a long day of white heat.

I looked at the monkey hanging down Agga's back, carried as casually as a rucksack, and was now repelled by the sight of the square-jawed face with its empty grimace. That death-haunted gaze. I had seen it before recently: newspaper photos, the Australians on death row in Malaysia – the sunken eyes, the vacuous, ironic smile as the grey faces stared from the newsprint, already almost skulls. I wondered if time had run out for them as well.

I stopped Agga before he could sit down. This was important: it was not right that gibbons should be killed, I told him.

'But the gibbon. He is different,' Agga said, scraping curls of mud off his feet with the parang. 'I never say they eat the gibbon, no.'

'They don't? But I'd assumed . . . But why not?'

Uhu came up. Immediately, I felt a strange vitality of understanding between us. We had been witnesses of a death together. He did not know a word of Indonesian. It did not matter. He had sensed what was troubling me. He said, '*Men-ong ka-le-leo.*' He raised a knee and patted it. The gibbon walked on hind legs. Like us. The gibbon by habit walked bipedally – unlike all the other mammals. He was also tailless, the only primate here that was an ape, like the human. He was almost one of us, so he was spared.

I leant myself against the verandah post, thinking of the primate that was not killed, and of the Gugu back on the mainland who were allegedly given gifts of tobacco. I had to have space to think. I scarcely knew the world was carrying on around me, that the little girl was laying blooms, Agga saying there was to be a party tonight – 'They believe that the spirits like pretty decoration. They invite the spirits to stay.' Tattooed people were streaming in from the forest under a marbled-blue sunset, I was shaking hands, I was down with the men on my haunches, sipping from a coconut-shell ladle. I was having hibiscus blossom planted in my hair, around me men's pointed teeth were working as cleanly as blades, drawing the red monkey meat off the bone. Now I was indoors, and Agga was nowhere.

The air was hot from a deep bed of faces painted yellow with turmeric. I looked up at the monkey skulls on the beams, the smallest of which was fist-sized, the largest of the three, the bokkoi, the width of a croquet ball. No gibbon.

I squeezed in among the cross-legged guests. In the central space of the room were the priest and his young apprentice; they had dressed themselves up with leaves – he had a cock's tail of them and more sprouting from his armband, crown and necklace. A couple of men were tuning palm-trunk hand drums, tightening the lizard skin with heat from the fireplace. They went outside and started a steady, easy beat whose echoes coughed back off the walls of the clearing. The guests carried on talking, but the beat became stronger, more insistent, pushing back the forest, forcing open a bigger human space. They came back in. Their drumming surged.

The young priest was suddenly off, shinning up a post. He reached out and swung up along the beam. He was being an ape or monkey – perhaps a joja, chewing his leaves. He swayed upside down; he swung and scratched his fleas. He was at ease in the air, and hopped lightly on the beam, while we thumped our heels on the floorboards. The air was a hot broth. The humidity of it sapped me, its vitality buoyed me up.

The creature turned up his nose at us. He plucked leaves, threw them as missiles. He pouted and he marvelled with black, child's eyes. Uhu tottered forward through the audience, being a gibbon, the primate that could walk on hind legs. He thumped his knuckles on the floor, sending up whoops. The joja backed off, panting. He crouched, musing, on his branch. Then he dropped down to us, and rolled out through the door, off to snuffle with the pigs.

The two priests sat face to face, swaying together, forward and back into each other's space. We drummed our heels, working harder and harder until the whole house clattered on its stilts and the thatch sheets chattered together. The priests got to their feet, gyrating, flicking their leaf flags over us. They rolled in a shared breath, flowing and ebbing. And they were chanting. It was a high note that coalesced in the air between them, swelled, grew heavy over us, and was sad. The men were trilling at the pitch of the night cicadas, but this was unlike any insect's mechanical itching; it was the expression of a broken heart. They were keening, the chant was a lament; the priests were like caged animals pining for freedom.

Theodore! I thought. You should be here! Whether this was a celebration of gibbons, warblers or wind spirits did not matter. This performance was for the sake of things basic, and the exact translation of the message was outside the confines of words. And how honest! These Siberuts have a truth here, Theodore. How right Father Stefano was:

This is high civilisation, but we think we've advanced beyond it.

The drumming and thumping was shaking us into unity, a cohesive mass. Whatever the purpose, the effect was a healing one. We were so alive. The blood ran more thickly in us. We were shaking, feeling the four elements strong inside. I noticed a woman whose head was drawn back, loose, her eyes caught in a splinter of moonlight, filling to the brim and overflowing, the silver tears running heavily. She was not sad, just responding to a pulse, the flux that was loosening our cramped-up emotions.

The priests were still singing. They might also have been crying; in the orange paraffin light you could not tell. The two dancers spun in the midst of our energy, supported by it.

At length, we quietened; the priests sang alone, lifted clear. They reached and lifted and sailed, up and beyond our circle. It was a plaintive wail that said that humans were unable to communicate freely with the spiritual world – the human, alone of all the animals, was always apart. Because the human was the one who was conscious of his difference, the species that was aware of his soul and able to express that awareness. The human alone felt the need to make these vaulting efforts to get from this world into the higher.

Quite unexpectedly, the older priest was gone; or rather his soul was. His empty body dropped like a sack into Uhu's arms, a whistling sound coming from inside it. The priest's soul rode, and his body remained down here – empty, a fleshy shell. Time passed, as he journeyed away from time. From time, 'the ultimate destroyer of everything'. We all watched as his soul ran free and clean, naked by itself, away from us prisoners, willing him on, helping him rise from our human isolation, our solitary confinement. The forest, I thought. The vertical trunks that were like prison bars. The two Australians who had been waiting on death row. Perhaps they had already been executed – released to freedom. The freedom of the unknown prisoner in *his* condemned cell. His escape, his ability to lift himself into another dimension.

My mind was raving, yet I could see cleanly. *Time is something of our own making – as insubstantial as matter itself. 'We' do not exist, as consciousness, in time or matter at all.* I felt I understood a little of what the prisoner had meant.

And these people also felt the prisoner's desire to leave this world. The more human-seeming primates were to be spared, because they reached out from nature and appreciated something of our isolation in the order of things. Segma had not been so wrong after all. The Siberuts did have a special relationship; the gibbons were more than just friends.

The younger priest drew up, exuding moisture. He spilled a coconut full of water on the corpse's breast, flapping it over the empty carcass, brushing it, cajoling back the soul, asking it with the help of the go-between leaves to come back. The priest snuffled. He was with us again.

Chapter Seven

Dogs, sifting around for last night's left-overs, woke me early, and I slipped into the bushes and set about my press-ups. *One, two, three* . . . Gnats and butterflies jerked around plants that had been enthusiastically gnawed by insects with big mandibles.

Seventy-eight, seventy-nine . . . Wheeze, pant. But I must think forward . . . Cough, splutter, wheeze. Onward to Sumatra. *Eighty-eight, eighty-nine* . . . Pant, pant . . . The Kubu are a motley lot, by all accounts. Cough, wheeze . . . Segma said they were hardly worth a visit. But there must be one Kubu left who remembered the ape-men tales of the Dutch days . . . Splutter, wince . . .

Ninety-eight . . . Gasp! *Ninety-nine* . . . Splutter, gasp! *One hundred!* I felt better after a good lie-down. 'Yes,' I said, from among the prickly bugs and wet leaves, 'if need be I'll find that last forest tribesman. See if he too has a half-animal friend, an extension back to his natural origins, an escape in time from his loneliness. Onward to the last Kubu!'

Agga and I caught a lift downriver. We scared a pair of pied hornbills; they steered off, cranking their wings over a treeshrub that had leaves like limp straps of seaweed. Frogs sang like finches in the high cane banks. We overtook canoeing girls with round reed hats, grass skirts and scoop nets, and then a man steering a spear into a bank hole that had wet lips. Fiddler crabs slipped in and out of other holes, waving glistening pincers.

I gave Agga his pay. He took the banknotes expressing thanks – not as a natural right as Uhu had, seizing all my remaining tobacco. We bit into the mangoes that we had brought along for the journey. Agga's was unusually sweet. He parcelled the stone in a leaf, stretched open his shorts, and dropped it down his crotch. 'No more sour fruits,' he said. 'It will be better and better.'

School, despite the classroom riots, had taught him well. Change, that badge of Western culture, was the key. 'Equilibrium with the milieu',

Father Stefano had told me, 'results in apathy towards progress.' He was right, and school's job was to destroy this equilibrium, this balance with surroundings. Only that way could man make progress.

Rulek was waiting. It looked as if he had been waiting, standing where the channel with bloody water split the village in half, for the two days I had been away. Agga shied, seeing Rulek all sprung, ready to pounce. The canoe nosed into the shore and chased Rulek a few paces through the water grasses. 'Afternoon!' I said. He played fitfully with the knot of his sarong.

While Agga tied up, Rulek said to me in English, 'I am not cross.' But he had folded his arms with grim determination and was finding it hard work forcing a smile. 'I am not cross because I'm your best friend.'

'I wouldn't go as far as that.' I stepped ashore.

'What present have you give him?' Rulek's eyes were on the bulge in Agga's shorts – the mango stone.

Agga kissed my neck. 'It will be better and better.' He waved the stone, and was off down the path. The children came to him. He showed them the mango and they listened to his plan for it. He was home again, and radiant, standing tall.

Rulek laughed. 'A seed only!' He offered a hand as he climbed the bank with me. But he slipped on the grass and I had to save him. On the path, he grabbed me by the shoulder, pulled me towards him, enfolded me in his arms and perfume. 'I am glad you are safe. I worry so much. At night I not sleep. I so worry that I take all your *barang* – luggage in speak English – and all your money and take care of this in my own house.'

'Taken my belongings? My money? Put them in your own house?' I loosened myself from him.

'Everything is safe in my house,' Rulek said. 'Do no worrying. There is plenty money left.'

I stomped down the path, through suburbia, to his house. Then I had to wait for him to catch up: doors and locks – I had forgotten about them. Once inside, I found that Rulek had taken only two small banknotes – 'A present from you,' he said gratefully.

Agga watched our loaded toy boat from the beach. He stood with a clutch of women, calling, 'It will get better and better!' and showing me his wrist, telling me he was saving up for a watch. The crowd did not wave us off, they viewed us. But I waved until they were no different from any of the branches or lumbering, sodden logs of the shore. I wanted to say a proper goodbye, knowing that you could not live in harmony with natural things if you measured your own rhythms by a mechanism of cogs, springs and ratchets. The Siberuts, like the Hmongs of Thailand, were finished as separate peoples. And I must not have regrets – not, at least, if Theodore had got it right; they were joining the rest of humanity, partaking in the one and only hope for our planet earth, the little dinghy in the eternal sea and space of time.

The island evaporated into nothingness as a mist of spray blew up off the green sea, and my mind turned to the Sumatran highlands, and the ape-girl that a peasant called Pastaran had said he had seen there. And to words that coalesced from the rainbow of so many recent memories. *We are greater than matter and can even create a shadow of it ourselves.*

Part 3

Hybrid Vigour

Chapter One

The roses of Elizabeth, the rose of the prisoner. The two were fused in my mind; I pictured their every detail – scent rising from a cup of cool petals, the tassle of golden anthers, the red-skinned thorns. The thorns especially; they were a spur for me. This was hybrid vigour and I would not be held back. I would not fail where Theodore had failed. I had that double edge. With this combined stimulus my energy could be neither deflected nor suppressed. Onward to the last Kubu!

'They won't come out of the forest and accept modernity,' Swartz had said about the Kubu, but I could think of only one man who might get me to them, as the Barisan Range came into sight, a perspiring giant asleep on his side, the heat-cloaked sprawl of Padang tucked tight into the small of his back. The man was contact number one, the elusive soulmate of Theodore, Father Morini, the malaria-riddled priest with a fag hanging out of his mouth.

I stepped ashore, paid off the crew and knew that I needed a drink. The boat had lost its rudder in rough seas, we had been marooned for days on a desert island while most but not all the missing structural timbers were replaced, and had shipped water every inch of the way home. I had nothing against rubber time, the relict from Sumatra's balanced, forest days. But when it came down to it, I had to get on. I was not here for my own sake. I was an ambassador. And, though a drink or two was required now, when all was said and done at least I had not stooped to Valium, yet.

I marched to the Muara Hotel – a pricey establishment for credit-card clientele, with bar tables arranged around examples of higher arts and crafts under thatched hutlets. In a land of rubber time, it was a stout, defended castle of prompt service. It was where Westerners who could not cope found shelter.

I ordered a beer, and a bowl of fish and rice. There was a spotlit stage and a bloated man with an electric organ trying to entertain us. Above the noise, I heard a familiar voice hacking across the restaurant through a dozen conversations. 'So there I was. She'd locked the goddam door, and I was out on the street without an item of clothing! That is, if you don't count what I was still holding – the Italian fruitbowl.'

Swartz! What was he doing here in Padang? According to his schedule he should be on to Bangkok by now, looking at the market potential for hand-painted umbrellas. Here he was with a tableload of Indonesians in impeccable Western-style suits.

'And – you're gonna like this – standing there in the buff, out on the sidewalk in the night, I heard police sirens. Yeah – she'd set the cops on me!' The Indonesians were bending forward politely, their eyes on Swartz's lips. They were checking that he had delivered the punchline before breaking into laughter. Swartz rolled his head, saying 'Boy!' four times.

Next to his beer glass were a handful of others, also empty. I was happy for Swartz. He had found a way of slowing his pace, of adapting somewhat to rubber time.

'Ever heard anything so funny?' His stomach, which was larger than I remembered it, kept him from the table, but he was sliding his feet apart for balance, and standing up with an air of importance, as if to propose a toast. A couple of the Indonesians were chuckling chaotically, skimming their hands over their mouths. Swartz's smile was weakening. He said slowly and sadly, 'No, I don't suppose you have.' The men thought it was an additional gag, and yacked some more.

'Come on, Mr Swartz, get a grip on yaself!' I murmured.

Just then he did. He flicked his fingers and a waitress came up. 'What's the deal?'

'Sir? I speak English but a little.'

'I want the check now please. That's all these guys included.'

'Yes, sir.' She walked smartly away, but slowed after a few paces and drifted to another table.

'That's what I like about you guys,' Swartz said. 'You take life easy.' But he was pale and sallow-browed. He lowered his shoulders and suddenly had the look of a refugee. The Indonesians glanced uncertainly around the table. But Swartz was amicable in defeat. He smiled good-naturedly and prodded his neighbour's chest with his forefinger. The Indonesians took it as a signal to squirt more laughter. 'You take life just the way it comes, ain't that right?'

While Swartz's guests cackled around him in Indonesian, he patted his jacket pockets, brought out a bottle, tapped out two white pills, chucked them to the back of his throat, pooled the dregs of beer from the five glasses, and swirled the lot down.

*   *   *

'Father Morini, here I come!' That was my cry out of the cracked window of the little bus, as we chugged north, the market women, my backpack, bow and arrows and myself compressed together in a hot, wet ball. The Italians in Padang had received a note from the Father; they thought I might just catch him at home today, a Sunday. The bus driver was cautiously optimistic. He might be able to get me right to the door. 'We shall see, John,' he said. 'John, we shall see.'

Heat shimmered off the road and fused my impressions – a forgotten tarmac roller on its side, damming a ditch; a fish-eagle pitching; a river slipping through the legs of washerwomen; stalk-billed kingfishers; water channelled this way, conducted that, sparkling through dull rice spreads. We were now higher and cooler. Some houses were not planked, but walled with plaited palm leaf. The patches of redundant jungle were fenced out by coconut palms, or diluted by orchard.

The zone of Javanese immigrants began. Smoke seeped across the straight gravel roads where any lingering forest was being cleared. A right-angled right turn, a hundred yards, then a right-angled left. The bus trundled on through row after row, block after block of box houses, chickens running a foot ahead of our loose bumper.

How I needed Morini's help. These carved-up hills were meant to be the Gugu homelands! Now there were just the Javanese immigrants, men like Pastaran the Gugu witness, doing their best, living back to back in shacks which went under names like Sampang I, Sampang II, Sampang III.

'John!' the driver shouted. 'The next stop is yours.' He was trying not to laugh.

'Here?' These were smallholdings with dirt yards scattered with chickens and tired women who looked as if they each had several children to spare. They had sticking plasters on their temples to ease their headaches.

'Here. The stop for Father John.'

'Father Morini is the one I want.'

'That's Father John to me, John.'

We drew up at a plank building with an unhomely, village-school façade, a functional verandah and none of the usual cacti in tin cans or birds in cages. There might have been boys knocking down rambutan fruit from leafy trees; however, no fruit trees grew here – just clawing, wounded jungle hunks. The passengers started unbuckling to make an exit for me.

Hell, I thought. I'm not sure this is such a good idea. A cow leaped

into the road out of the black ditch. Its eyes were rolling. It had found
something frightful in there. I squeezed out along the aisle, bludgeoning
passengers with my pack – 'Sorry!' – clouting them with Uhu's bow –
'Whoops! So sorry!' – and arrows – 'I shouldn't, madam, they're
poisonous.'

The bus driver said, 'Bye, bye, John.'

'When's the next bus?'

'Tomorrow, perhaps.'

'Can you wait a moment, while I see if he's in?'

'Of course, John.'

As I walked the plank over the ditch, the bus roared away. Thanks a
bunch, I thought. The cow from the ditch grunted and walked off too.
The mission post was shut up. No one answered my knocking. It looked
a godforsaken place. A man came by in wringing wet trousers, walking
his bicycle, swerving cow pats, steadying sheaths of long grass on his
handlebars.

'Good afternoon. Does Father Morini live here?'

The man picked up speed.

The noon insects were stuttering, boys were wrestling and tree-climb-
ing in the backyards, chickens were taking dust baths, ditches were
fizzing. I noticed that the electricity poles had sprouted buds and leaves.
Another cow stumbled by, this one tolling its bell.

After an hour I knocked again. This time a small Indonesian came out,
rubbing his eyes. I followed him down a corridor of loose wood panels
to an Italian who said he was Brother Robert. Morini would be here this
evening. I watched carefully, but Brother Robert definitely was not
hiding a smirk.

Robert sat me down with a bowl of spaghetti. He apologised for
Father Wittwer, who made honking noises from far down his throat and
spat about once a minute. Wittwer was French, from a Parisian mission.
He had caught a bug and left his bed only to dunk bread in a bowl of
coffee or to pray in the side chapel.

I sat like a tramp on the steps. Dusk fell around me very slowly as the
sun spilled over the trees. Wet men, women and children came from
hidden field crops and dropped themselves and their firewood on the
verandah. Instead of talking, the men rolled tobacco wads round their
cheeks. They, like me, were waiting. It must be for vespers.

Sure enough Brother Robert came out. He had not got into his vestments yet, but everyone rose to their feet. I thought I had better do the
same. There was a hush. I dipped my head in reverence. Nothing happened. When I opened my eyes I found my neighbours shoving for the

seats. My space had been nabbed. Brother Robert was unhitching a wooden flap in the wall. Behind it was a television.

A sports feature was on – highlights of last month's World Cup, interrupted at a crucial moment for coverage of a motorbike rally. The viewers were mesmerised – the children less so than the men, who looked dazed, as if they had been struck glancing blows on their heads. The motorbike item ended, all but the sound track, and we were back to football. We had missed the goal. The audience did not mind. They stared on, transfixed. I was so absorbed in the effect on the audience of the flickering screen that I had not noticed the bike soundtrack getting louder. Then I turned: the noise was coming from behind.

What with the full moon, the driver had not bothered with headlights. Nor had he bothered with a helmet. He was small and he had to splay his arms right out to reach the handlebars. His khaki sleeves flapped backwards into the helmet of the pillion rider, whose feet – long, pallid, hairy and bony – were in leather sandals.

The passenger eased off the saddle. The bike cackled away up the road and I looked at the figure left unstrapping his helmet. He had a dead cigarette sagging out of his mouth. *Thin, riddled, sunken-cheeked.* That was the description, and it matched. I stepped forward to meet Theodore's number-one contact.

'Good evening,' he said in English, trotting the four paces between us. 'Morini. It is nice. May I have the pleasure?'

I was retreating. 'Benedict,' I said. 'My name's Benedict. It's good to meet you at last – a friend of mine told me about you. He came seven years ago. An old chap – Theodore Hull. English, like me. Unforgettable.'

Morini had forgotten. He had big brown eyes which now turned upwards in their sockets and sank back. He was thinking. 'We talked about . . . ?'

' "Hope at Large". He was investigating the ape-men stories.'

'Ah.' He rasped his hand against his chin stubble. 'Ah. You come for the monkey-mens.' He flexed his lips. I took it as suspicion, and gave him time to look me over. Up on the verandah the Argentinian team had just put in a controversial header against England. The commentator was ecstatic; no one on the verandah so much as stirred.

Morini's face under the large moon shone out as white as a streetlamp. 'I remember. A strong old guy. A friend with him. I was ill, I think.'

'That's right,' I said, still walking backwards.

Morini picked at his damp silk shirt, unsticking it from his nobbly shoulders. 'Be of service?'

'I've come to find out about the ape-men for him. Can we talk?'

'Talk? I can talk and talk and talk!' I took another step back and my heels met the bottom step. 'You may try to stop me but you will not! I am famous because I talk of monkey-mens.'

So rumour had it. Morini clamped me in an arm and whirled me up the steps. 'We talk! We talk!' He was so excited. Any moment he might kiss me, but for now he was whisking me off down the corridor, darting into his office – the floor tiled with pamphlets, box files, worm-bored volumes laden with dust – then out, knocking over a paraffin lamp, kicking the broken glass under his door, and ushering me to a sitting room, a cage of insect netting. He pushed the magazines from the cane table, duffed up my chair cushions, sat me down, sat down himself. Only then did he take his backpack off. 'We talk.'

'But don't you want to wash yourself?' I said. 'Have a bite to eat?'

'No, no. I ate this morning.'

'It's night now.'

'Now we must talk. No time. How many days can you be here?'

'I must go tomorrow, if I can. Theodore's waiting.'

He forced one hand through his cropped hair. 'All right, so we talk all night through. Hey! You know? We are exactly on the equator, where we are resting. Bang on.'

'Really?' I opened my notebook.

'Very good. Writings.' He looked greedily at my notes. He wanted to take the book. I held it tight.

'To begin at the beginning. You believe the ape-men exist?'

'I suspect. I have so many stories. So many. These are only my collections. No time for special study, you understand. Only the stories.'

'Only stories?' But Morini had been Theodore's contact number one! A kindred spirit.

Father Morini biffed me lightly on the shoulder. 'But the stories! Listen. Where to begin?' He began with a German oilman who saw a Gugu with a baby Gugu nuzzling her breasts. The creatures 'had the hair of monkey, but already they were human'. These were the type which walked with backward-pointing feet.

'But—' I said.

'Yes, but the problem is verification . . .'

'Talking of which, what—'

'These are small men, *orang pendek*. There are *orang raksasa*, big men. I have tales of them smoking in the rivers, head above water. I am talking two metres, more.'

'Whereabouts was this?'

'Now, 1929, soldiers saw them beside the road—'

'If I could just—'

'Wait a moment, you know, because I try to give you something else . . .'

Father Morini, like Theodore, had been too much ignored by the world, and now that he had an audience there was no stopping him. He blew and blew. Decade after decade – he reeled off the unsubstantiated tales, words tripped up untidy rows of teeth, stumbled frantically out of the mouth. His top incisors dominated his face; perhaps it was the angle at which they leant left.

'And 1969 – a gang of these was in the plantation and steals the lunch of the peasants – they went to bed so hungry. And their children cry that night and in 1971 . . .'

As Morini raged on, the sick Pastor Wittwer coughed more loudly, like a sick cow.

'Now, what year is it? Yes. 1972; thirteen stories we have that year. A nun bicycles along the north road to give the comfort at the house of the madman . . .'

Ink poured from my pen. I had blisters on my fingers. 'Ooooooh, *mon Dieu*,' moaned the Frenchman every quarter of an hour or so, but Morini was talking too fast to hear. '*Mon Dieu. MON DIEU!*'

We were now getting to the present day – Father Morini was definitely slowing up. He said, with a note of finality, 'So, the disaster is five years ago. The building of the road comes.' I was taken aback by the abrupt silence. Morini had stopped. All I could hear were the French priest's groans and the insects rapping on the wire netting. 'But these are just stories.' He grasped my elbow – much more tightly and I would hear a bone crack. 'I want to give a week's talkings. But the proof. We need the proofs. You knows this, and I knows this. We need the proofs. And for this, you go to the Kubu. I met them one time, begging on the road to Jambi. Small gang. Yellow skin. Had a boy – a lizard carried on his back. Has no great fear. Pretty eyes. Nice smile.'

'Yes, Theodore also said we needed proof. I'm sure he said you had some.'

'Have not. No.'

'So how do I meet a traditional Kubu tribesman? I mean, the purest sort of Kubu would be wandering in the forests.'

Morini took hold of both my shoulders. I shrank my head back as far as it would go. 'You go to the Father in Curup. Hey! What is the name? I cannot remind the name.' He released me to smack his forehead with the palm of his hand. 'Moriceau. But watch out! Is a crazy man.'

'Crazy?' What, more than *you*?

'*Mon Dieu!*' The French pastor suddenly cried.

'Try Moriceau,' said Morini. 'French and crazy.'

We went to bed and, given the peace and quiet, the Frenchman was soon making only cattle-stall snufflings.

At 7.00 I jumped out of bed. It was not excitement, the scent of a fresh trail in the wind, but a noise like an artillery barrage. Children were smashing poles on the metal roof to scare fruit-pecking birds. Morini came out; the boys ran away screaming. I was to catch a lift in the mission's blue Toyota. We said our goodbyes. 'Once upon a time, we meet,' said Morini. 'Reunite.'

'That will be good.' I stepped back, lest I receive another Italian missionary's hearty back-slap. 'I'll let you know how I get on,' I said.

'Yes. We meet and we will meet.' I did not move fast enough, and he smacked me. 'God bless!' As the Toyota started off, Morini waving, the sick French pastor emerged – not a pretty sight. My last view was of him advancing on Morini from behind with a murderous look in his eyes.

Clear the way, because here I come! In the late heat of Padang I trotted along to the post-office telephone. A distant voice in Curup said he would get me to a Kubu. I should have no fear, 'It is but a minor operation,' Moriceau said. Then he broke into French. When he came out of it he had got on to the subject of the Vietnam war. 'Vietcong!' he said. 'I tell you, there were VCs everywhere.'

'Crazy,' I thought. 'French and crazy.'

Onward! Out along the seafront, where little fishing craft with dust-sheet sails lay like flotsam, and men were slopping white paint on tree trunks; then up and up into the singing, blue steaming hills towards Curup.

The journey of only a few hours took us ten. But no matter. We were getting there, and it was a fresh and bright morning among crop-striped hills. The sleepy-eyed boys on the roads had their sarongs pulled up to their shoulders against the chill. Last night's dead frogs were being prised from the road by chickens. The children's kites enmeshed in the power lines shook off their damp in the breeze. In the market the neck of a chicken was being wrung.

I stepped out on to the dirt. A trishaw driver put me, my baggage, my bow and quiver on the seat.

'Are you sure you can manage the weight?' I asked, because he had legs like dry kindling. 'The streets look uneven – and steep as well.'

'No problem, *bapak*,' he said. We rolled down the main thoroughfare and were soon out of control.

'*Awas!*' I yelled. 'Watch out!' We had missed an oncoming bicyclist, but now we were getting faster. 'Use the brakes!' I said. 'For heaven's sake, use the brakes!' But he *was* using the brakes. 'Use the bell!' But he was. The brass bell was dated. To sound it, you gave it a firm flick with a twig. The driver took both hands off the handlebars to do this, but even so managed to drop the twig. Old men stopped rocking on the balconies, and got to their feet. We missed a timber-lorry death by choosing the monsoon ditch instead.

From where we eventually stopped, it was twice the same distance again to the mission. We humped my luggage and the pieces of trishaw there together. 'That's ten thousand rupiahs,' said the driver, putting down his load. He peered suspiciously at his bloody ankle, which was bent at an unnatural angle. 'Excluding breakages.'

Beyond the metal bell-tower – like a prison-camp observation post – was a side door. The mission was thoroughly painted in caramel, but the cross surmounting the building was plain and simple. The garden flowered, the metal railings did not rust.

'Entrance *ici*' said a small cardboard sign. It was damp from the dew but the ink had not run – so the message was meant for me, put up just in case I had arrived in the night, on time.

Through the door was a small garden, with a lily pond and a scarecrow sporting a trilby. On the left a woman stooped in a kitchen door scrubbing white shirts. I would have gone up to her but another message said, 'Continue *à droit*'. I continued round to the right. '*Ici*' said a notice above an open door. At the kitchen table was a European, who was occupying all of it – elbows wide apart on the chequered Fablon beside liver pâté and a soupbowl of coffee. On the wall was a photo of Normandy coastline – a whitewashed lighthouse on barnacled rocks.

Father Moriceau, of the Paris Mission, MEP, was not crazy, just misunderstood. He was a man with a vision, like Theodore. But in Sumatra that meant he was a man harried by lists. They were a weapon with which to fight rubber time. You either gave into it, so the wisdom went, and eased into the rhythms of the paddies and jungles; or you fought it with rigidity and risked snapping completely. For Moriceau there was no choice: he had been sent here to change the world, to make it progress. But he knew the danger, and went about it according to his lists, a life of merciless rationality which kept him from the fate of so many that had come before.

While I had breakfast, I watched Moriceau's Indonesian protégés come for encouragement and advice. They went away quietly, examining file paper with headings like 'Hermann's saving scheme', or 'Rachet's first priority', or 'Inwic's objective of the month'.

My bit of paper read 'Getting Benedict to the Kubu (time allocation two days)'. The sheet was already waiting for me, pinned under the liver pâté. The first phase was already under way. 'While Benedict has breakfast – *baguette et café* – check with Kubu contact (Pastaribu).'

Moriceau cranked a lever on a black 'phone of historic interest. Then he pouted. 'The line, she is dead.'

Moriceau used the time in hand to answer my questions about himself. He had been a missionary among tribals in Vietnam. Most of his parishioners had disappeared at the hands of the invading communists, but some had turned up just lately on the Thai border. He showed me his snaps. These people were bonier than my Hmongs. Instead of embroidered jackets and black caps with silver coins they wore pillow cases caked with red soil.

'But now, monsieur, we hurry. As you see, we arrive, Jambi Province, midday tomorrow . . .'

After my shower – phase two – it was phase three: lunch. Moriceau sang grace from behind his chair. He warbled the tune at double speed – we were running behind schedule. 'What now?' I said, clearing the plates for the maid. 'We leave for the Kubu?'

'But you have not read the schedule?'

I looked up the next item: '(Two o'clock): journey to Muaraman church.' After that, it was 'Phase five (six o'clock): Mass (*vite*). Phase six (seven o'clock): to Kubu.'

'We go. It is time.'

Journey to Muaraman church. There were about twenty other Citroëns in Sumatra, all of them owned by French missionaries. One of Moriceau's two had been serviced here in Sumatra. We could afford no chances, and so we took the other.

We left in the 2CV, Moriceau humming '*Sous les Ponts de Paris*' as we tipped into the blind bends. 'Hold yourself tight, this is the Vietnam country. Who knows? The roads are mined perhaps!' I stayed quiet. I held on to my seat, and swung with the car. 'Look out for VCs!' Moriceau screamed. 'Vroom, vroooom!'

Curup was a fertile district, owing to the volcanic activity – the hill, Bukit Kaba, steamed from grey craters. The soil was like drinking-chocolate powder, but from it issued potato plants, carrots, haricot beans, cabbages and onions. We flew faster.

'Vroom, vroooooooom!' Moriceau cried. 'I am happy when I am moving.' He was not just moving. He was pulling the car round the bends with the force of his own weight, making roadside waterpitcher girls sidestep. 'Mademoiselle!' he warned, and they hopped into the ditches with the frogs. We were not stopping. Time was too precious. However far we had got tomorrow, at noon we would turn back. I knew because it was written into the schedule.

Cloves, coffee, ginger – we passed them all . . . Charge! We were well into the mountains; the slopes had recently been set ablaze and the remaining forest gutted. The landscape was looking war-torn, fought over. It was as if the army had been squirting napalm here, showering Agent Orange there. The bomb-crater holes were where the larger trees had once been rooted. 'Vietcong!' Moriceau aimed a cocked hand at boys with air rifles chasing pigs over the crops.

It was six o'clock – we were bang on schedule, but we had had to belt along madly to make it. Muaraman, I observed, had seen better days. The best of it was small and undistinguished, the lesser houses tiled with sheet metal, machine cogs and plates – all cobbled together from winding gear and digging apparatus. For this was goldmining country.

Moriceau got his vestments out of the boot, and looked enthusiastically at the church – it was like a boy scout's hall. I left him to it, walking up the open grass slope along streams that drove the ore-crunching tumblers. Europeans had been doing most of the mining, but they had already upped and left, leaving the hills hollow. The faces of rock were a jaundice yellow in the dusk, slashed with quartz veins and pockmarked with shafts. The heat of the rock slope blew over me, but the caves had a dungeon's old, tightly clinging air. *We are greater than matter and can even create a shadow of it ourselves.* I screwed the words up in my mind, and tossed them away like litter. They were an irrelevance, a distraction – nothing to do with Theodore's ape-men.

And with wispy tunes of the swifts inside the hills, I did eighty-five press-ups. No point in straining myself with the full hundred. Theodore was relying on me. I must pace myself. This was the final assault.

But, looking back into the cool space of this black cave, I could not help picturing that velvet rose. For a prisoner-of-war, the desire had been for a rose – the rose of England, symbol of beauty, cultivation, breeding. Suppose the prisoner did conjure the rose through the energies of his consciousness – the pricking thorns, the silk touch of the bloom, the smell of the perfume, the taste of its nectar. Suppose he really did create a shadow of that emblem of home and civility. Could humans who felt lonely and confined among nature, not create a Gugu? Call it Pan, or a yeti, an elf, a leprechaun, a centaur, that symbolic link and go-between with the free, natural world, his provider?

Chapter Two

Church was over. Climbing into the Citroën, I said, 'So we'll get to your contact, this man Pastaribu, by noon tomorrow?'

'If we are return *vite*, we find the Kubu. If we are not *vite*, you will not meet them. If you wish, you may pray. If you do not wish to pray, you return to England never seeing a Kubu.' He snatched at the air in front of my eyes. 'But I joke!'

Rain came with the dark. The roads were treacherous, but Moriceau kept his foot down. Pastaribu was only seven or eight hours away, but it was best to drive all night. In Sumatra if the going was good you kept on going.

We kept on going – faster. The roads were greasy with topsoil that was on the move downhill to the local reservoir, but Moriceau did not slow up. A Toyota was locked across the road, pitched into the ditch, but with judicious use of our bumper we lost only minutes. We ran out of petrol, but a Protestant churchman appeared to us out of the night and gladly sold us a can for a small fortune. Moriceau took off a sock to filter the rust and – '*En avant!*' – we were moving again.

But then, in the horizontal rain, we rounded a bend to find the road completely gone. The gleaming wet tarmac ended in a mat black void. 'Avalanche!' cried Moriceau, flicking to full beam. We were blocked by mashed trees, rounded chunks of hill and a crumpled wooden house. Clothing flapped in the glacier of mud. I braced myself for a corpse squeezed in half between two timbers. But there were no bodies, just the barrage beyond sheets of rain, and a smell of tree sap.

Moriceau clonked his head on the steering wheel, and said, 'The operation is failed.' He asked to look at my piece of paper, the schedule. He checked it was the right one, and then ripped it in two. He dropped the pieces out of the window, and I peered out into the black rain to watch them flow away. The remains of my expedition ... 'So, the situation is, you do not see the Kubu.' Moriceau climbed out of the car, into the downpour, and urinated in the ditch.

I felt betrayed. Moriceau's objectives, all set down in real ink on real paper, had looked so obtainable. The written words had promised to help me flout the natural pace, rubber time; now I had been let down by the unbalancing West, my very own culture.

But before I could reach for Swartz's Valium, I saw the first light of a silver dawn. Yet this was midnight! The light shifted. A forest-clearance tractor, a huge devouring glow-worm with cruel pincers, shuddered into view, head low, as if ashamed and owning up to the deforestation, the cause of the erosion. It buried its face in the mess, panted three times, then began chucking timber aside.

By the time the road was clear, we were five hours behind schedule. 'Can we still get to the Kubu?'

'Yes, it is possible. If we travel in the way of Vietnam.'

'Isn't that how you were driving yesterday?'

'But no! *That* was in the way of Paris.'

I should have known. And you could see now why the other Citroën had needed a new gear box. We charged on, as for guerrilla-war conditions, under a blue-and-crimson-dappled early sky, through the Barisan Range, north to Jambi Province and the land of the Kubu. We swerved to miss a creature that was golden and hairy and probably lived underground. We did not even slow as we took the villages, scattering the coffee beans laid out to bake in the road.

Cinnamon trees whirled by the window. On and on: men leant on their rakes, toes among the cash crops, and tipped back their palm hats to watch the swinging Citroën, or to listen to its mad whining. We plunged through a wedding group – a road blockage of men dancing on one foot, food plates balanced on fingers. Moriceau cheered, '*Bon appétit!*' but his eyes were on the road, scanning the tarmac for landmines. Now the only time that he waved was to children or goats ignoring the weak bleat of the car horn.

We were lower now. Hills sank without trace, sucked into the low forests. The sun rose high and strong, and midday seemed a breath away: two hours to reach Moriceau's Kubu contact, Mr Pastaribu. We took a sharp left, hardly slowing. Then, at once, the world changed. It was an end to cornering, and to gear-change jerks. The jungle, where it should have been beginning to unroll properly, had been parted, split by a jet-runway-sized road.

Theodore had said, 'I feel like Moses up that mountain, looking down at Canaan, and not able to get to the Promised Land.' The divide of the forest was a feat of Moses proportions, it had to be said. However, this Kubu land was no promised land. As Swartz had warned, things had changed. I was aboard the Trans-Sumatran Highway, the long, sleek, unbending snake from which all higher natural lifeforms fled.

We felt very small – the waves of naked parent rock curving up and away either side of us, gullied by water running like tears from the forest left-overs. Mostly the near forest had been burnt away. Blisters remained – thorny scrub plains of laterite bedrock, and a coconut-tree oasis or two.

Here and there I spotted the twisting remnants of the old road, meandering innocently to left and right. On one of those gravelly curves Millet had dented the bus roof with his head. Theodore had had to abandon *that* expedition. Time was running out for this one.

'On occasion, I see the Kubu doing the begging here. But this is always at the dawn. They come to the *marché*, with a fish to sell maybe, and then they walk back again to the forest.'

Father Moriceau kept the accelerator to the floor. There were speed restrictions of 40 kilometres per hour, but these were taken no more seriously by drivers than the no-overtaking signs. It was eleven o'clock. We should make it.

To the right was a sudden rash of duplicated concrete houses separated by bald soil, mudpats and trees that were dying lingering deaths. This was where vagrant Kubu had been settled, Moriceau explained. It was a government project which had not been the outstanding success which might have justified its cost.

Project Forest People Integration had gone quite well for a few months, rumours had it. The Kubu even expressed an interest in becoming Muslim – that was until the day they heard that Muslims did not eat pork. Then, not even contemplating Christianity, one daybreak they picked themselves up, grabbed their pig spears and left. Now Project Forest People Integration was accommodation for more Javanese immigrants.

Steam jetted from the Citroën bonnet, but we were there – Sukajadi, where Pastaribu, a church layman, lived. The town was a staging place along the road – only a bus stop and a market, and a soil-clouded river with fishing boys and mooring poles, and where we were now, this basic kind of housing estate. We clambered out. The car was bubbling and whistling. Moriceau patted it. Up the shingle path was a door painted with a child's mural, a marriage between two flags – the Union Jack and Stars and Stripes. The sun was vertical, our shadows shrunken – just black splashes chasing our feet. This was noon – turning-back time for Moriceau.

We did not have to knock; a woman was scrubbing a boy of about nine in the yard. She dropped her stiff brush, and ran indoors and through the bungalow to welcome us.

'*Bonjour, Madame!*' said Pastor Moriceau. He took the woman's hand and she was electrified, her eyes squeezed out by her cheeks. 'How are you?' he said first in French, then in Indonesian. He showed me to her. 'My *ami*, Monsieur Benedict . . .'

The woman was glowing all over, polishing her knuckles up and down her blouse, but so far she had not said a thing.

'Where's Pastaribu?' asked Moriceau. He had his arm extended indoors in a querying motion, and he sneaked a look at his wristwatch. She said her first words. 'As you know, Father, he sleeps a lot.'

I could not help frowning a little. A fat lot of use Bapak Pastaribu sounded.

'And his moaning?' asked Moriceau sympathetically.

'As bad as ever.'

'Sounds like a good sort of guide,' I muttered. But you have to look on the bright side of life, as Theodore would have pronounced if only he had been here, so I said, 'I like your boy's drawings – the British and US flags. He'll be quite an artist when he grows up.'

The woman looked wretched. Moriceau explained, with not as much delicacy as I might have liked, that it was Mr Pastaribu, her husband, who was the artist.

Pastaribu came to the door, flapping away a yawn.

'How are things?' Moriceau asked. '*Bon?*'

'Dreadful,' he said, and began at the top of a long list of complaints. During it, Moriceau looked at his watch twice. Then he could not stand it any more. He put out a finger and tickled Pastaribu's fatty chest. He explained what I had come for. Pastaribu pinched the skin of his thick neck. 'But why do you have to go to the Kubu? They're no better than animals.'

Moriceau smiled tolerantly. 'He jokes.'

'They've got snouts like pigs,' continued Pastaribu. His wife left hurriedly. She seemed to have heard what was coming next a good many times before.

The Kubu women sold their children for loose change, they came out at night and stole chickens, they dished out sex to any passer-by . . . Pastaribu went on and on.

'My *ami*, Benedict, is an important man,' fibbed Moriceau. 'He has to find them. And you say you cannot help a friend?'

Pastaribu raised his shoulders to his ears. He was going to laugh while pulling a grimace, say 'Sorry, but if you knew the Kubu like I do . . .'

But too late. Moriceau had already left. He was crunching down the gravel path, waving goodbye with his fingers. '*Merci, merci, mon ami.*'

Pastaribu stayed where he was, his head pulled forward, bent after us. He waved back, but rather slowly. Behind him, his wife was pummelling cushions and blaspheming. In front of him Moriceau was leaving, thanking him in a foreign language for something he had refused to do.

Teetering by his car door, Moriceau said to me, 'I am so sorry. This is all I can do for you.'

'Never mind.' I looked along the slat fence, beyond the lawn tufts dying there, to Pastaribu, propped on an elbow in the doorway. His wife was beating hell out of the washing-up. A family row was brewing.

'Maybe you can make something here?'

It looked as if I was going to have to.

Turning the Citroën would take too long. Moriceau backed the car through the palms, the hundred rutted yards up to the highway. He was half an hour behind schedule.

Chapter Three

To be fair to Pastaribu, he was not as bad as he invariably appeared to be. And there was his wife, who made up for him a great deal and who was a lesson to us all. She brought me cups of coffee while Pastaribu lounged in his easy chair, finishing his list of troubles. And look at the quality of shoes his salary forced on him. And the mosquitoes the size of wasps at night. And America was great. And Holland. And Britain. And the Prime Minister, the Metal Lady, must be so rich – could I get him an introduction?

There was not a hope of our getting to the Kubu this afternoon. We were not going anywhere. Night came, slowly, and, Pastaribu still yacking, I was introduced to his bedbugs.

In the morning, her husband's wallet now fat with my banknotes, Mrs Pastaribu filled my waterflask with coffee. We had struck a package deal that included an incentive bonus for quick results. He wheeled out a motorbike from his neighbour's garden. 'It's okay. He's a good Christian.'

The sun barely up, clouds stacking, promising rain, we toured through the stalls of Sukajadi market, looking for stray Kubu. A fruit boy said he had seen one at dawn, peddling bundles of cane. Now he must be out on the main road.

We cruised the mighty Trans-Sumatran Highway, keeping our eyes on the ditch scrub. No luck. Near Project Forest People Integration Pastaribu veered right off the road and through brittle grey grasses along a strip of hot bedrock. This split in the forest took you through an informal rubber-tree plantation which was also a Kubu road homeward. It led nowhere, Pastaribu said.

Leggy flies hit us and we had to squint. Sometimes they got into our mouths, and were gummed by saliva to the back of our throats. As we went along, through scatterings of scrub and rubber trees, the true forest looked less and less willing to compromise. It gathered in on the sides as if to heal itself over. Rubber-tree tappers were leaving, finishing their day's work. They appeared from nowhere, opening the drapes of foliage, pushing bicycles.

'You seen a Kubu?' Pastaribu asked each passer-by. 'Any primitives been this way?' The answer was always the same, no, and usually accompanied by a smirk, as if they had been reminded of a dirty joke.

Pastaribu was fed up. He wanted to go home. I reminded him of a cash penalty clause in our agreement. He bit his lip and we drove until we had to abandon the bike – the track was too knobbly with roots and had become just a narrow alley. From here, we walked.

This being a dry time of year, the leaves had drooped and withered back, opening up more space for the smells, and letting the sun in to burn away the compost fug. 'There are bare-foot prints here, Pastaribu. Women, children, men . . .'

'Rubber tappers.'

The adult tracks were wet but firm edged. Only minutes old. 'Why should a tapper head into the forest at dusk?'

'Someone forgot something. Went back for a bale.'

But children too? And the prints suggested feet unnarrowed by shoes. Another thing: the marks were becoming more numerous as the track went on. The light was now insipid, skating low through the leaves. Dusk; and we could hear rain blowing across the leaf canopy. We turned back and recovered the bike, just as the first raindrops got through the canopy and vine lanyards.

Pastaribu tore homeward. Half a mile on, the forest opening over-head, the rain was able to thwack at us. Mud squirted from the tyres on to the outstretching greenery. A man was coming this way, into the forest. At twilight! He ambled with a light, bouncy gait through the blades of rain. He was in no hurry, and had a fair distance to go – he had not taken his tee-shirt off to stop it getting wet, knowing he was going to get soaked sooner or later anyway.

'Slow down!' I said. Pastaribu had not seen him – it must be the rain in his eyes. 'Maybe it's a Kubu. Stop!' Pastaribu had his head down. He could not have heard. 'Slower! We're going to hit him!' The man had tightly curled hair, like a deserted bird's nest, and a blunt nose with round nostrils and black eyes which shone out. His head was raised, and his lips hard – stretched right open in fear. A motorbike was thundering out of the forest, smashing through the white rain, bearing down on him. He was right in our path.

'Pastaribu!' But Pastaribu was accelerating. Our handlebars were about to thump the man down. The path was walled solid by the tendril webs of leaves. He could not escape. I could not watch. This must be a Kubu we were killing.

I opened my eyes. The Kubu was not dragging in the mudguard or being tossed round and round, caught in the chain. He must have jerked aside. I listened for a waning cry of protest. There was none, only the unbroken hissing of the rain.

'Enjoy that?' said Pastaribu, slowing to a halt. 'Hee, hee!'

I stepped back, off the bike, and squinted through the downpour and up the track. The man was gone. 'You could have killed him.'

'A bit of fun. I'm afraid I don't see the problem.' He ripped a leaf from a bush and squeezed the mud off his black plastic shoes.

'The problem is that you almost hurt someone.'

'Climb aboard.'

I did not feel like climbing aboard.

'I know,' Pastaribu said. 'You're upset because you're after a Kubu, and we could be talking to him right now. Is that it?' He raced the engine. I wiped the wet seat with my hand and as a protest took more than my share of the saddle. 'Well, no damage done,' Pastaribu announced. 'And even if I *had* hurt him, there'd be others.'

I did not sleep. I did not and could not. It was not the bedbugs: it was an uneasy feeling about Pastaribu. There was definitely something wrong with him.

Chapter Four

This was a night full of stirrings and expectations. I would escape from here and make it to the forests; alone I would find a Kubu and an answer.

Pastaribu lay in the next bed, snoring in leathery, wheezing gulps. I slipped on my trousers and tore a leaf from Theodore's Blue Book. 'Suddenly have to get back,' I wrote, mysteriously. 'Thank you for all the help.' I folded up 30,000 rupiah and tucked in Swartz's Valium. 'PS Here's some medicine. Take one tablet next time you have a problem.'

It was my idea of a joke – give the man who saw time as money the Western medication for it. But joking was only a way of pretending that I did not care. And I knew I did: I was abandoning Western assistance – the lists, the contacts, the strategy of progress. I was leaving my last link, Pastaribu, right here, and disappearing into the forest. This was not really a laughing matter.

I flipped the rucksack on to my back, and took up the bow and quiver, and my shoes. I was midway to the door, when Pastaribu's bellows-action breathing stopped. I waited. This was freedom. No one must take it away from me. An insect ran over my toes, prickling them, and leaving a tickling wetness. Pastaribu's lips were nuzzled to the bedsheet. I heard a cough from next door, where Mrs Pastaribu and all the rest of the family preferred to sleep. Pastaribu snorted, and then wheezed again. I counted five of his breaths in and out, then tiptoed to the door.

Outside, the motorbike lay shining in the path, crumpled on the gravel like a giant, trodden-on beetle. Pastaribu had not bothered to return the vehicle to his neighbour, just a fence away. I slipped on my town shoes in case of a scorpion or snake. I was going to miss the protection of my jungle boots.

Without looking up I knew there was a half moon. I could trace the path between the looming black palms. Nearby, a dog released a small yap. A second dog barked. It triggered a third. I was pleased – they seemed to know the importance of not letting me escape. Too late. I was well away, and I wanted to maintain this sweet thrill of freedom. I started into a trot. My shoes clattered gravel on the bushes. Chickens scattered in backyards, and flapped in tree roosts. They thought I had come for them. I had come for the forest.

The highway was as smooth as a whale's belly, a gleaming black skin under the hunk of moon. The tar sucked at my town shoes, and its warmth rose up through my clothes. Then I swung right, by Project Forest People Integration and up the Kubu track. I was hurrying. In the dark my world seemed to have less power over me, and so I ran on out of it, escaping under the black felt sky while I still could.

By first light, the air fresh and cold and the scrub muddy red, the last mathematical lines of the rubber trees were behind me, some dribbling from this dawn's milking, others waiting. I had heard coughs and the men's parangs dinging saplings, but I had not seen any rubber workers. That was good. It was a secret thing I was doing; something between me and the Kubu.

Our motorbike tracks of yesterday stopped here, by the shrub that Pastaribu had crushed when he dropped the bike. Now the crumpled leaves had swollen out and lifted themselves again. Not much further, I saw the gouged mud where we had turned on our heels and headed back.

This forest was tidy, the leaves arranged in orderly strata under colour-stained light. And it was huge, not bearing down but hoisting itself – branches vaulting over me a hundred feet up. The bed of the track was getting narrower but clearer, fashioned by an increasing number of feet. I was heading towards something – some sort of Kubu camp in a clearing, I imagined. And that answer? *We are greater than matter and can even create a shadow of it ourselves.*

A whiff of woodsmoke. That was the first sign. But ahead there was no clearing, just a space between the buttresses of two trees. Here was the Kubu camp – a crumpled lean-to hung with silence. Weaving through the last blue trees, it looked as if a sick traveller had been this way, heaped together a few branches to spend a night here, hardly bothering to make a fire to keep warm because dying of double pneumonia would be a relief anyway. Maybe the Kubu camp had been deserted some time ago – this was more of a hope than a fear because if Kubu lived in this shambles they were going to be a grave disappointment.

They *were* here. A dog gave a puny yap, and sappy wood crackled, freshly laid on a fire. The Kubu were all around me – for what it was worth – women propped up with the help of the broken lean-to, and men crouched about the fire like lichenous boulders. Some of the Kubu looked up – most did not bother.

I waited awkwardly for a welcome of sorts. A handshake, that would be nice. The four wiry old men – one blind, with scratched-pebble eyes – had nothing to say. They were curled remnants of themselves. In the lean-to, two toddler girls hugged a woman's ropy arm and a baby lay by itself on the bamboo-pole floor, looking happy to be abandoned.

These people had enough on their hands without my questions. They moved, but only to scratch their itches or to pick at cuts which were like wet mouths – flies on the lips. Different flies were wanting to play on the Kubu eyes, and the Kubu let them.

I had to say something. I tried 'Good morning' in Indonesian. It seemed to be a mistake – the men were pricked by the two words, and hunched down even lower, as if in pain. The women pulled themselves to their feet and adjusted cane backpacks. They were expecting to be rounded up.

It was not as if I was interrupting any activity. No one had been dancing a jig, they were not packing bags, they had not been baking roots in the fire ashes, not even a banana. Then I understood. They were waiting for their fit young men and women to come home. This family cluster was just those who were too infirm to hunt and gather properly.

I propped my bow and arrows against the nearest tree and put the pack down gently. The men threw rude stares at it, as if it was a stranger who had sat himself down for lunch, uninvited. We waited in this dumb silence. I thought to myself, You think I'm a preacher, don't you? Come to drag you off to a mosque or church. Well, I'm not. Here, have some of these. I extended a packet of cigarettes to the camp, passing my hand in an arc that began at the circle of men around the fire and ended at the line of mud-blotted women's faces in the lean-to. Dry, brown, tired eyes looked at the cigarettes. I snuggled them into the uninterested, curled fingers. The men's eyes grew small, confused. They were wondering what the catch was. I squatted down a little way off. They smoked, but stiffly, not enjoying my gift. Then, in a swift, decisive action that was alien to the atmosphere here, the smallest of the men swung about on his haunches to face me.

He was showing me something he had – several eels lashing out on a plastic wrapper, tarnished silver bodies in a gluey slime.

'*Beli?* Buy?' said the Kubu, talking at the fish, not at me. It was the first word anyone had spoken out loud. By now I was pleased with anything. 'Buy?' he repeated to the fish. His teeth were grey and chipped, like knapped flints. He had a sunken mouth, hair like greybeard lichen, dark, deep pools for eyes. He was not like the other Kubu, desiccated of spirit. They were like quashed children. Their eyes worked hard to evade mine; his were placid and secure, those of a person who had seen too much, rather than not enough of the world. And I knew him. He was the man that Pastaribu had tried his level best to run over.

Ants had already got wind of the eels, and were dabbing antennae in their direction. 'All right,' I said. If you insist . . . The Kubu rolled the eels into the wrapper and left them on the ground. I put them down on my rucksack. Then I made to toss a packet of fags to him – an exchange. He stiffened, as if I had offered a clenched fist.

Time edged by, as we waited hour after hour in silence for the young to come back. The women carried themselves like beggars. All except one. She was much younger. She looked about thirty and must have been about twenty. Her face was round, almost a perfect circle, and forward leaning, lips outstretched, as if she was going to whisper something. The Kubu nose was, in general, short, high and flared, but hers was poised delicately on her face. Her shoulders were held well back; her tee-shirt was buoyed upwards and outwards by her high chest. I took rather a shine to her.

Soon it would be too late for me to return to the road – I noticed it in the dulling of the forest that precedes the dusk cicadas. And the Kubu saw this too – they were beginning to murmur and fidget. They had not been waiting for their healthy young to return. They had been waiting for me to do whatever I had been intending to do to them, and leave. They had no healthy young to come back.

I looked at these people, with their slow, empty stares, their peeling-bark skin, and thought of Pastor Stefano's words. 'Civilisation is the distinctive mark of humanity. Persons in the natural state, "savages" in whom Linnaeus believed, are nowhere and have never been.' He was right if the Siberuts were anything to go by, but *these* raggle-taggle humans looked a mess, and you could quite understand why the outside world believed civilisation lay in churches and home comforts and buses running on time.

St Elizabeth give me strength! This was not good enough. I needed these people. Yes, it was true that I was an intruder – but I was a temporary one. Besides, these Kubu might well profit from my coming. For them, death was only a kiss away.

'Look, I'll share everything,' I said. I moved. The Kubu froze solid. The camp flies swirled. I pummelled my rucksack, and dug out rice, coffee, sugar. I spread them all about me. 'Look, you can have these.' I waved to the man who had offered me eels. 'Here – it's yours.' He got up. He was almost a pigmy. He slowly reached out. An old woman creaked to her feet and took a rice bag from him. Her skin was clean, but it had a corpse-like opaqueness and looked damp and cold. You felt she was rotting from the inside out. Her flesh would come away easily, like that of a dead fish.

She opened the bag, and finger-tapped the grain like a scuffing chicken. The rice seemed to please her, and she made a noise. 'Henn-aaaa.' What did it mean? Perhaps it was not even a word. Perhaps she was clearing her throat. She seized a tin pot and scuttled away with it. This told me the direction for clean water. When she was back, I got up and rummaged for my soap. Everyone watched my fingers for what else they might produce.

'Bath time.' I mimed scrubbing my back. The Kubu eyes chased after the soap as I walked out of the camp. 'Don't go away!' I laughed alone. They had eyes only for the bar of Imperial Leather.

I would not have privacy this near by, so I followed the water course for thirty yards, to where it spun round a pelt of moss. I pulled away my shirt, my lace-ups, draped my trousers on a shrub. I raked the water down my legs, and dabbled my white toes. I dug deep into the stream, and pulled scoops of it over my head, letting the soap lather flow down the length of me. This was invigorating – the cold water had more life in it than the Kubu camp.

I put on my shirt and trousers and got straight on with the day's press-ups. At forty I stopped. I felt a presence. I was being watched. I looked up along the stream, the black-hatched leaf flags and green and yellow spindles. It was the man with the flint teeth, high on the bank. Now he was hopping lightly down through the blunt rocks. He nodded at the spot where I had been doing my press-ups.

'You do this for the like of who?'

'For myself. It helps me get things done.'

'And for God?'

'God?' What had this got to do with religion? 'Not really for God, no.'

'I', he said, very deliberately, watching the stream water run from my hair, 'am called Telee. And you pray to your television. You think I do not know the television. I know.'

He was absolutely correct – I had been assuming he had never even heard of a television. There could not be a functioning set for miles. He nodded. He had a confidence; he was unafraid of truth and this honesty shone out sadly from his eyes. I looked for more shirt buttons to do up. I felt spotlit – yet physically he was such a helpless figure. His hair looked like a mat kept for wiping muddy feet. Standing there in the forest, in his home, he looked down and out. But why should anyone be a drop-out in his home? I suddenly felt the urge to talk to him, not just to chatter, but to exchange ideas.

'Yes,' I said. 'Some people worship cars, radios, videos. Material things. Other people – like the Kubu in fact – get along without that. Isn't that so?'

He did not look impressed. He grated his flint teeth.

'You live according to a balance with the natural system. Yes? I met the Siberuts – they're on one of the Mentawai islands. I'd guess you might be similar in that respect.' How could I be doing this, standing in a jungle rivulet, nibbled by mosquitoes, talking about balance with the ecosystem?

'The people in the camp do not know why you come.' He spoke as if the other Kubu were not of his kind. He must have been whisked away to a missionary school, I thought. Been given a classroom education.

'I'm trying to learn something from you – your beliefs.' Maybe I was talking freely just because I liked him. He was a decent bloke.

'Yes. I see already that you do not come to trade, and you do not come to move us . . .' He stopped what he was going to say, and abruptly frowned. He said, 'Sad people. We is sad people.'

I visualised the squatters' camp, the grizzly hags with their potato skins, fingernails black and long, teeth short and occasional, rags that might be shorts, might be loincloths – you could not tell. I said, 'Sad. Yes, I thought you might be.'

'Many problem.'

I had thought it extraordinary to be talking like this here, but this stranger was loosening his trouser buckle! His shorts dropped to his ankles. He reached for my hand, and took the soap. He smelt it, rubbed it on his arm, leaving a white smear, and wiped it under his armpits as he must have seen me doing. He sheathed himself in water and, streaming, pulled up his trousers, and looked bleakly around at nothing in particular.

'Do you ever make gifts to any forest animals? Or gods?' I was manoeuvring – rather skilfully I thought – towards the Gugu.

'Gifts. Yes, gifts.' His eyes were puzzled suddenly – a boy's in such an ancient face. But he was not foxed by the question; it was the soap bubbles in the stream.

'You leave gifts for monkeys ever?'

'Monkey. No.'

'Nor apes? No. So you don't know of the *orang pendek*, the little people?'

'Little?'

'*Orang pendek*. Half man, half ape.'

'Ape?'

Patience, I thought. I'm sure the truth is there in your compact head, somewhere. 'Do you know of the Gugu?'

'Gugu?'

I was on the very brink here. Any minute now Pastaribu would stumble out of the leaves – armed with a kitchen knife against tigers – and ruin it all.

Telee said, 'Tell me.' He pocketed the soap in his shorts.

Patience. 'You see, there are stories that Kubu people leave presents of tobacco out at night to stop Gugu bothering them. Was that ever true?'

The man was like a shrunken reflection of myself, then – his face all bunched up with the tension of waiting. He was not emulating, as Agga had done. He was empathising, absorbing my mood to help me reach him.

'You are an asking man,' Telee said. It seemed to be a criticism, not a compliment.

'Can you just answer that one question, though?'

'Asking, asking.'

So I had to leave it at that. For the moment.

I picked up my town shoes. The Kubu took my other hand. He was inviting me back into the camp. I felt like a child being led by another, slightly older child.

Back around the fire, nothing had changed. The blind man peered at me with his dead eyes, open mouthed, as if tasting the air for my smell. The others were only shadows that occasionally scratched and spat and detached themselves from the shelter. I kept an eye out for the young woman, but in this light she was only a rounded shadow that slipped between the slower, long ones.

I gutted the eels and lobbed them into the fire to cook. By the fireside, down on my haunches, my head wrapped in my hands, I wondered about Theodore's passing comment about them not having yet blossomed into a fully human state. Their possessions were basic, and ornamentation in the camp was accidental – a feather which had slipped down through the branches, or a bracelet from a twist of string being kept aside for future use. Their hair was chaotic: they had no combs, and even if they had had them they would have left them here when they moved on. But this was because material things were a burden. Theirs was a smooth operation, not the total shambles it had first seemed. They could get by with only a backpack-worth of valuables each.

Everyone was having an early night – maybe they would be moving on tomorrow, Telee said. He was not certain where. They curled up in the shelter, or sat sprawling, women at one end. I bagged a space at the other for my mosquito net. Telee fingered each knot as I tied up the supporting strings. He gaped through the fine netting, and blew through it. 'The mosquito will not travel to you. She will not know you in the night.'

'Oh, you want to borrow it?'

'I have never leave the forest, sir, but I am a complete.'

I went to bed, wondering, A complete *what*? A complete person? Did he have that sort of confidence, when his world was collapsing, his friends were ragamuffins? Or was he a complete fool? I did not sleep a wink. My bed was alive under me. Too many questions needed answering. *We can even create a shadow of matter ourselves.*

I went to crouch with Telee near the resinous light of the fire.

'You are lonely,' he said, as an opening gambit.

I searched his eyes in the weak light. 'Why do you say that?'

'You are lonely for a woman. You don't have peace till you have the woman.' He meant I was a wanderer, restless and so wifeless. 'You want my wife? If you want, you may have.'

'I beg your pardon?' What was this? Telee was a friend of only a few hours. Had he just offered me his wife? I thought of the handsome circular face pitched forward in intimacy.

'She is so beautiful. She will make fine love for your manness.'

I said it again to myself: He's offering me his wife! 'It's an honour, I'm sure. And I do appreciate it. But I couldn't.'

'She swells for you.'

'Does she?'

'Look.' Telee cocked his head over his shoulder. I copied, turning so fast I almost crooked my neck. There, uncovered and lit by the amber fire, were a woman's breasts – both of them. I could not see the face, just the two orbs. They looked specially taken out, polished up and arranged. 'You may have.'

'I couldn't do that,' I said. 'I really couldn't.'

'She is too old?'

'Of course not.' But Telee's proud eyes were not on the girl with the whispering face. They were on the scrubbed-clean woman who was going rotten inside. The living corpse. 'If you want, you may have,' Telee repeated.

'I really couldn't do that,' I said, more firmly this time.

*   *   *

The Kubu were losers. Even their popular name was one given to them. 'Kubu' meant 'stockade for war', Father Morini had thought. In centuries past, the King of Jambi had ousted them, and they had retreated into the forest.[12] The forest was their stockade. That had been centuries ago, and they were retreating still, tomorrow morning even.

But the Kubu must pull themselves together. It was time for answers. One way or another, these people held the key to the Gugu. And in Telee I had someone special. He was a thinker – yet he was not familiar with soap. A man of wide experience – yet he had obtained it all in the forest. I said to him, 'What is God, Telee?'

He replied pat, as if expecting us to move on to theology now. 'God is here. He makes us.' He suddenly released an unpleasant raucous cough. 'Maybe he loves us, like the Christian man says.'

'He loves you? But look around you – you're on the run. You're in measly rags. What has God done for you?'

'He has given me all.'

A squatters' camp, I thought. A corpse for a wife. God has blessed him with ruin.

Telee said, thumping his heel on the ground, 'If I strike the ground with a spear, God is hurt. *Ground* is God.'

'Is God all around us, then?'

'Good God and bad God.'

Hmmm, I thought. That's right. He's an animist, like the Siberuts, the Hmongs and all our human ancestors. Believes God is in everything. God is nature – not just made in man's image. I said, 'And you've never seen my Gugu?'

'Them is spirits.'

'Ah!' The dog snapped fitfully, then collapsed back to sleep. 'So!' I clapped his shoulder. 'You believe in them.'

'I believe?'

'My friend Theodore believes they are real flesh-and-blood creatures, not spirits. And there are so many eyewitnesses.'

Telee scratched his chin. He had no need to ask these questions. But I pressed on. 'Are the spirits visible?' The fire was dying, and I could not see Telee's eyes, only the creased surrounds.

'Benedict, *you* never have *kesempurnaan*.'

This Indonesian word meant 'perfection'. What exactly did perfection have to do with it? We were puzzling to each other. His answers certainly did not dovetail to my questions, and now this scruffy stranger – *not yet in a fully human state* – was saying that I could never have perfection. Did he understand what he was saying, this forest man? Because our Creator, something all-powerful, must be the only perfection – God, the Goddess Nature. If so, it was true enough: I, a Westerner, could not have perfection with nature. I had been brought up to tell the time by clock, to extend the day with light bulbs designed not to last a year. The Siberuts were balanced with the world, the elements, I was not. I was out of balance, I saw that.

'So what has perfection to do with Gugu, exactly?' I asked.

'Them is perfection. Them is now all near dead. I seen 'em. Spirits? Maybe they is part God. I don't know.' Telee sniffed. He was crying. His cheeks were as shiny as glass. Without Gugu there was no perfection – the things he had in mind *were* a route to a balanced state, or a state of being at one. Something to relate to nature with, like the gibbons of the Siberuts.

'Kerinci – ten days' distance – I can take you where the Googs is. The mountain explains, sir. She explains. I think you cannot see the Googs. I can.'

But I thought of the prisoner's rose, the petals gleaming from the black of the dungeon. The man had manufactured them out of stale, acid air. *We are greater than matter and can even create a shadow of it ourselves.* I said, 'Isn't there even a chance of me seeing them?'

'Me can sometime see them. But you is too without the peace.'

'But I *need* to see them. I need to take a photo – for proof.'

'Is too late for you. You people seen them long ago – but they got no visibility to them any more.' As he spoke his head did not move an inch, only the shadowy cords of muscle in his jaw. This was the most precise attention he was giving.

'White people *did* see them though?' Our words clicked back and forth, slowly. The intensity of the blackness gave each one weight, and slowed our conversation down.

'Stories say.'

'And why can't we see them now? Are you saying that they're animals, and almost extinct. Or definitely spirits?'

'The Googs is little now, sir.'

I *must* know more. 'Listen. There's another explanation. Now this might sound an odd question, but do you think it's at all possible' – don't laugh, please – 'that you believe in the Gugu so much that you have created them yourselves? Out of nothing?'

Telee had never had a sense of humour. There was no chance of his laughing. 'Sir, the mountain knows what the Googs is.'

'Telee, is there actually any point in me going to this place? It sounds a bit late, to be quite honest.'

'I take you – I can feel good by them if they is not angry.'

If they is not angry. But I was too excited. I did not take in what he said: Telee was going to get me to the Gugu. Within days I would know what they were.

'What about the bus service?'

'Bus?'

'You haven't been on a bus, have you? Well, I'll take you on one tomorrow. Does that suit? I'll give you plenty of food. Cigarettes, a parang.'

I was on the home run. I would not fail as Theodore had. Hold tight. Here we go!

Telee said, 'At light time, sir, we get off.'

I was already packing my bag.

Chapter Five

We got to where the track spread into a patch of desert, and I was relieved to see that the highway, up ahead, was empty. We would be almost unobserved. This was dawn – blue crystal light, a few lone trucks, a boy scratching in the grasses for frogs with his toes. We looked ridiculous; I knew we did. Our height difference begged other comparisons – my slippy size-twelve lace-ups, his crusty, rectangular jungle pads; my loping gait, his short, hopping one. All this was made worse by my shirt sagging on him like a loose bell tent. I had thought that wearing a clean shirt would make him less conspicuous, but seeing us the boy in the ditch abandoned his frog pot and ran for the cover of the mist.

Here we were, out of the trees, on the tarmac. I took the lead now. This was more my world than his – the concrete, the timetables, the wristwatches, the factory clothes and the cars with fashion lines and built-in obsolescence.

'We eat now?' Telee asked. 'Sir, you know someone here?'

'I do know someone,' I said, thinking of the slug, Pastaribu. 'But we're certainly not calling on him. We'll go on to Bangko.'

The first spectators were crowding in on us. Mercifully, a local bus scooped us from the roadside. It was not a direct bus, and it orbited the region, scaring me with sightings of Pastaribu's bungalow and, the second time round, with a view of Pastaribu himself, kicking dirt off the trail bike, his neighbour fuming and looking on with his hands on his hips.

To Bangko, then, the town with a road branching off to Kerinci mountain. Somewhere between the mountains of Kerinci and Seblat, you said, Theodore, and maybe you were right.

The market in Bangko was packed with browsers. We were tight in there with the throng, but we were not hidden enough. The stares Telee got were the cold, fascinated ones that people give the disfigured. I kept him moving – right up to the threshold of a cheap restaurant. There

Telee was split off from me by the waiter and steered in the direction of the chicken stall. 'He's with me,' I said. Every face swung around and took a closer look – the giant, the tramp, our packs, my bow, arrows, dirt-smeared jungle fatigues, the sodden town shoes . . .

I laid down my baggage with Telee's cane backpack, tucked his spear away so that it would not trip so many customers, and took a table near the exit. The set menu dishes were already laid out. Telee carefully duplicated my table manners, sipping the soup with a spoon. Then he lost patience. He grabbed a peppered fish, bit off its dorsal fin, spat it on to the tablecloth, chomped into the fish's flank, reared his head back – the chilli was burning – and spat that mouthful out too. He dropped the fish back into the bowl, and the juice squirted across the lap of our neighbour, the bus driver. But the man was staring too hard at Telee to notice.

Now everyone was gawping. Meals were forgotten. Ash dropped from cigarettes and spoiled food. Telee had got through a dish of chicken legs in red ooze. 'What an appetite!' I said. I ordered another round of soup, the blue and silver mackerel, and more chicken. Telee finished these as well. The bus driver clapped – few people could help admiring the achievement. The waiter quickly brought more plates.

But we had a journey ahead of us. I washed my fingers in the bowl. 'Right, let's go.' I got up, paid the bill. Telee had not budged. His eyes would not leave the left-overs. 'What's the problem?'

'Sir, the food is left.'

'I'll buy something in the market to take with us. Rambutans, tangerines, those strange triangular packs of banana leaves with steamed rice in – whatever you want.'

Telee stood up – but only so that he could reach all the plates. He fished the chicken legs out of the ooze and stacked them on the table. Some of the meat was juicy, some was not so juicy, some was grey. He scooped out the whole lot.

'People are beginning to stare, Telee.' They certainly were. Telee was grappling with the mackerel. He slapped them down on the chicken mound. From the base, a circle of beautiful liquid, glittering with loosened mackerel and tuna scales, expanded like a yellow dawn across the tablecloth. Anchovies were boating in it. Suddenly the woman behind the till was waving her face at me and screaming at the waiter and anyone who came to calm her.

'Why is she sadness?' Telee asked.

'I think she must have swallowed a fish bone,' I said.

Telee was untying a waist band to stash the food away in it. I said, 'If you have to do this, please hurry.' The waiter was closing in, hesitantly, as if Telee might bite. 'As it is, I'll have to pay over the odds for this.' I went over and satisfied the till woman with large notes.

'He's with me!' was a phrase I used a lot at the bus terminal. As each bus came in I checked its destination and sprinted back to make sure that Telee was still in the waiting room, folded up like a vagrant beside a child who could not take her eyes off him. Her fascination scared me. I had a dread that somehow Telee would disappear. Someone would fear that this mangy little man who smelt bad held a new, greater knowledge of our existence, one which said that we in the West were backward in our loss of harmony and so were not more advanced. That we had no right to inflict change, even if, as Theodore argued, it was our 'obligation' to improve. This claim of tribal peoples to an equal, but natural, civilisation might make Telee a threat to the established vision of our future, and also to the alternative, 'Hope at Large'. All, in fact, that went by the name of progress.

But no one kidnapped Telee. No one even spoke to him. He kept himself to himself, dazzled by this outside world – the buses sweeping in, guzzling passengers, belching smoke, roaring into the dust – and the remaining, heaped travellers, an island lapped by food-tray boys with never-ending treble songs, and assorted spectators and pickpockets. After an hour it was too much and he fell into a sleep. Nothing would wake him.

We missed one bus, but, past midnight, I coaxed him on to an unscheduled one that would take us through Sungai Penuh and right by a shoulder of Mount Kerinci. The window seat fitted Telee's child frame perfectly. I slotted him into it, and the bus carried us through the night.

By first light we had been going for five hours, the road surging around the lower hills, in and out of the potholes. Of the mountain itself, there was precious little visible through the mist. Much of what I could see was uninspiring. The slopes were blocks of sallow yellow–grey paddy, or the dark-green etched lines of tea, coffee, bananas and cinnamon. What forest there was left did not look the least interesting – cords of it, glimmering bowls of it, but always soulless, violated. The farmers were not to blame – how could they be? They were striving for their loved ones. But now the forest had been systematically robbed of spirit, its integrity dismantled plot by plot.

Telee lay with his head cradled between the window and the seat. Rising up the pane there was a fan of condensation from where his mouth was squeezed against the glass. At last we were in forest, some high saddle of Kerinci, which ran high to the right. I thought I had best wake Telee. I jiggled his shoulder. When his eyes had opened fully I asked, 'Where do we get off?'

He blinked, slowly. I tried to remember this many times afterwards. I'm sure, though: he did not so much as glance outside. He said the one word, 'Here.'

'Er . . . here?' As it happened, this steep forest had been left aside, unwanted, so far. It *was* feasible that Telee had seen something of interest here. 'Are you sure? We won't get another bus to pick us up. This is the middle of nowhere.'

'Here.'

'I'd better stop the bus then . . .' I hesitated, half out of my seat.

'Yes.' There was no doubt in his eyes. He was strong, in control. He was not looking to me; he was a separate force. He was back with the forest, about to be the leader again.

I called to the driver. He slowed the bus, and gave a satisfied smirk into his rear-view mirror as we got entangled with my bow and arrows. He revved the engine as we jumped off. Telee's shopping bag released our oranges down the steps. As the bus roared on uphill, they were massacred under the wheels, every one of them.

'Now where?'

Telee looked about dreamily, as the bus climbed onward and its blue fumes settled over the ditch leaves, adding another oil veneer. To the right, the forest spilled over the road, and downhill, to the left, it spread down and down, a slung quilt, towards the sculptured-out paddy valleys and sheens of mists. Telee padded off back down the road, the Kerinci highlands on the left.

Despite his bouncing gait his feet pressed silently on the road; my town shoes clacked. A lorry crawled up towards us cradling a tree trunk the width of an airliner. A car in its lee was timing an overtake. We stood in the ditch and closed our eyes for a dust bath.

'A spirit?' I said afterwards, meaning the tree, and hoping for something illuminating from Telee. 'A bit of God, do you think?'

'Tree,' said Telee. 'God is finished with him.'

How did his mind work? I felt too young to understand him. I said, 'This God – what is He? Is He a She?'

'You are an asking man. Asking, sir. Too much. Fighting to God.'

'Meaning that God is a state of mind? Not the Creator? What about a chief spirit?'

'Sir, God is everything.'

I stopped, opened my rucksack and jotted it down in Theodore's blue notebook. 'RESULTS OF GUGU EXPEDITION: Conclusion 1. God = everything.'

Good. And hopefully we would be able to be a little more specific about God, Gugu and the universe for Theodore before the day was out.

My feet were wet from perspiration and the leather chewing into my heels. 'Telee, we must have walked two miles. I'll be whacked soon. Where's your path into the jungle?'

Telee said, 'Cigarette?' He stopped in the road and went down on to his haunches. He breathed out the smoke in jets from between his knees. Suddenly he was as bad as Father Fernando; he really needed that cigarette. This look of weak craving on Telee's face was a disappointment. He was more than an ape-man guide, he was something of a mentor. But, I thought, he was only human and I should be pleased he was taking the trip so seriously. I thought nothing more of it.

After two cigarettes' wait, I said, 'Right, can we get on now? Don't get me wrong. Rubber time is good. Rubber time is all about keeping the balance – taking life as it comes, allowing space for intuition. It means less asking, more being. But I'm champing at the bit, longing to know if Theodore got it right. I want to dive into that forest – so that I can report back, you see.'

Telee spun his cigarette stub away, and we went on down the hill. We sauntered on like this for another half-hour. I had no hat and the sun was removing my nose, layer by layer. If I squinted hard enough, I could see the tip glowing, as thin-skinned as a carrot.

'Telee?' I tapped his shoulder. 'What's going on? Where's the path?'
'Path?'
'The path into the forest.'

He said, 'I think you call the forest *her*. Definite. You like it more that way, sir.'

'If you think it will help . . .' In the Blue Book, under 'God = everything', I wrote, 'But for my purposes = female'. I kept my pen in the page as a marker, then packed the book away. 'Right. So I need a path inside her.' *Her*. I pointed at the face of forest – at the indifferent organism: eyeless, seething trees holding no purpose; not asking, just being. Then I said to Telee, 'And what's at the end of the path? For instance, are you taking me to a beautiful spot to help me understand perfection, and that the Gugu are a state of mind? Or are you saying we have real relic apes here?'

No answer – we had arrived at the right entry point. Telee went for a closer look. While he opened up the straggly drapes, I squatted in the broken shade with my pack, and watched the spiders laying traps in the storm ditch. Pebbles and wet brown soil tinkled down as he hoiked himself inside the forest, inside the God that I must see as a woman.

I said softly, lost in myself, 'Telee is right. In the Amazon I *did* get the feeling God was a Goddess. Then in New Guinea, it was the same. God was Mother Nature.' And Telee had perceived this. Or so it seemed.

Ten minutes later Telee came out of the forest. He was wet with steam, as if he had been broiled. This was not what I expected from a forest man at all. He should slip, fawnlike, in and out. He was blinking and silent, as if unexpectedly released from a punishment block. He stopped and turned his feet over for leeches.

'Well?' I asked.

'Here.'

'This is the place you remember, is it?' The forest was dark and thick, drooling its life waters on to the road. The mass of greenery looked defensive and uptight. Telee was humming and nodding at it, as if recalling details and piecing together memories.

Another spasm of doubt: had he really wandered out to this lonesome spot from Bangko? Entered the forest here of all places – just where it was at its worst? But the man had offered me his wife, and I had never seen anyone with such molten brown eyes, so deep and exact, waters undisturbed, rippleless. 'Fair enough,' I said, and raised my parang.

Telee just kicked the road and shuffled. Now what? I wanted to peel the forest open, enter her. I was impatient. 'Sir, the forest is wrong.' Telee rolled road pebbles with his toes.

'The forest?' I said. 'Are we still in the wrong place?'

'Right place. This *right* place.'

Telee was stiff-shouldered. I had not seen him like this before. A guru should not be so highly strung as this, *should* he? Now he was settling down for a think. He could have sat in the shade; he chose the withering sun. I put a cigarette in his lips and got the matches from my shirt pocket. They were damp from my perspiration and the first three heads crumbled like clay. Telee's arms were slack, fingers lying dead, sprawled on the road like the split end of a run-over snake. I was standing over my leader, a man of the forest who was afraid of it.

'It's to do with your Googs, is it? Are they angry?'

'Cigarette,' he said to my town shoes. In traditional Western role terms, I considered, Telee was strong in the female, in the intuition, but weak in the rationalising male. He could not rationalise away his apprehension.

'You must get a grip on yourself.' I squeezed his shoulder. 'You've got all this spiritual power. You can't have everything. So don't worry about it. They're only apes – or ghosts of them at the worst. *I'm* not scared.' I've been brought up in a male, patriarchal society that rationalises *everything*, I thought. That's my problem. I took the cigarette from his mouth, and put it in my own – a sharing gesture, reminding him of our friendship. 'Come along!'

'I is afraid because I know. You is not afraid. You do not know.' I smiled hopelessly to show that I accepted my ignorance, and that my senses were duller than his. I yanked off my town shoes, demonstrating my trust in his forest. Together we came within the shadow of the forest, the hem of nature's skirt, opened her a little, and went in.

At first, as we forced our entry through laced cords of leaves, our feet picked up spikes lying loose like carpet tacks. But properly inside, we were in a basin of clear, dark light. There, Telee scraped the leaves off his toes, as if coming indoors. It must be only his professionalism, a tracker's neatness, but to me it seemed an odd procedure, like a mark of excessive respect, as if we were approaching a feared shrine.

Though we were climbing a slope, we were scrambling down almost as often as going up; we were working round to the east, through the land where, Telee had said, ape-men 'lived' on. Yet I now guessed that Telee had never been in the Kerinci highlands in his life. Why trudge all the way out here from the Kubu lowlands? And there was not a human print or cut branch in sight. *No one* had left a mark here.

We were driving deeper into the forest. As deep as we could go – as close to the Googs as we could. Telee parted the leaves in a kindly way, picking through the mud like a heron, and lifting his head to sniff the air with patient understanding. He had a great freedom here. I felt that his access was not limited to the world I knew – his senses pushed up and out into other planes. My mind was closed. His was open, exposed. He was accepting, being. Beside him I felt cold, inert. Like Uhu, this man moved through a different forest. He knew heights and depths unknown to me. I put my feet in his footsteps. I wanted to be something like him. That way I might see his Gugu.

In dryer parts the forest scattered its glades with palm stands, red jungle fowl thrashed through undergrowth, orchids were bedded down on bark shelves which were snake and frog homes. That was in the *dryer parts*.

Here and there, even on the slope, the trees stood drowning in dead water. The trees wore more fungi than bark. Frogs and shrimps should have made homes in the pools. They did not. Even mosquito larvae gave them a miss. The water's life was its bubbling. It was lukewarm and stale, and laid with silt like black soot.

I bumped into Telee. He had stopped in front of me. 'Where now?' I found that I was whispering.

'Here.' He made it sound the most obvious answer in the world, as if he had been aiming for this precise spot all along. And I could believe it. He could have sniffed his way through the trees, over streams, through clouds of fat gnats, down slides of clay, homed in precisely on this spot, to where he felt that the last Gugu, and *kesempurnaan*, 'perfection', was.

'Sir, we stay night time, by water.' He indicated with his blunt nose that he meant further up the cobbled brook. 'Special place. Tonight I take you to the Googs.'

'Why not now?'

'I is not ready, sir.' He drew a quick breath: 'You're scared, sir?'

'Why should I be scared?' Besides, I would have Telee know that I had knocked around rainforests a fair bit, been adopted bloodily by a Melanesian tribe. I did not scare easily.

Telee's face said that I had not grasped the situation one bit.

We sat on the boulders of the brook, watching the silent water glinting around us. I showed Telee how to remove leeches with salt. He watched them rear and convulse and seem to spit. Then he played with my skin, stretching and pinching it. This intimacy – it was so much like him, so like the Siberuts. Probing and sensuous and open. 'You is so soft. Like a woman – but body so strong.'

'Poor-quality covering, this white skin.'

'Breakable for the forest. But your head will not break.'

He was right – my thinking mind was my weakness; it was something I had brought along with me from beyond the trees – not Christianity or Islam, but pure mathematical rationality. Telee was telling me he saw this, my lack of intuition – lack of ability to feel. Why had I ever doubted him?

'Let's have something to drink. It'll refresh us for the march.' I unstrapped my pack, and brought out a brown-paper pack of Sumatran coffee. It would have to do. Telee snorted. He would not say what was wrong, but he was disgusted with me – as if it was a superficial thing to have a brew-up before approaching the Gugu. Why the fuss – the hissing and tutting? It was not as if we were going to enact some sacred rite.

'Sir, you must not eat. It is right that you do not eat. I want you to be clean for the Gugu.'

'If you say so.' I did not mind. I was close now. Close to the time I could write a conclusion in my notebook, below 'God = everything. But for my purposes = female'.

The forest lulled through the heat of the day. Telee sat alone on a stone, head between his knees. He was not at rest. His mind was racing. He talked to himself. If I had not known better, I would have thought he was chanting a prayer. I wanted to tell him to stop. It was unnerving me. Then he lifted his eyes to mine. 'I am so sad for you, sir. You not being knowing.'

'Never mind me. I'll know what the Gugu are soon enough.'

Small tears spilled down his face in several different rivulets. My innocence was really distressing him. 'You are not scared, sir?'

Chapter Six

He left me for half an hour, then surprised me by appearing from upslope through the peeling grey bamboo stands.

'We go,' he said.

'Do we?'

'This is not the good place for *kesempurnaan*.'

'Oh. I thought you said it was.'

'No.' He was uptight again. His cheeks had lost all colour. I gave him another cigarette. I did not like it in him, his dependency on a drug. And he was fast becoming a chain-smoker.

We started off towards a spot where this intuitive man thought we would find the Gugu and perfection, this place that still had the power to reach to him. Up and up this slope, along the stream bed. Telee was getting faster and faster. Soon it was becoming a challenge to keep up – all this scrambling in bare feet over loose shingles and hummocks of dry weed.

Telee halted. I stopped dead beside him – it was his face that made me freeze. He stood in front of me, face skyward, his body rigid and displaying a kind of physical agony. His mind was curled in on itself. His eyes were distant, empty, inward, apparently directed at a new searing pain. A few paces away there was an animal salt-lick – stream banks had been trampled and gashed by deer. We could smell their urine, and so could the butterflies – blue skippers with speckled hazel rings which formed owl faces.

Telee sat down for another of his rests. He placed his head on his wrists, and watched me inspecting the splinters in my feet. The next thing I noticed was that he had picked up my parang from beside my pack. He began mindlessly sharpening the blade on a stone.

It made me lonely, seeing Telee distracted. He was not here with me. 'Let's make a fire,' I said. He moved. But not towards kindling. He moved to hold himself tight in his arms. His jaws were locked together – the muscles at the hinge protruded and were hard. His eyes were fixed

on the forest ceiling, but only as an aid to his other senses. 'What is it?
Tell me. I'd rather know.' This was getting beyond a joke. Telee knew
the Gugu forest, I did not. He must snap out of this. 'Don't worry about
the firewood,' I said. 'I'll do that. Sort through the stores we bought.
Tinned fish? Fruit? Take your pick. You can even share my Golden
Honey Crunches – I hunted a packet down in Padang.'

A vein like an earthworm slowly rose in the skin of his temple.

'The Gugu? You can sense the Gugu?'

'We go,' said Telee. I was too unsure to question him. We went, Telee
travelling fast, as if he was late for an appointment.

It was understandable that no one had cultivated this forest. No one
would want to buy these bamboo screens, the dells lined with black soup
or hatpin-sized palm thorns. At times the air smelt rotten. It gave the
whispering trees a cadence that was eerie, as if tainted by the residue of a
past horror. With any luck I would get accustomed to it soon, but it did
not seem localised – a foul-breathed swamp, a carrion-strewn glade. It
was everywhere we went, as if closely pursuing us. I started thinking
hard, working my brain, trying to stay rational, to keep my head out of
Telee's forest.

Telee stopped. I came right up to him. He was grateful for being able
to stand close. He looked up at me, then slipped his hand into mine and
took a firm hold. He was taking comfort from my growing fear. Our
foreboding was a thing in common. It drew us closer. The strangeness of
it unnerved me. 'The Gugu want more presents perhaps,' Telee said.
'They is not happy with what I bring.'

'You haven't brought anything very much. Except me. Anyway, when
the time comes, give them what bits of our luggage you think is right.
Excluding the Honey Crunches, if possible.'

We climbed. But were we not going the wrong way? We would be in
cloud forest before long. As far as I could see, Telee was simply following his nose, driving himself at whatever stimulation was provided him –
spiky saplings, leaf showers, root humps, the soapy mud. Yet he was not
using the sharpened parang. It was as if he was reserving the keenness of
the blade for a later, more important task.

There was only two hours' good light to be squeezed from the sun. I
called after Telee, 'Where to now? Are you trying to get to a good
camping site for peace? Is that it? I really must know now. Suppose we
get separated. Where to?'

We dropped a hundred feet, skidding down crumbly leaf-litter shoots,
into a huge but dry gully. Then Telee stopped tight, frozen to the core.
Away, far away, was the whooping of a gibbon troop – not a pure

sound, but an echo, cradled by the canopy layers.

I said, 'Gibbons. The dark-handed race, I should think, but there's a chance it's the white-handed variety. That's the type I saw in Thailand, but its range extends to Malaysia and north Sumatra.' I gabbled on. If necessary, I wanted my rationality to blot out his intuition. I had come here believing in him, but now I was strangely afraid. I did not know enough about this man. Why should he want to help me out, bring a white man here?

'Gibbons.' I came in close to Telee. He looked at me; his eyes seemed to be focusing not on my face but beyond, somewhere towards the back of my head. The fierce penetration of his stare frightened me. He was judging me, measuring the precise difference between us, and reading the answer out loud – showing me the severity of that gulf.

You don't understand what's got to happen, his fluid eyes were saying. You simply do not understand.

One hundred per cent correct. I did not. I said, 'They remind you of your Googs. But they aren't. Look, I know you've been brought up in the forest all your life, and you know better than me, but these are gibbons. I don't know why they are calling just now, but I promise you, that's what they are. It's your state of mind.'

'We go,' said Telee, going. I saw it more clearly now: his running was a fleeing act – his motion was away from, rather than towards. He had an ear out for those gibbon sounds. He kept them on his back, climbing higher up Kerinci.

I must not be left alone here, I thought. If he lost his nerve and bolted, I would run after him. Never mind my Kleenex-soft feet, my indoor-fashioned body. I would chase him for all I was worth. He knew the forest better than I did, and he was afraid of something here. Something that was unhappy with what he had brought. *I* was all that he had brought.

'What's going on, Telee? Stop and tell me!'

The gibbons whooped on, and though they might have been five miles away their calls vibrated from the other side of the mountain. 'Are they sensing the Gugu? Are they upset? And by the way, can I have my parang back?'

Telee did not stop. We skipped over a black stone with a beard of moss, intent on getting away from the lower gibbon forests. I now remembered that Telee had said, that first day, 'I can feel good by them if they is not angry.'

And they *were* angry. I paused, now fully smelling Telee's cold fear and feeling it in myself, seeing it in the quivering of my fingers. 'Listen, the gibbons have finished,' I said. The leaves high above trembled in the open sky. Somewhere a palm leaf shuddered down through the storeys.

I must have looked flustered, because Telee stopped and said, 'You have seen the Googs?'

'There aren't any Googs,' I said, wanting to believe it.

Telee smiled at my dismissing the Googs. It was one of the few times he ever smiled.

'There aren't any Googs,' I repeated. I did not want to give the Gugu access to me. I wanted no part in what Telee believed.

'Sir, the Gugu are angry with the world.'

'I'd rather gathered. Isn't there a present we can give? Tobacco might be an idea.'

'They is too angry to smoke. They do not want my present.'

His present. Did he mean me, a white man? White men had built the road and the Gugu needed appeasing. But this was nonsense, and I knew I would laugh about it later. All the same I would feel better if only Telee would hand my parang back.

The sun had been up, and now it would be tilting down. Telee crumpled down on the ground. I joined him, but was immediately wanting to be on the move again.

'Telee. You offered me your wife. That makes us the best of friends, doesn't it?'

Telee said, 'Sir, I seen you hexacise.'

'Yes, we have seen each other naked. That makes us the closest of buddies. You'd never mean me harm.'

Telee said, 'I know why you hexacise. You hexacise for a woman.'

What? I had misheard. I must have. This was the man who had led me to a wet mountain after ape-men. He understood me. That was why he had agreed to help me to here. That was why it was nonsense thinking he had brought me as a present to the Gugu. He *must* know I exercised only to keep fit.

'Because I see you hexacise for a woman, I give you my wife.'

The living corpse, I thought.

'Sir, you were wanting to love my beautiful wife so much.'

Wrong. Absolutely, completely and utterly wrong. 'I'm your friend,' I said slowly, looking at the blade that he was testing on his thumb.

Telee said, 'For you, I charge only five thousand rupiah.'

'Really?' I felt like a ruined man, bankrupt and cracked to the heart.

'Normally she is ten thousand rupiah to white men,' Telee said, raising his chin with pride.

Too expensive, I thought. Far too expensive.

The dusk closed in. I lit a fire and kept talking, now usually in English. He might not understand a word, but maintaining that human link bolstered me against whatever it was that was out there in the forest, demanding.

Hampshire in midsummer – scabious blue downland, bracken hardening to bronze, the dew ponds and their crested newts. I weaved an aura of hard rationality around the two of us. 'There's nothing out there,' I said. And, wondering again why I was trying to believe this when I had traipsed round the sixth biggest island in the world wanting to believe the opposite, I snatched back my parang.

'Phew!' I said. 'That's *one* less being to worry about.'

I'd hoped to see in Telee relief, a look of responsibility shouldered. He hadn't really wanted to use it against anyone. But no, he just looked more scared than ever of the Gugu. His eyes chased the blade desperately as I moved to slip it in my belt. He was blinking at the trees, bewildered, frightened. He had let the Gugu down.

Telee curled into a ball, nestling in the leaves. I patted him as one might a nervy dog in a storm. I closed my eyes and tried to breathe slowly. An hour to go before dark, and the Gugu were out there somewhere, perhaps watching.

I listened as the forest swung in the breeze overhead, the giant bamboo pipes giving it the creak of a galleon. This forest didn't have quite the throbbing insect vitality of the lowlands, and the comparative quiet should have given us peace. But Telee's fear seemed to infect every branch. He put an end to the tranquillity that should have settled on us from the moss sheets, the cobweb skeins.

Then it changed. The forest became a new place; I was aware of it immediately. And I knew, somehow, that if I opened my eyes Telee was not going to be with me.

'Telee?' As expected, there was no brooding, curled Telee there – just a space, an invisible hole in the damp air where he had been.

I was on my feet and running. He could not have gone far. I yelled. The sound came out like a yelp. He must not leave me in this forest alone. I crashed on downhill. Where I was going became less important than the movement itself. Losing my way was not a worry – I was lost already.

I reeled and scurried on through the weak light, the mist in it a silver dust. My bare toes were flaking bark from logs, scattering pebbles. The wet wool of spiders' nests was smearing me. A soldier ant dug its head into my left calf and hung there, but I did not care. I ran on, ducking boughs from which lichen trailed in grey beards. And all the time I was expecting to meet the face of a Gugu.

Suddenly the scum on the curved stones skidded under my feet. I was falling. The forest was bringing me down. My view of it – white and green chinks, brown ropes – swirled. A hand of palm thorns reached out to slash me. I swivelled from them. They opened my shirt across my chest. I knew I had been caught. It was the sudden wetness on me. But I did not feel the pain. I hit the cobbled floor on my back, and lay catching my breath, tickled by the warm liquid running down my ribs. It was a two-and-a-half-inch slash – just one, the track of a single thorn.

I kept my right hand there, pincering the wound closed. My shirt was soaked. I ripped off the cuffs and used them as swabs. The blood churned out, and was not going to stop. I remembered the needle and thread tied into my belt for emergencies. This was an emergency. There was not much choice. I threaded a needle on the third attempt and began the first of five stitches. I must start in the middle, and get most of the cut closed. I went about it with my fingers shaking – a knot for each of five separate stitches, closing the gash with five tugs, wondering how I had, despite my best endeavours, achieved an expedition even more catastrophic than Theodore's. What were the Gugu? I was not waiting around to ask them.

Postscript

Now I am back here in Hampshire and the scar from the thorn is almost gone, only a two-inch raised crease. The wound, the puzzling Telee, the return flight from Sumatra are a year away. Since then I have not set foot outside Europe.

In the end, before I came down off the mountain, I recovered my backpack, the bow and arrows. And the Blue Book, with Theodore's label on the front cover: 'Journey'. From time to time, sitting here at my desk, I give the book a flick through. I always slow as I get towards the end, the conclusion, and those penultimate words: 'God = everything. But for my purposes = female'. I pause before the words that follow, and take stock. Then inevitably, inexorably the memory looms again: that last night in the highlands . . .

I had been deserted. I had that fresh gash high across my chest. The light was failing, and I was lost. But dropping back down the slope, my shirt heavy with the wet blood, I was oddly calm. The forest was no longer aggressive. It was as I had found it before, when alone; nature's strength was easier for me to perceive as female.

Around me, the shoots of giant bamboos rocketed to the ceiling of the forest, providing umbrellas for open space. I laid myself down, shaking but steady. A wind was picking up, spinning around the range, and the bamboos were beginning to move. The hundreds of poles and tubes bent as if by their own will, like the spikes of a sea urchin. The heavy, hollow cracking of the stems was like the snapping of the last tense fibres of my defence, my rationality. But this did not matter. The fear in this forest had vanished with Telee.

And this confirmed my thinking about the nature of his Googs. The Gugu should be vengeful, he had felt. And that was how he had created them. *We are greater than matter and can even create a shadow of it ourselves* . . . The Gugu were potent, visible once, maybe, but never made out of flesh and bone. He had created for himself a shadow of fear.

The night closed in, tightening off the world above and beyond the forest edge. Algal fluids came to me down the bamboo poles, sleek dribbles that snaked down and dropped, tapping me like the fingers of the forest's consciousness. Tap tap, tap tap. I was rising in myself, coming to the surface, as the restraints of my rationality were weakening, dissolved by the wet air, the breath of the forest.

The growing warm dark was the very essence of my origins, the tapping pulse of life. A mother. She was folding over me; I was quivering here inside her, an embryo enclosed in a tissue of leaves. Tap tap, tap tap ... I heard the pulse and, transported in the darkness of the old mother forest, lost all time. *Time is something of our own making.* Time began to blur, and now matter – the forest around me. I had been here, I thought, in the centre of my origins, the hot core of the infinite, for ever.

The sensation was of being lifted in a vortex, a cycle that was seamless – no clear beginning, no obvious end. I was journeying as the forest priests had before me; I was being hoisted out of my lonely human prison state. Into an expanse of freedom.

Now Mount Kerinci is a long way away. Even after all this time I believe my impression was a true one, no trick of the mist. What were the Gugu but messengers of hope? To the forest people, to the world. To Theodore, who had wanted them as a genetic, evolutionary product. One way or another, the shadows were saying we are only caged by the limits of our perception. We *can* escape from this planet of ours, our little dinghy in the sea and space of time.

I see it written there on the final page of the Blue Book – the last entry, the final conclusion, below 'God = everything', I scribbled, 'Gugu = Hairy Angels'.

Theodore took the result very well, really. I broke it to him quickly, as we drove the Old Crate back from the airport. 'It's bad news, I'm afraid. I've had a very nice ... interesting time. But as far as your evolutionary hypothesis goes, I've found nothing. No clues whatsoever. I really am truly sorry.'

He was silent a moment, heavy fingers flapping on the top of the steering wheel, as we sped by the State Mosque. 'Don't bother yaself, Benedict! No sense in being depressed about it. We'll go back together. Look properly this time.'

'*Properly?*'

'We'll get back home, have a glass or two. Get out the maps.'

As I dragged my luggage into the sitting room Theodore took Uhu's bow from where I had left it propped against the Buddhist-monk lampstand, and ran his fingers over the grain of the black palm. 'How do ya string this?' With a deft flick of his knee he bent the wood, tugging the string.

'Careful. It's irreplaceable.'

Crack! The bow was in two. Splinters lost themselves, skidding off across the tiles, under the barrel table and the cane chairs. 'Giant, I *am* so sorry.'

We had a drink. Then a second. Theodore said that he would get me a brand-new bow on our return. 'Are you booked up at all next year, Benedict, you mad fellow?'

Fully, I said.

Notes

1. One of Hull's sources seems to have been Bernard Heuvelmans, *On the Track of Unknown Animals* (London: Paladin, 1965), and I gratefully acknowledge the publisher's permission in allowing me to use whatever might have been directly quoted by him.
2. A brief survey of the threat to the Hmong's way of life can be found in Nicholas Tapp, *The Hmong of Thailand: Opium People of the Golden Triangle*, Anti-Slavery Society Indigenous Peoples and Development Series Report No. 4, (1986). This a short incisive read.
3. A more exact, slightly less grammatical version of the account is given in *On the Track of Unknown Animals*.
4. Winston S. Churchill, *The Second World War*, Vol 4 (London: Cassell & Co. Ltd, 1951).
5. An ill-fated escape from Padang, which, like Theodore's, ended in capture and a railway camp, is given in Ernest Gordon, *Miracle on the River Kwai* (London: William Collins Sons & Co., 1963). See also Richard Gough's more documentary *The Escape from Singapore* (London: William Kimber and Co. Ltd, 1987).
6. John Bastin, *The British in West Sumatra (1685–1825)* (Kuala Lumpur: University of Malaya Press, 1965) is the source for all the related quotations which follow.
7. Stefano Coronese, *A Primitive Civilization* (Holliston: St Francis Xavier Foreign Mission Society, Inc., 1985).
8. Portraits of the Batak, Nias, Siberut, Kubu peoples as they lived with cultures more or less intact may be found in Edwin M. Loeb, *Sumatra, It's History and People* (Vienna: Institut für Volkerkunde, 1935).
9. It later turned out to be Sjovald Cunyngham-Brown, who is mentioned in my previous book, *Into the Crocodile Nest* (London: Macmillan London, 1987).
10. Recounted fully in Sjovald Cunyngham-Brown's splendid

autobiography, *The Crowded Hour* (London: John Murray, 1975).

11. See Tony Whitten, *The Gibbons of Siberut* (London: J.M. Dent & Sons Ltd, 1982). Regarding the environmental threat to Siberut, see *Saving Siberut: A Conservation Master Plan* (Bogor: WWF Indonesia Programme for the Government of Indonesia, 1980). Also, *Siberut Nature Conservation Area, West Sumatra: Management Plan 1983–1988* (Bogor: WWF, 1982).

12. A light book on the Kubu is M. Jasin Jacub and K.A. Soedarmanto's Indonesian *Mengenal Masyarakat Kubu di Jambi* (Bandung: CV Rosda, 1979).